D1436142

The Trial of
JOMO KENYATTA

BY THE SAME AUTHOR

The Trial of
JOMO
KENYATTA

Montagu Slater

London

SECKER & WARBURG

1955

Printed in England by
Western Printing Services Ltd
Bristol
and
first published 1955
by
Martin Secker & Warburg Ltd
7 John Street, London
W.C.1

Contents

1

Queen against Kenyatta and others

JOMO KENYATTA and four of his leading supporters have been convicted and are in prison in Kenya on charges of "managing Mau Mau". The first hearing of the case against them occupied some five months; appeals and a petition added another fifteen months; the transcript of the proceedings runs to nearly a million words. Yet, since length and wordiness are not the same thing as significance, we have to ask what is true importance of the case?

A simple answer might be that it was a political trial of decisive importance to the immediate future of Africa: but this was something the prosecution was anxious to deny. "It is a criminal case," declared Crown Counsel at one stage of the proceedings, "*Queen against Kenyatta and others*, for what is a crime. It would have been the same if *Queen against Kenyatta* were for a felony or picking a pocket; to describe it as a state trial would invest it with a halo it does not really possess." To Crown Counsel's mind such a description would bring "pictures of Westminster Palace and the Earl of Essex with the axe edge turned towards him, and Warren Hastings. But in these humdrum days," Counsel went on, "there are no such things."

The legal distinction between a criminal and a political case is difficult to draw, but historically there can be no question that Crown Counsel was wrong. Forensically, it is proper for Counsel to do what he can to avoid any association of dignity or drama with the men it is his duty to prosecute, but whether we like it or not his six prisoners will become historical figures. Whether they will rank with Parnell and Casement or with Thistlewood and Guido Fawkes is another matter: what is beyond doubt is that they will appear before the bar of history, and history will have to make up its mind.

7

Jomo Kenyatta was known in Europe and America long before the trial. His life had been so closely bound up with the growing political problems of Kenya, that to describe one is to describe the other. In his evidence he gave a very full account of his life and his political beliefs, so they can be left in very broad outline here. He described himself as "about 50". Coming to Nairobi in his twenties he worked first in a minor post in Government Service— according to Crown Counsel, as a meter-reader in the gas depart-ment. At his time, Kenyatta says, he was a sympathiser with the East African Association which was busy denouncing what was described as forced labour for Africans. In about 1922 or 1923 this body was replaced by the Kikuyu Central Association which took over this and several other topics of agitation. By 1925 Kenyatta was an official of the new body, and by 1928 he says "I took up political work as a full-time job".

The Kikuyu are the largest tribe in Kenya. At the 1948 Census it was found that the population consisted of 5,252,753 Africans and 154,843 of other communities. Of the Africans 1,026,341 were Kikuyu. They inhabit the fertile, highland region which is roughly bounded by Nairobi, the Aberdare Mountains, Nyeri and Mount Kenya, and by a line drawn thence to Thika and back to Nairobi. Their geographical position brings them into the closest contact with the settlers, and many Kikuyu believe that the land occupied by the settlers originally belonged to them. What is as much to the point, the Kikuyu—like the Ibo in Nigeria—are the go-getters, the men of enterprise, of their part of the world; and in times of political agitation they tend to lead their neighbours. The Kikuyu Central Association—KCA for short—as good as announced the fact in its title.

In Kenyatta's own account it was not till the late 'twenties that the KCA became aware of an event which had taken place during the first world war, the passing of the Crown Lands Ordi-nance of 1915. This Ordinance (No. 27) defined as Crown Lands, among others, "all lands occupied by the African tribes of the Colony". Under the same ordinance the Governor of the Colony was empowered to "grant, lease or otherwise alienate in His Majesty's behalf any Crown lands for any purpose and on any terms and conditions as he may think fit". The Kikuyu were already complaining, to quote from a pamphlet by Mbiyu Koinange, of the "alienation of 16,000 square miles to 2,000

European settlers and the reservation of 50,000 square miles for
5½ million Africans". Now they seemed to find themselves on their
own land "tenants at will of the Crown". A point of agitation had
arisen which from the point of view of the African farmer trans-
cended all others. From this time on, the land agitation had an
important influence on Kenyatta's career. The Ordinance was
changed in 1938 when lands which had not already been alienated
were given a new status, but Kenyatta, in his evidence, insisted
that the change by no means met Kikuyu demands.

Kenyatta's own account as he gave it in court slightly simplifies
the story. The land agitation had been in progress ever since the
war and from 1922 onwards one Royal Commission after another
visited Kenya to hear evidence. It was in 1929 after the sessions of
the Hilton Young Commission in Kenya that Jomo Kenyatta was
approached "by my people who asked me to go to England to
represent them".

He came to England to discuss three questions: the first was
land, the second was female circumcision. By a singular twist in
the story female circumcision now becomes a motive force. At this
time many of the Kikuyu schools were run by the Church of
Scotland, and the Presbyterian missionaries now refused to admit
circumcised girls. The custom of female circumcision has a significant place in Kikuyu culture: Kenyatta himself several times
describes it as "a beautiful custom". The missionaries' reaction
produced the first impulse towards the foundation of independent
Kikuyu schools. Thus on his first European visit in 1929 Kenyatta's
mandate was to discuss the land question, to discuss female circumcision, and to obtain permission to found independent schools.
On this last point he gained concessions. The Kikuyu were told
that if they could build the schools and train the staff they could
have their independent schools. Kenyatta went back with this
concession, but returned here in 1931, gave evidence before the
Carter Commission on Kenya lands in 1932 and did not return to
Kenya till 1946. During the intervening years he travelled extensively in Europe, studied in several academic centres including
Moscow University and the London School of Economics, and in
1938 published his book *Facing Mount Kenya*, the fruit of his
studies with Professor Malinowski, who found this study of the
tribal organisation of the Gikuyu (this being the spelling of the
word Kenyatta favours) "a first-hand account of a representative

A*

African culture . . . an invaluable document in the principles underlying culture-contact and change; last, not least, as a personal statement of the new outlook of a progressive African". During his wander-years Kenyatta was more or less consciously preparing himself for leading the education movement among the Kikuyu. When he returned to Kenya in 1946 he found "over 300 schools educating something over 60,000 children". He became the principal of the independent Teachers' Training College. He also found that during the war the Kikuyu Central Association had been proscribed.

This caused him to enter into personal negotiations with the Governor, Sir Phillip Mitchell, on the question of lifting the ban on the KCA. Their conversations at first seemed promising but later broke down. Sir Phillip made a wise and friendly suggestion that Kenyatta might do well to become re-acclimatised before undertaking much political activity, so many things had changed in his long absence, and Kenyatta took the advice. A year passed before he became President of a new body, the Kenya African Union.

From now henceforward KAU—the three letters are usually run together and pronounced *cow*—became a predominant force in the politics of Kenya. The evidence given in this case pieces together a very clear picture of its activities and size. It had about 100,000 members paying a subscription of five shillings a head a year—a large sum by African standards in a Colony where a Government clerk will be paid from £2 to £5 a month. The night before it held an outdoor meeting it would be an evening's work for two of its officers to make out enough receipts for the five-shilling payments of its new members. It was gaining as many as 4,000 recruits at one meeting. People would travel far to hear Kenyatta. At one meeting, as Crown Counsel said, forty coach-loads went out from Nairobi. Audiences at meetings addressed by Kenyatta were from 30,000 to 50,000 strong.

Kenyatta and four of the other accused were the leading members of its executive committee, the sixth was secretary of one of its biggest branches. They form a significant cross-section of the African population of Kenya—for though the Kikuyu were still predominant there was by now a deliberate attempt to include members of other African communities. One of these committee members is a trade union leader who had become interested in the Oxford Group even to the extent of attending one of its conferences in Switzerland. Another is an editor, a political journalist. A third, Kaggia, is an independent religious leader. His own account of himself (pp 192 *et seq*) makes instructive reading. He too had been in England, and his studies there drove him to the conclusion that the religion the missionaries taught in Africa was not true Christianity. (He found for instance a colour bar in churches in Kenya.) He entered into discussion with the missionary societies but, in the end, despairing of root and branch reform, he broke away and went back to Africa to preach true religion, though he insisted repeatedly that he had no intention of forming a new sect. Five of the prisoners, including Kenyatta, are English-speaking intellectuals. The sixth, Karumba, is a local leader evidently of great influence, who has no English. He gives his own account of himself on pp 200 *et seq* and gives the reader, I think, a clear feeling that Kungu Karumba is very much the Kenya man-in-the-street.

The policies of KAU covered as wide a field as its personalities. The land question was naturally the basis of its agitation; but KAU also occupied itself, like Kaggia, with religion; like Fred Kubai with labour questions. And, as a nationalist movement, it aimed more or less consciously at producing a synthesis, a way of life which, as Kenyatta several times explained, would take the best from Europe, Asia, and America, while rejecting what was less suitable to the African. For instance, English beer and English hats were both considered bad things, to be resisted. And even this is not quite as trivial as it sounds. Both in Asia and Africa —in Nigeria as well as in Kenya—the danger that the snob attraction of European and American clothes can make the African or the Indian lose dignity and become ridiculous, has been recognized by the nationalist movements. The Indian nationalist has a "Gandhi hat": KAU had a "no English hats" campaign. The attempt at synthesis goes deeper. Female circumcision has been mentioned. It can perhaps stand for a symbol of an attitude of which Kenyatta is perhaps the most eloquent exponent: a poetical and sometimes a mystical veneration for tribal or national tradition and character. And here, manifestly, is the cue for the entry of Mau Mau.

These two syllables which, as Defence Counsel was to put it, are "of no meaning and of unknown origin" seem first to have appeared in the settlers' newspaper, *The East African Standard* in 1950. Kenyatta, in his evidence, declared that no such phrase occurs in any of the half dozen African languages he knows. By all accounts Mau Mau is a secret society, with savage ritual and a terrorist programme, but little evidence was produced in the trial—or indeed anywhere else—to throw light on the origin or early stages of Mau Mau. Terrorist crimes against both Europeans and Africans, murders, mutilations and hut-burning, occurred in 1950, and in August that year Mau Mau was proscribed. Accusations that KAU was behind Mau Mau increased in frequency and Kenyatta and his associates found several public occasions for disclaiming any connection between the Kenya African Union which "worked in daylight" and the terror that struck by night. In August 1952 Kenyatta joined with a group of other Africans, including several chiefs, in a meeting which was not of KAU but called by an *ad hoc* committee with the express object of its being an anti-Mau Mau demonstration. Kenyatta was the chief speaker and he denounced Mau Mau in a solemn curse derived from Kikuyu mythology. His speech was recorded on tape and film, and formed a part of several official broadcasts intended to win the Kikuyu from Mau Mau's evil ways.

The growth of the terrorist movement occurred against a background of unusually rapid advance by the open political movement, represented chiefly by KAU but also by other organisations such as, for example, the East Africa Trade Union Congress. The war had given momentum to African grievances and African nationalism. The settlers' organisation was so disturbed by the growth of KAU that in 1948 they demanded that Kenyatta should be deported. In 1949 there had been a general strike in Nairobi led by some of the six accused in this trial. During the short-lived second Labour Government the Colonial Secretary, Mr James Griffiths, felt it necessary to visit the Colony. Emergency was in the air. There was talk of a crime wave. Yet in September 1952 the Chief Native Commissioner said, "There has been a certain amount of trouble but it is confined to a small area and is not as serious as newspaper reports make out", and indeed police statistics of crimes against the person showed a decrease in comparison with the previous year. But by now Government with all possible precaution was making preparations to declare an Emergency. The African member was not present at the Executive Council of the Colony when the effective resolutions were passed;

nor were these resolutions discussed in the Legislative Council till some time later. Government kept its intentions dark until military reinforcements arrived. Then a State of Emergency was proclaimed and arrests began. These were in three waves. First to be arrested were the top leaders of the KAU, the trade unions and African religious bodies, some 130 in number. The next two waves were of mass arrests for the purpose of screening. In a short time more than 50,000 Kikuyu were in concentration camps. Native grain stores, cattle, sheep, goats and money savings were confiscated. All the independent schools were closed. The whole process has in our day an only too familiar air. These swift moves were followed by a new wave of terrorism. Mau Mau murders and atrocities swept across the colony. Frequently the victims were settlers on isolated farms, whose servants either joined in the crime or were themselves murdered, sometimes with ghastly mutilations. Previously it had been possible to argue, as many did, that Mau Mau was a vague and undefined body which perhaps did not even exist, at any rate as a single entity. But after the emergency measures there was no question about it. A year and a half later, in January 1954, a parliamentary delegation was to report that:

> Mau Mau orders are carried out in the heart of the city. Mau Mau "courts" sit in judgment and their sentences are carried out by gangsters. There is evidence that the revenues collected by the gangsters, which may be considerable, are used for the purposes of bribery as well as for purchasing Mau Mau supplies.

Despatched to the scene by the *Sunday Times*, Mr Graham Greene was to write with characteristic vehemence:

> "Where is the man of courage who will see that so long as able men like Kenyatta or even Kimathi are excluded from effective political power ... ?" The voice drones on in the gallery. From there you cannot see the group of burnt huts, the charred corpse of a woman, the body robbed of its entrails, the child cut in two halves across its waist, an officer found still living by the roadside with his lower jaw sliced off, a hand and a foot severed ...

But this is to anticipate. Jomo Kenyatta and four of his fellow accused were arrested in the first wave. The sixth was in prison

already. Nearly all the atrocities—on both sides—and the minia-
ture civil war that followed, occurred after the arrest of the KAU
leaders. On 17 September 1952 they were charged with managing,
or assisting to manage, Mau Mau.

We can now perhaps see in clearer perspective the significance
of the charge and of the trial. Kenyatta and his colleagues were
the leaders of an open, constitutional and in every sense legal
political movement, and, even more clearly, a movement which if
it followed its peaceful and constitutional course was achieving so
much support that its final success seemed reasonably near and
certain. Not only were the KAU leaders the representative men of
the current political drive, they were manifestly the inheritors of
all the traditions of East African nationalism. To identify Kenya
African Union with all its educational, religious and progressive
policies with the dark, barbarous and terrorist Mau Mau was a
charge of a gravity that can hardly be overstated.

In his last speech in court Kenyatta argued that "this case, from
our point of view, has been so arranged as to make scapegoats of
us in order to strangle the Kenya African Union, the only African
political organisation which fights for the African people." In his
eyes the trial was a machiavellian political manœuvre. Others went
farther and hinted that the whole policy behind the Proclamation
of Emergency was of a similar character. Certainly, from the point
of view of the settler, if KAU could be identified with Mau Mau
and shot down, there might be less to fear for a long time from
the roaring success of Kenyatta's KAU and its political campaign-
ing. Thus, whether the case was political or criminal, the issues it
was to decide were of supreme political importance for Kenya.

To the situation thus presented there are of course numerous
historical parallels. Nationalist movements normally begin with
open political parties but in moments of stress it sometimes happens that a secret terrorist movement starts a shooting war. Then
the questions have to be asked, Does the open political party
know what the terrorists are up to? Is it secretly involved? Is it
denouncing, or is it tacitly encouraging? Is it standing apart or
what is it doing?

The classic case is that of Parnell and the Phoenix Park murders. In the 1880's the agrarians, "the dynamiters" and "the
Invincibles" created a terror in Ireland. There was a veritable
network of secret societies with oaths, ritual and all the para-

phernalia. Parnell was leading the open political agitation of the Land League—very like the KAU. This did not stop Gladstone accusing him, as the Crown accused Kenyatta, that he "stood between the living and the dead, not like Aaron to stay the plague but to spread the plague". In 1881, 4,439 agrarian outrages were reported and Gladstone said, "with fatal and painful precision the steps of crime dogged the steps of the Land League!" The parallel with Kenya is surprisingly exact. In 1882 the new Irish Chief Secretary and the Permanent Under Secretary were murdered in broad daylight in Phoenix Park, Dublin. Parnell publicly denounced the murders, but six years later *The Times* reproduced facsimile letters purporting to show that he condoned them in private. There was a libel case and later a special commission of inquiry opened investigations which produced the result that one Richard Piggott confessed that he had forged the letters and sent them to *The Times*—then he shot himself.

If an open, legal and constitutional nationalist movement brings a campaign of terrorism in its train, can the crimes that follow be laid at the door of the political leaders? When Gandhi's campaigns of civil disobedience were followed by terrorist acts the pacifist leader went on hunger strike, removing himself temporarily from active life but not solving the problem. Dan Breen, by his own account the leading terrorist of the Irish troubles of 1919 and 1920, became in later life a senator and a respected figure in Eire. In 1924 he wrote in *My Fight for Irish Freedom* a classic autobiography of a terrorist, and here we can see the "open political movement" through the eyes of the gunman. His campaign began after the general election of 1919 when Sinn Fein swept the board in Ireland. At the very moment when constitutional settlement seemed round the corner the gunman broke loose. In Dan Breen's own account it was at first a purely individual effort by himself and a couple of friends in Tipperary. After their first two murders their fellow Volunteers tried to ship them to the U.S. They refused. "To leave Ireland would be like an admission that we were criminals, or that we were cowards. Now, more than ever, we declared that ... Ireland's fight would have to be made on the hills and at the crossroads of Ireland, not with printer's ink in America or any other country." And this, Dan Breen bitterly complains, "was apparently regarded as a breach of discipline". Throughout his story he is the tough guy against the namby-pamby leaders. He pours contempt on political action, "drawing room politicians", all forms of peaceful action, "cheap heroes" who go submissively to gaol without shooting a way out. The habit of gunplay is catching. Terror on one side produces terror on the other. Dan Breen was soon faced with the Black and Tans. Atrocity begot atrocity.

The point is a simple one. Terrorists, whether in Ireland or Palestine or India or Kenya, are a recognisable form of life and their separation from the open political movement is often as complete as that of the Indian terrorists from Gandhi or Nehru, and Dan Breen from de Valera or Griffiths. Terrorists are sometimes *agents provocateurs* but as often they are simple, impatient men who ruin the plans of the political leaders. Certainly this is what happened to Parnell. As one historian puts it, "the Phoenix Park murders did more than any other incident of his time and career to frustrate Parnell's policy and render Home Rule impossible". They helped to delay Irish independence by something like forty years. And, turning back to Kenya, this will perhaps give us a measure of the importance of the case *Queen against Kenyatta and others*, a measure of the weight of the charge and the significance of what had to be proved.

.   .   .   .   .

Two questions must be put to any record of a trial. The first is: Were the findings justified by the evidence? The second is the related but rather different question: Did the accused have a fair trial? In the nature of things the evidence in this case was difficult to get hold of. Terrorist organisations issue few manifestos. If British justice is to live up to its great name this makes it all the more necessary that what evidence there is shall be the more scrupulously weighed. The circumstances of the trial, the fact that it was held in a Colony in full state of Emergency, made it at once more difficult and more important to maintain the judicial attitude. The mental discipline to which lawyers subject themselves should be seen at its best when it is under strain. So we have to ask not only how did the protagonists behave, the prisoners and the witnesses, but how did the Magistrate and Counsel acquit themselves too.

The charge was managing Mau Mau—but not in general terms only, the offence was dated. The management was said to have been exercised between the dates 12th August 1950, when Mau Mau was first declared to be an unlawful society, and 21st October 1952, on which day all the accused "ceased to be free agents". To establish management the Crown relied on a series of incidents which were finally numbered by the Defence under 21 headings and set out in a table, produced in court, which is reproduced at the end of this book. Of the twenty-one incidents tabulated five took place before August 1950, the date when Mau Mau was proscribed. This led to argument whether the earlier evidence was admissible: to which the reply was made that if membership of Mau Mau before the date of proscription could be proved this made management after proscription seem more probable. The question is of more than technical interest, as we shall see.

Four of these "pre-proscription incidents" concern initiation ceremonies: they serve well to begin the story.

The first was on the face of it a fairly straightforward story by a certain Rawson Macharia that on an afternoon in March 1950 he drank with Kenyatta and some others in Joram Waweru's shop, and afterwards they went to Joram Waweru's house where Kenyatta initiated at least two of the company into Mau Mau, exacting from them a ritual oath and a fee of sixty-two shillings and fifty cents. The ceremony as described was mild and faintly Masonic in flavour, the only eerie detail being the eyes of a goat stuck on two sticks, which was afterwards described by a Crown witness as an old Kikuyu custom in oath-taking. The initiates had to take off their shoes and socks and pass through an arch of banana leaves. Mild as the ritual was, the words of the oath contained the criminal formula, "If you see an African killing anybody you must help him". There were not strict measures of secrecy. Rawson Macharia for instance had not been initiated, yet by his own account he was admitted to the ceremony, and later when he refused to take the oath himself no one seemed to be much put out. In cross-examination certain doubts were thrown on Macharia's story. He seemed obviously self-important and claimed close friendship with Jomo Kenyatta who on his side inferred that the witness was a pushful man and only a distant acquaintance. Macharia made a stupid mistake in his facts, insisting he had heard Kenyatta giving evidence before the Carter

Commission in Kenya in 1932 when in fact Kenyatta gave his evidence in London. The Crown called no witness to support his story but he mentioned a number of names and from this list of those present the Defence was able to call no fewer than nine people, plus of course Kenyatta, all of whom denied his story. Macharia by his own account had witnessed a crime yet he had to admit that he had kept the whole transaction "a secret in his bosom" for two years after it had happened.

Another initiation ceremony was mentioned by the next witness who, however, had the misfortune to leave before it took place. This was a tea-shop proprietor of the name of Muthondu who lives just less than a mile from Kenyatta's house. He told how one evening after a public meeting he went with a crowd of people to the house where he saw three dead goats, but he left before anything happened in order to put his chickens to bed. He was kept awake at night by the singing, seven furlongs away, and could report the sense of one of the songs which he had never heard before or since. Next morning a number of people came to his shop for tea and they had cuts on their hands from which he presumed they had all been initiated into Mau Mau. Again he was uncorroborated and again the Defence was able to call a number of those mentioned, all of whom denied his story.

A third initiation ceremony, also in March 1950, was the story of one Njui. This time the offence was reported without delay. Witness told his Chief, and later he made a statement before the District Officer as a result of which a man called Kiruki was arrested, though he was afterwards released on the grounds that there was no case. When the Defence eventually got hold of the record of the abandoned case and the statements made by this witness to the police, it turned out that he had not mentioned Mau Mau, nor had he implicated Kenyatta, though now in the witness box he swore that Kenyatta had initiated him personally. In his statement to the police at the time he had told exactly the same story about another man altogether, one Dedan Mugo, treasurer of the Kikuyu Age Groups, an organisation of some anthropological interest which was being used as an agency for collecting funds for the Independent Schools. Njui sought to account for the changes in his story by saying he had been threatened that his life would not be worth living if he mentioned Kenyatta to the police. Asked whether it would not be just as dangerous to mention Dedan Mugo, who was almost as prominent a politician as Kenyatta, he said yes it would but he happened to mention Dedan Mugo just the same. What made his story even weaker was that he admitted the alleged threats came *after* his statement to the police, not before. The Defence dubbed Njui "the season-ticket witness".

There was one other story of an alleged oath, though this was of a different kind and concerned only the accused Karumba. In this story a self-confessed police-informer said he was seized one night and made to swear on magic meat that he would give no information about Mau Mau, in other words he was not so much initiated as subjected to magic blackmail. The Defence claimed that when he ran into difficulties in his story he calmly changed its date by a whole year, and to the last it was never quite clear whether the incident should be dated June 1951 or June 1952.

There are certain common factors in these initiation stories. The terms of the oath and the ritual described by these witnesses are mild, except for the phrase already noted in Macharia's story. Taking off shoes, passing through arches and eating magic meat are common to most ceremonies of oaths—bride and bridegroom frequently pass through an arch after the taking of the European marriage oath. Judicially the important common factor is that none of them is corroborated except the weakest, Njui's, "the season-ticket witness", and his story to all intents and purposes was dropped.

So far then there was evidence of three oath-taking ceremonies before, and one after, Mau Mau had been proscribed. They are all rather insubstantial stories and none of them is supported. What Crown Counsel said about this was that though each by itself might mean very little they added up: the Crown relied on the "cumulative effect" of these stories in seeking to prove that before it was proscribed Kenyatta and his associates were managing Mau Mau.

About half-way through the case, and conspicuously during the cross-examination of Kenyatta, the Crown sought to strengthen this part of the case by adding the rider that Mau Mau was in reality the continuation of the proscribed Kikuyu Central Association. In 1948 when Kenyatta's negotiations with Sir Phillip Mitchell looked as though they might be successful he thought of calling together the former leaders of KCA to tell them what was going on. When in 1952 his papers were seized—in such quantity it took the police three weeks to sort them out—a draft circular signed by him was discovered. It was addressed "to all the leaders of KCA Kiambu" and said, "I want that you should come here on 20.8.48, together with four elders from each village" to discuss these things. Kenyatta said he afterwards changed his mind and the circular never went out. But the Crown case was that this showed he was managing an unlawful society in 1948, to wit the KCA, and that he continued to manage it under the name of Mau Mau. The reason for the change of name, Crown argued, was that Dedan Mugo had about this time been arrested and put in prison for administering an illegal oath binding those who swore it to the KCA.

There was one more incident in the period before proscription. An old acquaintance of Kenyatta's—he had known him years before in Paris—was making a deal to sell corrugated iron for roofing some of the Kikuyu Independent Schools, one morning in 1949, when in the course of conversation Kenyatta asked him to join "my society". When he asked "which society?" Kenyatta did not reply as might have been expected, "The Independent Schools Association", but "Mau Mau". When the witness was asked, Surely in 1949 the words Mau Mau were unknown? he replied, "The name was not known but the plan was known."

This then was the evidence on which the Prosecution had to build. The theory so far is that there was an organisation, the Kikuyu Central Association which was banned, went underground and, when detected again, changed its name to Mau Mau. Into this society Kenyatta was said to have initiated members up to a date some six months before proscription. The rest of the evidence came within the period mentioned in the charge sheet.

In the spring and early summer of 1952 KAU planned a series of meetings all over the colony, "a sort of stump campaign" was Crown Counsel's description. One of the reasons for this campaign according to Kenyatta's evidence was that allegations being made about KAU branches getting involved in Mau Mau activities made it desirable for him and his officers to make a round of personal visits to the branches. Official permission had to be given for all public meetings and the District Commissioner Kennaway, in whose district several of them were to be held, tried to impress on Kenyatta, when they discussed the permits, that denunciation of Mau Mau should be on the agenda. According to the District Commissioner, Kenyatta rather brushed this aside, saying, "They know about Mau Mau but these things they don't know about"— "these things" being the constitution, policy and proposals of the KAU. The District Commissioner was asked when cross-examined whether this meant more than a sensible decision to emphasise the positive aspects of KAU policy, and he had to agree that a political organisation could stultify itself if it spent all its time trying to refute any false charges its enemies liked to make.

Out of the so-called "stump campaign" came two blocks of evidence on which the Prosecution most relied. It turned out that when Kenyatta called on the District Commissioner he asked for permits for nine meetings but was granted only six. At the same time he was told there had been an outburst of local enterprise and a small branch, at a place called Limuru, had arranged for three meetings on its own. Kenyatta, who said he had never heard of the Limuru Branch, was curious to know what was going on, so along with Fred Kubai, editor of the KAU journal *Sauti ya Mwafrika*, he turned up at the third of the Limuru meetings.

They had to search for the meeting, it was not in the market-place where they would have expected to find it, but people heard they had arrived and began to gather, till eventually there were some two hundred round them sitting on the grass. Then the Limuru Chairman, Vice-Chairman, and Secretary turned to Kenyatta and each in his own words spoke to this effect: "People say you are the leader of Mau Mau as well as of KAU. Can you do something to clear this up?"

The main story was told in Court by Ephraim, the Secretary, whose version was that Kenyatta evaded the question and was indeed so incensed that he ordered the office bearers to come to head office in Nairobi where they were closed down as a branch. Rather late in the day, and by chance, the Defence came on a report in a vernacular newspaper of this meeting—the find was a piece of luck for the Defence since Kenyatta's papers had been seized by the police, the trial was held three hundred miles away from Nairobi, and there was little chance of consulting files. They found that in this report in *Mumenyereri*, the branch officers' questions and Kenyatta's answers were faithfully recorded. Kenyatta, as asked, dissociated himself from Mau Mau, saying "I don't know the animal—if you can find it, hit it with an axe-handle", which he said later was a stronger metaphor in Kikuyu than it sounds. Traditionally the axe-handle is the weapon kept till last, and it is as much as if we said, "Club it with a rifle butt." What was more, the report went on to describe the Limuru branch in terms to which its officers took such grave exception that they threatened legal action. It was this, according to Kenyatta, that brought Ephraim and his colleagues to Nairobi head office, and Ephraim admitted that this was indeed one of the things they came to complain of. The report said they belonged not to KAU at all, but to something called "The Association of Those Who Wait", and in court they admitted membership after some hesitation. Indeed, in the end, it came out that it was not being called members of this sect that they objected to, but the fact that the newspaper report said they took their oath on a chicken. Ephraim had said that in head office Kenyatta came out with the phrase, "Leave Mau Mau alone, it is a *dini*"—that is to say a religious sect. To this Kenyatta replied that they were not talking about Mau Mau at all but about "The Association of Those Who Wait" which is a *dini* and proud of it. The episode is small in scale, but the Prosecution and the Magistrate found it important in implication: indeed it is perhaps to the point that the Magistrate found it almost the strongest evidence against Kenyatta that the trial produced.

The rest was more indirect: indeed the next episode was the tale of Tabitha, a young woman described as a police agent (an informer, the Court was told, acts for money but an agent acts for love). Tabitha listened outside a door and heard Kenyatta telling a group of people not to use so much violence in taking the oath, or the police would get on their tracks. Kenyatta was still on his speaking tour; those he was supposed to be warning were comparative strangers; and, according to Tabitha, they included a young woman called Wambui who was later discovered by the Defence to be the mistress of the local police inspector. Tabitha said Wambui came out just after Kenyatta had spoken the tell-tale words and Tabitha went in. There was some natural dispute whether in fact Tabitha could have heard anything of what was said from where she described herself as standing outside the closed door. According to Tabitha Wambui was in the room, but the Prosecution did not call Wambui, indeed the police inspector was cagey about her till the Defence interviewed and then called Wambui. Wambui said she was not in the room at all.

The rest of the evidence against the chief accused was derived from his public speeches and the words from a set of song books which later came to be called "hymn books". Prosecution set out to prove that in his speeches Kenyatta was anti-European. In this they ran into the danger of proving too much, for Kenyatta was thus given the opportunity to show that the struggle of the Kenya African Union for the rights and dignities of the African had sometimes a look of statesmanship. So much for the "anti-European speeches". Another batch remains to be considered which may be called "the anti-Mau Mau speeches". Here the Prosecution had to prove that the speaker really meant the opposite of what he said. In one case he was said to have denounced Mau Mau publicly but to have added in Kikuyu "Take a pinch of snuff" from which the witness, a self-declared police informer (professional this time), concluded he meant "take a pinch of salt—you can go on taking Mau Mau oath". When the Prosecution called an expert witness on the Kikuyu language he thought the phrase had only its literal meaning and not the figurative meaning it has in English.

From the beginning Crown Counsel had emphasised that "failure to denounce" Mau Mau was no part of the Prosecution's case, but from the Limuru incident onwards it inevitably became part of the case, and in the Magistrate's final judgment it moved near to the centre. Now it so happened that in August 1952, at the end of the "stump campaign", Kenyatta joined with a group of other Africans in a sort of united front anti-Mau Mau demonstration which has already been referred to. This was the big public meeting at Kiambu. The Prosecution at first seemed to forget this meeting. When the Defence adduced evidence, Crown Counsel again had the task of trying to show that this solemn curse administered by Kenyatta to the crowd was not what it seemed, while the Magistrate favoured an ingenious argument that it was really a method of telling Mau Mau to go underground.

Last came the "hymn books" or political song books sold by KAU members. To these the Crown attached a good deal of importance—indeed Crown Counsel sometimes seemed to think this evidence alone would be decisive: the Magistrate on the other hand chose to pass over the "hymn books" lightly. Perhaps he was

justified, for what we get even in the sort of translations that came
out of the heated court-room are two or three poems of a kind
familiar in many a nationalist movement. They bring to mind
Irish songs like "The Bold Robert Emmett", or even "The Wearing of the Green".

The evidence against Kenyatta only has been given in this preliminary outline, for the additional evidence against some of the
other five prisoners complicates the picture without changing it.
Against one of them Paul Ngei there was evidence that in a
drunken row with a District Officer, and later in a letter, he as
good as admitted membership of Mau Mau. The evidence against
the others was a great deal less definite than this. Were they
guilty or not guilty? This is what the reader will have to decide.
He will first have to make up his mind whether the slightness of
the evidence is the result of innocence or cunning. If the evidence
is thin, is there perhaps a good reason for this?

The case is strongest in the period before Mau Mau was proscribed—that is to say in the period before 10th August 1950, the
date mentioned in the charge sheet. We may or may not think that
the witness Rawson Macharia was bumptious and unreliable but
at least he says (though without corroboration) that he saw
Kenyatta administering a Mau Mau oath. We may think what we
will of Njui whom Defence called "the season-ticket witness" but
at least he says he saw Kenyatta administering the Mau Mau oath.
We may or may not think that Muthondu the tea-shop man was
rather an unconvincing witness but at least he says he heard singing in the middle of the night and people came to drink tea next
morning with cuts on their hands. If it is argued that these witnesses prove that Jomo Kenyatta was administering the Mau Mau
oath and running nocturnal sing-songs before Mau Mau was proscribed, Defence might well reply—and did—"Very well, for the
sake of argument you might assume this for the moment, but we
would then say he stopped these activities the moment Mau Mau
was made illegal," and the reader now looks for the evidence of
accused being active in the affairs of Mau Mau after proscription.
He finds that it turns, so far as Jomo Kenyatta is concerned, on the
evidence of what Tabitha heard outside the door, plus whatever
can be made of Ephraim and the Limuru incident. Defence argue
that after cross-examination the most that can be made of the
Limuru incident is that if, like the Magistrate, we believe all the

Prosecution witnesses and disbelieve all Defence witnesses, the three office bearers asked Kenyatta to denounce Mau Mau to their branch; he did so and the press report is produced, but his denunciation was considered insincere. Later in the head office they say he told them to "leave Mau Mau alone it is a *dini*" that is to say a religious sect. Manifestly this would be an insubstantial foundation on which to base charges of managing Mau Mau.

Moreover, it is clear that during this period, after the proscription of Mau Mau in August 1950, Kenyatta was the most notorious or—we can take our choice—the most popular personality in Kenya. Running his "stump campaign", touring the country, a spell-binder with audiences of 50,000 at a time, the leader of the Kenya African Union which was reaching the height of its influence, growing in numbers and popularity every day, Kenyatta was living in a floodlight of publicity.

A public personage like this has little private life. Thus if the Crown, or anyone else, wanted evidence about what such a notorious individual was up to, it ought to be easy. Wherever he went the crowds followed. Wherever he slept there were Tabithas outside the door. If he had really been managing Mau Mau at this time would there not have been some evidence better than Tabitha's? Or is this a sign in itself of effective security measures by the Manager of Mau Mau?

Finally the Crown Counsel collected all newspaper reports that could be found of Kenyatta speeches, particularly the numerous reports in which there was no mention that he denounced Mau Mau, and put them one after another to the witness with the question, Was this report fair and accurate? and—not surprisingly —always got the answer no. The politician does not exist who would agree that a ten-line summary of his speech got in all he said! The process of putting these newspaper reports to Kenyatta in the box went on so long that it began to seem interminable. The point intended—and effectively scored—was the small amount given in the reports to denunciation of Mau Mau. What was perhaps not so clear was that by implication Kenyatta was being asked to prove himself innocent, and a mighty denouncer of Mau Mau, or in default he would be presumed guilty as one of Mau Mau's managers.

In asking were the accused guilty or not guilty the reader will find it difficult not to take a glance outside the court-room. The question, Was it a fair trial? comes within a narrower compass. Certainly to some degree the traditions of British justice were maintained. At a time when passion and prejudice were beating with hurricane force on the walls of the court-room the form and order of British justice was maintained—by and large. But this being admitted, a number of other questions remain. Formally it was a trial properly conducted in the British way of law. But in detail can we say that the Magistrate acted judicially? The Defence said no, They claimed that "The Magistrate accepted practically every application, motion or submission made by the Prosecution . . . and rejected practically every application, motion, or submission" by the Defence. He "accepted as truthful every witness called by the Prosecution, no matter what their character or history, however improbable their stories were, how gravely they contradicted themselves, or how badly their stories were shaken in cross-examination": and at the same time he "rejected as untruthful every witness called by the Defence, no matter what their character or history, however fully they were corroborated, or however intrinsically probable their stories were." The Defence found the Magistrate's judgments "perverse" and his mind prejudiced. The Defence claimed he admitted such a large body of legally inadmissible evidence that his findings of fact were untenable. They complained, too, that he held up the trial for three weeks while the leading Defence Counsel was tried for contempt of court—a charge which the Supreme Court of Kenya dismissed without hesitation. On appeal, the Magistrate was supported by the Supreme Court of Kenya, though with some remarkable comments. The Privy Council in rejecting a petition from the accused took their stand on a refusal to reconsider the case.

Here then, for the reader's inspection, is a full summary of *Queen against Kenyatta and others*. It should be emphasised that it is no more than a summary, for the whole of this book amounts to only about one-tenth of the transcript of the trial. This naturally raises the question of the fairness of the summary. And here I have had to take account of the fact that my own normal sympathies would be more likely to be on the side of the leaders of the Kenya African Union, though not on the side of the leaders of Mau Mau, and I might therefore have a more pronounced tendency to differentiate between the two than we should find in, say, Prosecuting Counsel. How was I to ensure that this attitude would not be reflected in the selection of evidence to be given verbatim and that to be given in précis form? One fairly obvious rule to follow was to give the Crown most of the verbatim reporting while summarising the Defence evidence more drastically. Of the following pages some 100 are devoted to evidence for the Crown, and this represents 644 pages of the transcript. To the evidence for the Defence I have given 60 pages, which represents 1,100 pages of the transcript. The whole transcript fills some 2,000 pages, the remainder being taken up by Counsel's speeches.

In addition, I have had full discussions with friends who have read the typescript and with the publishers; and, listening to their comments, I have twice gone back to the transcript and carefully revised the account of the trial in the hope of avoiding any feeling that points may have been glossed over, or incriminating evidence not given due weight. I am now convinced in my own mind that the summary is not only as fair as I can make it, but is in fact a true account of the trial.

.   .   .   .   .

One of the incidental features of interest in the story is the vivid cross-section it gives of life in Kenya before the Emergency. Do you want to know what it felt like to be running a political campaign in Kenya at that time? What kind of person was a trade union organiser in Kenya and what sort of life did he lead? What was the climate like and the transport? How much pay did you get—or more accurately, how little—as a night watchman, a Post and Telegraph clerk? Where would you buy your London Sunday newspaper in Nairobi? (The answer is Woolworths.) It will even answer such questions as, What was it like to be a prostitute in rural Kenya at that time? What sort of person would the prostitute be and what sort of life would she lead? More important it has a great deal to tell us about how the Kikuyu were building up their education system and their schools; and of their attitude to European customs and Indian customs.

Most of the stories are self-explanatory, and there is no need for footnotes, though perhaps one or two small points should be made in advance. The currency in East Africa is in shillings and cents—ten cents are a penny and there are no pounds. Brought up on

"Westerns" we are apt to think of a Chief as some sort of heredi-
tary nobleman. The Kikuyu like many African tribes have no
chiefs. The Chiefs who appear are official personages appointed
and paid by the Government with the status of something like a
parish clerk or even a Town Clerk. The spelling of African names
is a little hard to settle since we depend on transliteration from
another alphabet and the systems of transliteration vary. By and
large names are spelled as they sound, though a thing to remember is that the frequent prefix M or N should be pronounced Um
or Un, so we get Njui pronounced Unjooey or Mbari pronounced
Umbahri.

2

The Case is Opened

On 17th November 1952 an acting Superintendent of the Kenya CID, Special Branch, Supt. K. R. T. Goodale, applied before a District Commissioner, who was also a Magistrate, for warrants to arrest Jomo Kenyatta and five others on charges of membership and management of Mau Mau. He made his application in a remote country station near the northern boundaries of Kenya, 280 miles from Nairobi and the homes of the accused. The place chosen was Kapenguria, a station so little known even to the officials in Nairobi that when they came to appoint a Resident Magistrate to hear the case they appointed him to the wrong province by mistake. For while Superintendent Goodale was getting his warrants from the DC in Kapenguria, the Governor of Kenya was in Nairobi signing letters patent to appoint a retired judge formerly of the Kenya Supreme Court, Mr R. S. Thacker, QC, as a Resident Magistrate in the Northern Province especially to hear this case in Kapenguria which is in the Rift Valley Province. But this was excusable since few people had heard of the place before the Special Branch picked it out for notoriety. The six prisoners—five of them were already detainees and a sixth in prison on a previous charge—were moved as fast as possible to Kapenguria where next day they were brought before the DC and remanded in custody.

Outside the houses of the DC and the District Officer there is not much to see in Kapenguria. There is a big prison and a small court-house, and two miles away a school of agriculture. The Suk people who live there are a pastoral tribe. There is little cultivation, there are no settlers, and the desert begins only ten miles away. Kapenguria lacks amenities and the distractions of a busier world. There are no telephones—no railway, no hotel and the road is poor. When a car overturns the first man you tell is sympathetic but he will add something like, "Oh, that hasn't happened to me for nearly a month."

Outside the DC's house is a small court-room but plainly it was insufficient to accommodate this trial with its counsel for prosecution and defence, court officials, interpreters, court reporters, military escort for magistrate and lawyers, and a large number of witnesses and journalists. But there is still the agricultural school and it was decided to make this do. True the biggest room in Kapenguria school house was so small that everyone seemed to be sitting in each other's pockets, and when leading Counsel whispered in the ear of one of his juniors, Prosecuting Counsel and the Magistrate could hear what was said, and quite often the whispered aside got itself incorporated in the verbatim transcript of the proceedings. Still, space was found at the back of the room for members of the public, divided into two parts, officials and their families, and "the rest". "The public" in this court was practically all European, for Kapenguria was a closed area. It was as much as a Kikuyu's life was worth to come into the area without a pass, passes for Africans were hard to come by, and most of the local Suk tribesmen were too canny or too shy to appear. The crowd of Europeans at the back of the court-room made its presence felt from time to time by applause which made no pretence of being anything but partial.

At Kitale, 24 miles away, there was hotel accommodation for the European Counsel. Defence Counsel however were not all European, indeed they were preponderantly Indian and Nigerian. These last were prevented by the colour-bar from visiting or eating at the hotel. They lived at first with Asian merchants, who sometimes complained that the settlers were boycotting their business as a result, and later in the proceedings the lawyers were offered a virtually unfurnished bungalow for their accommodation. When leading Defence Counsel wanted to hold a consultation with his colleagues they would go to a non-colour-bar hotel and experiment with Asian or African food, or tax again the hospitality of the Asian merchants. To add to their discomforts, after the first few weeks, they had to be guarded night and day by police who apparently feared unpleasantness from the settlers. The boundary of the closed area was nine miles from Kapenguria, and, when a Defence car crossed the line, things began to look a little film-like. In front drove a fast police-car in a cloud of dust, a little way behind the Defence car followed with dust-bespattered lawyers or witnesses, then came another police car. If there happened to be a Kikuyu in the Defence car there were extra precautions, and the car was instructed "to proceed without halting from the frontier to the court". Hence, naturally, minor difficulties. Witnesses waiting to be called had to be fed, which meant that food had to be fetched from outside the closed area. More trouble, more passes, and, what was still more awkward, one of the cars had a Kikuyu driver. Defence, again, were short of money, and the cars they had to use reflected this. The daily journeys, sometimes twice a day, back and forth on 24 miles of spectacularly bad roads, told their tale. Defence cars kept breaking down. All these things affected in their small but searching ways the atmosphere of the trial.

What was still more important was the knowledge that, from now on, Kapenguria was news. The world's press crowded the court. Whatever happened there took place, so to say, under the eyes of interested or merely curious readers all over the world. Sometimes Defence Counsel found it to the point to refer to this invisible gallery. Once, at least, Crown Counsel got rather cross about such references. But whatever anybody felt about it, Kapenguria remained news to the end of the trial. For all the long five months it was given full coverage.

This international interest in the proceedings was to be seen too in the composition of the Defence team. From Nairobi came a Punjabi barrister, Kapila; a Sikh, Jaswant Singh; a Goan, De Souza; and from Tanganyika a Jamaican, Dudley Thompson. H. O. Davies, of Lagos, the only African counsel, was a key member of the team and bore a major part of the burden from the start. From further afield came D. N. Pritt, QC, from London to lead the Defence, and he was assisted by Chaman Lall, a distinguished lawyer from India, who, until just before the trial, was Indian Ambassador in Turkey. Two or three volunteered to come from the Sudan but they were told they would not be admitted. One or two did come from the Gold Coast but on their arrival at Nairobi they were refused entry into the Colony. An Indian lawyer, Sethi, also arrived at the airport but at first he was not allowed to enter, later he was admitted—but only on the unhelpful condition that he must not go anywhere near the case. The refusals were based on

an argument that the Government were not satisfied that the
accused wanted the services of these Counsel, which brought the
prompt reply that nobody had asked them, and if they had been
asked the answer would have been certainly yes. And later the
Defence argued that all this was a remarkable demonstration of
solidarity—and of Government obstruction to the elementary
rights of Defence. For as the case opened out Defence Counsel
found that its complexities called for much legal manpower. They
wanted something like three lawyers on the spot to conduct the
case, and four or five to travel about Kenya finding more witnesses,
investigating facts and tracing documents. For not only was the
case colony-wide, embracing events and persons all over Kenya,
but proceedings—and this again was a cause of repeated protest
—were what are in England called "summary proceedings", in
the sense that there were no preliminary hearings or exchange of
papers, none of the elaborate preparations which in England
precede the hearing of anything but the lightest charges. And this
meant for the Defence that the case was being unfolded from
hour to hour: and, as Defence Counsel was to put it later in the
trial, until the day's instalment of the serial story had been told,
and late in the afternoon he had the chance to consult his clients,
until then, he was "as ignorant as any beggar in Nairobi—perhaps
even more ignorant"—about what his clients were going to say.

This is to anticipate a little, but it is perhaps useful in giving
the reader some notion of the form the proceedings are going to
take. This form essentially means that the case comes out in a
series of surprises—which perhaps helps to keep the story interesting, but makes a certain amount of anticipation necessary if it
is to be clear.

It began quietly, in the pidgin-English phrase, "small small".
Mr Thacker took his seat on the improvised bench in the schoolroom in Kapenguria on 24 November 1952. Two counsel, A. R.
Kapila and Dudley Thompson appeared for Defence. The Crown
was represented by Deputy Public Prosecutor Somerhough. (The
"deputy" in his title is deceptive, for he is in practice the Public
Prosecutor though the title itself is reserved for the Attorney General of Kenya who is also the Member for Law and Order. This
tripple-wigged official does not appear in court himself but appears
in the person of the lawyer commonly known as "the DPP".) The
interpreter from Kikuyu was Dr S. L. B. Leakey, well known for

his anthropological researches among the Kikuyu. Dr Leakey's main work on this subject was not yet ready for publication though he had recently edited some of the material in handy form for a short book which was published during the trial and later was cited by the Defence as one of the reasons for questioning the interpreter's impartiality.

The first session was brief. All the accused pleaded not guilty and Mr Kapila applied for an adjournment, saying the Defence would be led by Mr D. N. Pritt, QC, and he asked for two week's adjournment for Mr Pritt to get there. In these days of air travel DPP Somerhough thought two weeks too long ("Pritt can get here in three or four days") the Magistrate compromised with a ten days' adjournment and listened to an application from Defence Counsel Mr Kapila for "further and better particulars of the facts".

These, the Magistrate formally refused. "To order the Crown to give further particulars would, I consider, be equivalent to order-ing the Crown to show what evidence it proposes to give, and that I am not prepared to do." This became a point later when Defence argued that it was almost without precedent that a case of this importance should be launched without preliminary hearings.

On 3rd December Mr Pritt appeared in the Kapenguria school house and asked for bail for at least five of his clients. (Paul Ngei was already serving a short term of imprisonment.) "It would be of substantial convenience if bail could be granted on terms which permitted the accused to go to Kitale," 24 miles away where the hotel was, but failing this Counsel asked for a schoolroom to be allotted where Counsel could meet their clients. He was refused the bail but granted the schoolroom. Now Mr. Pritt said he was not going to ask for an adjournment, it would be no use to him until he knew something about the Crown case. "My clients and I know nothing about it whatsoever. We have a charge sheet and a refusal of any particulars." For the present he limited himself to asking, "in order to save inconveniences to many people who have been brought from their natural bases that for the first few witnesses at any rate evidence-in-chief shall be taken and cross-examination postponed" until he had had time to consult with the accused. "Perhaps today things could be taken a little slowly and there should be an adjournment at say 3 p.m. when at any rate we shall know something about the Prosecution case." This was

B

granted and the case opened, by Deputy Public Prosecutor Somerhough.

> May it please Your Honour ... The charge is that of managing an unlawful society ... I would ask Your Honour to take notice of the prohibition of this Society published in the Gazette of the Colony, and its effective date which is 12th August 1950. The dates between which the charges are set are 12th August 1950 and 21st October 1952 the date on which the accused, or at least five of them, ceased to be free agents.
> The Crown cannot bind themselves to any particular place in the Colony where this society was managed. The Society is Mau Mau. It is a Society which has no records. It appears to have no official list of members. It does not carry banners. Some details of its meetings and its rites, the instruments of which are got from the local bush, will be heard later in the proceedings. Arches of banana leaves, the African fruit known as the Apple of Sodom, eyes of sheep, blood and earth—these are all gathered together when ceremonies take place.

After this colourful introduction Counsel dropped into prose. The society first came to notice in late 1948 or early 1949, becoming more active in late 1949 and very active in 1950: "so active that it was proscribed". "Fundamentally it is a Kikuyu society." The first block of evidence aimed to connect Jomo Kenyatta with the society in late 1949 and early 1950, though at that time it was not an unlawful society. "The Crown will argue that if they can show that Jomo Kenyatta was actively concerned with it then, if this is taken together with his activities afterwards, the result will be to prove that he has been a member all the time." This was the first statement of what came to be the most discussed features of the case, that is to say the use of what came to be called "pre-proscription evidence".

The Prosecution's first character sketches of the accused threw light both on the accused and the mental climate of the trial. The DPP opened with Kenyatta. "His name is stated to be Johnston, John or Jomo Kenyatta. As far as the Crown knows, and subject to correction as the birth dates of Africans are always rather misty, his date of birth was 1893." He was educated at the Scotch Mission at Dagoretti and worked at one time for the Nairobi Municipality, "it is believed as a meter reader". Later he went into politics and travelled extensively in England and on the Continent and was at the London School of Economics. He returned to Kenya in 1946 and entered the political field again. At that time the leading African political organisation was the Kenya African Union. "I will henceforth refer to this as KAU (pronounced *cow*) as everyone else does in this country." KAU succeeded the Kikuyu Central Association. Very soon Kenyatta became a dominant figure and interested himself in African education, schools and the management of the African Teacher's Association at Githunguri. In 1947 he was elected President of KAU and still held this office. "I think it would be fair to describe Kenyatta at this stage as an exceptionally widely travelled and educated African who has had the advantage of contact with a great many people of standing both in Kenya and in Europe, and who has interested himself in politics, in his fellow countrymen and so on, particularly through his connection with education and his presidency of KAU. Perhaps the shortest and best description of Jomo Kenyatta is that he is in a class by himself."

The rest may be summarised. *Fred Kubai* on the Executive Council of KAU was a labour leader and former President "of an organisation which no longer exists called the East African Trade Union Congress." *Richard Achieng Oneke*, aged 32, an African Councillor on Nairobi Municipal Council in 1949, has lived in London and Paris, was "the present substantive secretary of KAU."

Bildad Kaggia was in the British Army from 1942 to 1946, a former clerk in the National Bank of India, an ex-editor of a Kikuyu journal, member of the KAU executive, and chairman of one of its branches. *Kungu Karumba*, "of a slightly different calibre from the others", knew no English, was secretary of a local branch (the Chura branch of KAU). *Paul Ngei*, one of the two accused who was not a Kikuyu—belongs to a tribe called the Wakamba and was said to be their leader in KAU

At this point Crown introduced an argument which presently became crucial.

> The Crown case is going to be that Mau Mau is part of KAU —a militant part, a sort of Stern gang, if I may borrow a phrase from another country. It is possible to be a member of KAU and have nothing to do with Mau Mau: yet Mau Mau itself is a definite limb or part of KAU as it existed in 1952 when all the accused were closely connected with KAU as high office bearers.

Later, the Defence was to argue that from this moment this became a political case, though the Crown maintained to the end that it was an "ordinary criminal case".

The first block of evidence to be outlined concerned a political campaign. Early in 1952 Jomo Kenyatta held a series of meetings all over Kenya.

> It was a sort of stump campaign. At that time the authorities were becoming more and more concerned about the more violent activities of Mau Mau, and were finding it difficult to separate it from the normal procedure and proper activities of KAU. So, as many members of KAU were saying that it had nothing to do with Mau Mau, and as Jomo Kenyatta was professing, as he is doing even now, not to know what Mau Mau is, some encouragement was given to the office bearers and branches of KAU to make public announcements and to make it clear that KAU and Mau Mau were nothing to do with each other.

In accordance with this policy when the office bearers of a branch of the Kenya Africa Union in a place called Limuru applied to the DC to hold a series of KAU meetings denouncing the activities of Mau Mau, they were given permission to do so, and in fact held three meetings. The first two "passed off peacefully". They "said their pieces", denouncing Mau Mau and said it had nothing to do with KAU, and KAU must come into the open and say so. But at the third meeting there were two unexpected visitors.

> Jomo Kenyatta and Fred Kubai turned up. They were asked by the office bearers at the meeting to take a stand about KAU being nothing to do with Mau Mau, and the Court will hear what happened.

> They summoned the three office bearers of the Limuru branch to the KAU headquarters in Nairobi, where it seemed there was an Executive Committee of KAU, and all the accused were present. Very briefly, what was said at the meeting was that they repeated their protest about Mau Mau, and they received instructions from Jomo Kenyatta that Mau Mau was a religion and not to be interfered with. They were also told that they should join the Chura branch of KAU.

The branch officials protested, the DPP went on, that all who joined the Chura branch were forced to take the Mau Mau oath—it was apparently a condition of entry. They were over-ruled and told they must join the Chura branch or close down.

Your Honour, I claim that this was an act from which membership can be inferred and management can be inferred, and that it showed a close alliance between KAU as run by the organising committee, and Mau Mau which was then running like wildfire through the colony.

Other meetings followed and, according to the Prosecution, crime followed the meetings.

The Crown will call the DC from Laikipia, and he will tell the Court of the circumstances immediately following the meeting of KAU—a very big meeting—at Thomson's Falls on June 29th. Immediately after this there was a wild outbreak of Mau Mau activity in the neighbourhood. It is the business of these gentlemen as everyone knows to govern their districts and to know what is going on in them. If there is a wave of outrages and murders, they are the first to know about them, this is their business.

(When it came to the point this evidence was disallowed.)

The political campaign was continued after that. Crown Counsel went on. There was a very large meeting at Nyeri which was covered by the police, and at that meeting Jomo Kenyatta and Achieng spoke "and considerable feeling was whipped up". In July 1952 Jomo Kenyatta "told the public that he did not know what Mau Mau was".

MAGISTRATE: When did he say this?

DPP: He was addressing a local public meeting. It was a very large meeting, and the people came from Nairobi in crowds, I understood there were 40 bus-loads from Nairobi alone.

This brief passage gives some notion of the scale of open political activity in the Kenya of 1952. Naturally as well as speeches there was literature. The DPP described the printed exhibits he was to produce, a number of song books, which later came to be called "hymn books", at which Defence protested, and still later they began to be known by the Kikuyu word for hymn book, Nyimbo. These songs books, said the DPP, made their appearance at the Thomson's Falls meeting, or to be more precise, after the meeting, when Jomo Kenyatta was accommodated at the house of the local chairman, and crowds of people gathered round and sang mission tunes with new words. There were several editions of the songs, a Yellow Edition found in Kenyatta's house when his papers were seized; and in this, the Yellow Book, was a song or hymn which referred to Mau Mau by name. The names of the accused, especially Kenyatta, Kubai and Achieng frequently appeared in the songs. Moreover, in Kenyatta's house was found a black exercise book in which versions of these songs appeared in manuscript. Moreover, there was a Grey Edition, a Red, a Purple, and a Pale Blue.

MAGISTRATE: These are the colours of the covers?
DPP: Yes.
Q: Is any significance attached to the covers?
A: I think not. They are by different hymnologists if I may coin a word, and there is evidence that Kaggia, when stopped, was accompanied by 100 copies of the pale blue edition which he had apparently been distributing.

There were six prisoners and six variations of the Prosecution case. Crown case against Kenyatta had been outlined.

The evidence against Kubai is that he is a very prominent figure in the Transport Workers' Union. The principal members of this union are taxi drivers in Nairobi. The Crown will be calling a witness to say how Kubai endeavoured to introduce the oath into the ranks of the taxi drivers' union. Indeed, according to Kubai, if one does not take Mau Mau oath one's taxi-driving days are over, or at any rate limited.

(This witness from the Nairobi taxi-drivers never apeared. Nothing was heard of him after the Crown opening.)

Against Ngei the evidence is really his own declaration. He has on two occasions made declarations about Mau Mau; on one occasion when he was taken into custody on some minor offence, he was extremely violent, announced his membership of Mau Mau and the fate that would overtake all who opposed it. On the other occasion he composed a little song in praise of Mau Mau which he suggested should be set to the music of George Formby.

(Perhaps it is an example of the powerful appeal of George Formby's films in Africa that henceforward this song is referred to by all parties in the case as "the George Formby song", a little unfairly since it is quite clear that, apart from singing it, George Formby had about as much to do with the song as he had with Mau Mau. For when the evidence was heard Ngei described himself in a letter from prison as singing "Bless Mau Mau" to the tune of *Bless 'em All*, the charming folk-song, which we owe like so much of our current slang less to George Formby than to the RAF. Nor, surprisingly, did it occur to anyone to point out that the song is ironical, and that though in respectable versions we use the word "Bless", the real word is ruder and shorter by one letter.)

And now, said the DPP, he had given his learned friends an idea of what to expect, and he sat down; but rose again to ask that when a witness did not wish his name to be disclosed the Magistrate should request the press not to disclose it. The Defence objected that this would be a convenience to witnesses wishing to commit perjury and thought witnesses' names should be given, and the press allowed to use its own discretion. To this the DPP replied that it was not a question of witnesses committing perjury but committing suicide, and had his way. From this moment every Prosecution witness was asked if he wanted his name suppressed. If he said yes his name was not given in the newspaper reports of the trial at the time. In the following pages, however, all names are given. Practically all the Prosecution witnesses asked for their names not to be used, though for a moment it looked as though the first witness was going to be an exception.

3

Oath-Taking

THIS was Rawson Mbogwa Macharia who appeared in the box
and announced his intention of giving his evidence in English, "as
it would be less cumbersome than Kikuyu and he was afraid of
giving a wrong impression."

"He would be just as likely to give a wrong impression in English," commented the magistrate, drawing the reply: "Some words
in Kikuyu take three to make a word in English."

MAGISTRATE: Very well, you can give your evidence in English.
 You seem to speak it very well. Are you a Christian?
MACHARIA: Yes.
Q: Do you object to your name being published in the press?
A: No, sir.

A trader, 33, a member of KAU from 1944 to 1949, he claimed
to know Kenyatta "very well, he is my neighbour."

Q: Have you known him long?
A: Very long. The first time I saw him was in 1932 when he
 came to give evidence before the Commission, the Carter Commission. And my second contact with him was in 1946, the last
 time he came from England. I live one and three-quarter miles
 from his house.
Q: Did you know know him socially as well as politically?
A: When he first came from Europe he found me as general
 secretary to the branch of KAU. I know him socially too.
Q: In the course of these years when you held office in KAU
 did you in due course hear of an organisation called Mau Mau?
A: Yes, in 1950. It was during the month of March, on the 16th.

Defence objected that evidence of association with a society
when it was not unlawful had nothing to do with the case. Objection overruled.

SOMERHOUGH (to witness): Go slowly through it, and tell us
 about the 16th of March 1950.

MACHARIA: I was at a place called Kaimwange in the Kiambu district. It was round about 3.30 p.m., when I saw Mr Jomo Kenyatta and another person called George Waiyaki. They came in the latter's boxbody car. They found me with another three people in a certain man's shop. It was Joram Waweru's shop. After arriving we greeted them and then we sat down all together. I bought three bottles of English beer for Jomo Kenyatta. We started drinking. When drinking of course we had general conversation. The general topic was whether Africans were up to the standard or ready for their self-government. Then I saw a person called Solomon Memia a few yards from the place where we were sitting. Then George Waiyaki asked Mr Kenyatta whether that chap was initiated.

Q: You mean Solomon Memia? Will you please use the Kikuyu word for initiating.

A: Yes. Ruruithio—it means initiation. Then Mr Kenyatta stood up and told George Waiyaki "that is what I am trying to find out myself". Then he called Joram Waweru and then they went a few yards, about fifty, from the place where we were sitting. They had a private talk for a few minutes, roughly 30 minutes. Then they came back together.

Q: Was there any more discussion about oaths?

A: Mr Kenyatta did send for Samuel Kihara, Harrison Gachukia, Stephano Kamugu, William Kibera and someone called Ephantos Waithaka. Then we were put in a big house.

Q: Tell us what happened.

A: Immediately when we arrived I saw the head of a goat and blood mixed with earth and stomach contents. These were in a calabash. Also goat's meat roasted, and there was an arch which was made of grass and banana leaves and sugar cane leaves.

Q: How high was the arch?

A: About four feet. The goat's meat and blood was next to Mr Kenyatta. Harrison Gachukia was sitting on the other side, on the left side of Mr Kenyatta. George Waiyaki was facing Mr Kenyatta, opposite.

Q: Now, you told us about seeing a goat's head and stomach contents, etc. Did you notice anything peculiar about the goat's head?

A: The tongue had been taken out.

Q: Anything else?

A: And the top end of the neck, and the eyes were taken out of the head. These eyes were placed on the side of the calabash and were stuck on thorns . . .

Q: After that, what next did you see or hear?

B*

A: The next thing I heard was Solomon Memia was asked by Samuel Kihara to take off his clothes and shoes. He took off his clothes and remained only with short underwear.

Q: Who told him to take off his clothes?

A: Samuel Kihara. Then he was asked by Mr Kenyatta to stand stationary, and told he was going to be initiated, and then he would become a true Kikuyu. He was then ordered by Mr Kenyatta to pass through the arch, and then to respond to the following words: "When we agree to drive Europeans away you must take an active part in driving them away or killing them."

MAGISTRATE: Jomo Kenyatta said this?

A: Yes, Mr Kenyatta said this. "If you see any African killing anyone, you must not disclose it or tell anyone. If you shall see an African stealing, you must help him. You must pay sixty-two shillings and fifty cents to this society." Then he said: "And that is Mau Mau, and you must not ask how this money is used, and if you shall be asked whether you are a member of this society you must say you are a member of KAU." When responding to these words, in every single word he had to pass through the arch and eat a part of the meat. That is, the chest meat and the Ngata. Also, the eyes were being re-pierced, and the water in the eyes had to be put to his lips at each time he passed under the arch. He had to swear seven times and to repeat what Jomo Kenyatta had said.

SOMERHOUGH: How many times did he pass through the arch?

A: Seven times.

Q: Then what happened next?

The Magistrate here asked what the man had to swear seven times, and what he had to say.

MACHARIA: He had to swear those words which Jomo Kenyatta had uttered. He had to repeat exactly what Kenyatta had said. Then after that was complete he was ordered to sit on a Kikuyu stool and put on his clothes. He was cut on the forearms, at the back of the neck and also near the navel.

Q: Where on the forearms?

A: (indicating spot just above wrist) Here.

Q: With what was he cut?

A: With a razor blade.

Q: How many times was he cut in each of these places?

A: Seven times. Then in every part which was cut a sort of leaf, Kikuyu word Mukengeria, was put on the place where he was cut so as to have the blood taken off on the leaf, and the

leaf again was dipped in goat's blood, and he had to lick it and
swear the same words which I have already uttered. Then the
process was completed with Solomon Memia.

Q: After that had been done, what happened next?

A: Samuel Kihara asked me to take off my shoes and clothes. I
asked him why. He told me I must be made a true Kikuyu.

Q: When this was said to you, were all the same people present.

A: They were all present, including Jomo Kenyatta. I protested,
saying that I did not belong to the Kikuyu Independent Schools
Church, and they knew that I belonged to the PCA Church,
that is, the Presbyterian Church of East Africa, and as such I
was not prepared at any rate to take such an oath. He (Kihara)
tried to force my shoes from my feet. He succeeded, but still I
insisted that I must not take the oath. We had an argument, and
it became so heated that I thought to address Jomo Kenyatta
himself personally. I told him in English: "Look here, Kenyatta,
if you force me into this society against my will I will hold you
responsible, and no doubt I shall expose everything to the
Government." When Mr Kenyatta heard that he asked Kihara
to go outside the kitchen, and they both went out.

Q: How long were they outside?

A: Roughly 30 minutes.

Q: Who came back?

A: They came back together, Jomo Kenyatta and Kihara. Jomo
Kenyatta sat down at the place where he had been sitting, then
Samuel Kihara told me: "You Macharia, you can go outside on
condition that you will not reveal what has been going on to
anybody." I undertook not to tell anybody, and then I was
released. I did not go back to the house where Charles and
Stephano were, but straight to where we had left Charles's car.
I got inside it and remained there for a short time. Then Charles
came. I went with Charles to his home, where I spent the night.
I did not go back to my home that night.

Asked again whether he wished his name not to be published
the witness vehemently declared that if his name was published
he would be a dead man. Cross-examined the following day, he
said he was under police protection and had been since 11th
November during which period he had been interrogated by the
police four times. "I first said the press could publish my name
because I did not understand the judge. I misunderstood."

PRITT: If you do not understand English why choose to give
evidence in English?

MACHARIA: I elected to give evidence in English because I thought I could express myself better in English than in my own language.

Q: Did the police interrogate you in English?

A: Yes.

Now witness insisted what a good friend of Kenyatta's he was:

It is not true that the only time we met was when he once gave me a lift. I am his neighbour and more friendly than his full brother. It is not true I was never in his house. I saw him once when he gave evidence before the Land Commission at Kiambu when I was a schoolboy. That was when I saw Jomo Kenyatta. I read in the Kenya Carter Commission report about his giving evidence—I heard he gave evidence in England and also in Africa.

The point of this part of the cross-examination was that Kenyatta did in fact give evidence before the Carter Commission in 1932 when the witness was a schoolboy, but Jomo Kenyatta's evidence was heard not in Kenya but in London.

Witness went on with his story:

In 1946 Jomo Kenyatta came back to the country. I went to his house on the very day he came back. Very many people were there. I was just one of the crowd. I greeted him and shook hands with him. Nearly all the persons there shook hands with him. I was present when he was elected President of KAU.

I have often drunk with him. He is the heaviest drinker in the world. We have drunk ourselves silly together several times, I cannot say how many times. I paid for it. The 16th March was one of the occasions when we got drunk together. Harrison Gachukia does not drink. I said yesterday he was present and he administered an oath to Solomon Memia. He is a minister in Kikuyu Independent Schools—a Christian minister—administering a Mau Mau oath. Ephantos Waithaki was there too. He does not drink either. I never said yesterday he was drinking. Yes, he is also a Christian minister of Kikuyu Independent Schools. He stood by whilst his son was initiated into Mau Mau. Yes, I saw blood mixed with soil. It was in a calabash. The usual colour of blood was not prevalent; that is why I said it was mixed with soil. I attended only that one Mau Mau ceremony. I refused to be initiated and I made a personal protest to Jomo Kenyatta. He let me go. I have seen him since then several times. I have drunk with him several times since then. Usually when I am with him I do not get drunk. Since March 1950 only once have I been intoxicated with him. I kept this secret in my bosom until 6th November 1952.

The full team of court reporters had not yet arrived, and the transcript in the first day or two is not anything like as full as it later became. In the above quotation it will be clear to the reader that he is getting the answers to cross-examination without the questions. The last sentence, for instance, is apparently an answer to some such question as this: Q.—Did you tell anybody about this criminal oath at the time? A.—I kept this secret in my bosom until 6th November 1952.

This was the end of Macharia's evidence for the moment, though he was to be recalled for another brief cross-examination. Now Crown Counsel moved on to Incident Number 2—another story of an initiation, but a story at second-hand.

The witness was Muthondu, son of Nduti, a Christian, from a village called Gathundu, an elder of a Native Tribunal—a position which gives him some local eminence.

Muthondu said: "I know Jomo Kenyatta well. He lives close to me in Ngenda area—about a quarter of a mile away from me. I have known him ever since I was a child." Witness went on to explain that he belonged "to Ndege age group", which in itself needs a word or two of explanation.

The age group structure in Kikuyu society was fully explained later by Kenyatta in his evidence, but not by any of the Prosecution expert witnesses. Most African tribes have some sort of age group organisation. Sometimes it is simply that all the boys born in a particular year, say, 1930 are initiated together, and retain through life a sort of attachment to "the men of my year". In many African towns and villages there are "age group club houses" where eighteen- or nineteen-year-old boys make a great din all evening. Women are usually in three very broad age-groups. In Nigeria a District Officer of some local fame once dubbed them "Marrieds, unmarrieds, and old trouts", and he formed, with great success, an "old trouts club" with an OTC badge and a member's privilege of immediate access to the District Officer. Among the Kikuyu the age groups include men and women and are fixed by the date of circumcision. Circumcision ceremonies for both men and women take place at irregular intervals, not necessarily every year. Thus, sometimes the boys and girls born in two or three different years will be circumcised together, but henceforward they will all belong to one age group, which will be given a name. Muthondu's age group, as he says, was given the name Ndege.

He continued:

> In 1950 I remember a meeting of age groups in Gathundu market which I attended. It was the 3rd month of 1950. There were many people at the meeting. There were leaders of the Kikuyu present. Jomo Kenyatta was there. Dedan Mugo also. Kubai also. I see Kubai in this court. He is next to Jomo Kenyatta. I do not know Kubai very well because he does not live near me.

The mention of Kubai is significant, for later Defence were to argue that Kubai, not being a Kikuyu, would not attend an age group meeting.

Muthondu went on:

> The meeting started about 1 p.m. Dedan Mugo was in charge of the meeting. It lasted till the sun was setting. People started separating and going to their houses.
>
> A man called Samuel Kihara stood up. Jomo Kenyatta was still here. Kihari said: "We the people of Kahuguini School—we the grown men and women are going to Jomo Kenyatta's place, because we are going to have visitors there and we are going to sit down and chat with them." This affected me because I belonged to that group. The school is very close to my place. It is a Kikuyu Independent School.
>
> When Samuel said this we left Gathundu market and set off to our home area. I went right to Jomo Kenyatta's homestead with other people. When we got there the sun had gone down, but it was still a little light. When I got to Jomo Kenyatta's place we found three female goats in the process of being slaughtered and cut up outside the men's houses.

In a Kikuyu homestead there are a number of huts or houses—"the men's houses", "the wives houses" and so on.

At this point Defence again objected that this evidence of events before proscription was inadmissible. The Court ruled "for the same reasons as given yesterday" (for we are already in the second day of the hearing) that the evidence could be heard. So Muthondu went on.

The goats were white. The door of the men's hut was open. There were people inside the hut. Jomo Kenyatta arrived after we did. He had gone a longer way in a car to show someone a garden. I arrived at the hut before him. Kubai arrived with Jomo Kenyatta after I did. When Jomo Kenyatta and Kubai arrived they first showed some of the visitors the home gardens. There were quite a number of visitors. Kubai was one of them. Of the people like me who took the short route there were nearly 400 of us.

I stayed there until it got dark and I wanted to go back to my house and shut up my fowls. I had an eating-house and a bicycle repair shop. I wished to return to the eating-house to shut up the fowls. The eating-house is about a quarter of a mile from Jomo Kenyatta's house.

After shutting up the fowls I stayed there and had food and went to bed in a room behind the shop. I spent all the night there until the morning. I did not go out. I heard a great deal of noise. There was singing right until dawn over at Jomo Kenyatta's house. I heard what was being sung. They were singing new kinds of songs or hymns—one I had not heard before and heard for the first time then.

On the following morning I got up early to light the fire in my eating-house when it was just getting light. I opened up my shop and straight away about forty men and women arrived at my eating-house. I know them—they were from all around, and from our school group. I saw they came along the path from Jomo Kenyatta's house. They came along the path and they were looking at each other's hands, and when they were inside the eating-house they went on looking at each other's hands. I saw they had seven cuts on their hands—on one hand —the right hand. I looked at the hands of more than five people. They looked at each others' hands and drank tea. Then they went home. The women went away singing and the men went away.

Up to that time, 1950, I had never seen people with cuts on that part of the hand.

The witness demonstrated cuts below the wrist and between the wrist and knuckles, and he added:

This was not done before so far as I know.

Muthondu ended his evidence-in-chief there. Defence Counsel proposed to reserve cross-examination till the following morning, so Crown turned to the next block of evidence, one of the most important episodes in the case, that of Limuru.

4

The Limuru Incident

ONCE a petition reached the British Parliament which opened
with the words, "We the people of England"; but when the signa-
tures were examined they turned out to belong to three tailors of
Tooley Street. The three officials of the Limuru branch whom the
Defence later dubbed "the three tailors of Tooley Street" came,
led by their secretary Ephraim Gichereri. Ephraim explained how
it was decided "to hold meetings in our district in order to show
people that KAU and Mau Mau were not the same thing". At the
third meeting, early in 1953, Jomo Kenyatta and Fred Kubai
attended. "We welcomed them to the meeting. The meetings
were on the grass. Jomo Kenyatta was given a chair near the
Chairman who addressed him as follows: 'Mr Kenyatta, very
many people in this part of the country say you are the leader
of Mau Mau. It would be a good thing if you stood up in front
of this very large crowd and made it clear that you are not the
leader of Mau Mau.'" But before he could answer the Vice-
Chairman stood up in front of this crowd of some two or three
hundred and made a speech (as Ephraim put it) "about all the
evil things Mau Mau were doing, burning houses down, committing murders, causing mistrust among the people and making
them go against Government". Then the Treasurer of the branch
spoke saying much the same things, and next the witness himself.
"I said to Kenyatta: 'Since KAU is an organisation which meets
by day and in the open, I cannot see why people should
have to go and take an oath secretly or at night, because I
do not see how doing this sort of oath business will help to
get land or self-government.'" Still another speaker went over
the same ground "at considerable length" before Jomo Kenyatta
replied.

48

"Then Jomo Kenyatta did stand up and began to speak and he said: 'I did not know, Ephraim, that you would call upon me for something like this.' He was speaking in Kikuyu, and he said: 'You leaders of the Limuru branch are like the Fort Hall branch leaders. I was up there in connection with a case—one of our people was before the Court charged with trying to prevent cattle being inoculated—and it seemed to me that the Chairman and Secretary of that branch were like detectives for the CID. And it is quite clear to me that you know nothing really about KAU. I have found that at a time when we are fighting against the Europeans, you are fighting against your own people, and because of that, this question you are asking me about Mau Mau, I am not going to answer it for you.' And he went on to tell us that since it appeared to him we were unworthy to follow the rule of KAU we were to come down and report to head office."

Obediently they went on April 19th to KAU head office in Nairobi and were told to come back on the 21st. "We got to the KAU office about 2 p.m. The office was still closed and we waited outside, and Oneke was there before us, waiting. The others then came except Karumba. We all entered together. We went in and Jomo Kenyatta took the chair and he opened the meeting by asking us who had given us permission to start our branch and we told him Tom Mbotella was the person who opened our branch when he was Vice-President. He then wanted to know why we had been given permission to hold three meetings in our district from the District Comissioner whilst he, as President, had tried to get permission from the Provincial Commissioner to hold meetings without success. He said he would have had nine meetings but because the DC had given us permission for three, these had been deducted from the nine he wanted.

"Then Jomo Kenyatta said, 'You have been given permission to hold these meetings. Are you all the enemies of Mau Mau?' We said 'Yes'. He said, 'Well, I see you've been given permission because you are the enemies of the people and want to fight against the black people instead of the Europeans'. He then repeated what he said at the meeting, that they, the KAU, had sent a petition to England asking for self-government and the return of the land, and how we in the Limuru branch definitely ought not to be fighting against the other people, the Mau Mau, because Mau Mau was a religion. He then went on to say our branch had been opened wrongly and we ought to be under the leadership of Karumba."

To this the three branch officials replied: "We would not agree to be mixed up with a branch under the leadership of Karumba because we knew well that Karumba was the leader of Mau Mau in the district." Kubai (according to Ephraim) said, " 'You people of Limuru branch are the ones who are preventing people from entering into the association of the country'. We understood him to mean . . ."

The witness was stopped by a Defence objection that what the witness understands somebody else to mean is not evidence.

SOMERHOUGH: For what it is worth his understanding should be given.

MAGISTRATE: I think the witness is entitled to say what he understands. An explanation of this understanding does not at all mean that his explanation must of necessity be the correct one. The objection is overruled.

EPHRAIM: I understand his expression to mean Mau Mau. Everybody knows that "association of the country" is a common alternative for Mau Mau and the Kenya Central Association (KCA). I know they use the term *Kiama kia Bururi* as a secret cover name for Mau Mau and KCA which is the same thing.

That KCA—the Kikuyu Central Association—was a predecessor of KAU was common ground, but this remark of Ephraim's was the first suggestion that Mau Mau was in fact KCA under another name. It seemed to pass unnoticed at the time but later became one of the cornerstones of the Prosecution's case.

Ephraim and his friends had had a bad quarter of an hour at head office. It seemed that the meeting where Kenyatta addressed them had been reported in a vernacular newspaper, not the official KAU journal but another which was apparently edited by the printer of the KAU journal. This was *Mumenyereri*, edited by one Henry Mworia, and after reporting what Kenyatta said at the meeting, *Mumenyereri* had gone on to give particulars of the so-called Limuru branch. This newspaper report asserted that they were not so much members of KAU as of a religious sect which the reporter named a *Dini*, and which he said swore its oath on the entrails of a chicken. Ephraim and his office-bearers had been so incensed by this report that they wanted to take legal action against the editor, and they said so repeatedly at the Executive Committee meeting. But, added Ephraim, "Kubai said we shouldn't do this when KAU was agitating for more freedom of the press. Kubai spoke of many things I can't remember but he finished in the end by telling us our branch was closed." And, Ephraim added, somebody else had said, "These people had better get out of here, they are stopping us from working".

5

Muthondu and Ephraim
Cross-examined

THE fact that at the begining cross-examination was nearly always held back until Counsel and clients could hold one of their classroom consultations, produces a slight discontinuity which would be easy to correct in this account of the hearing, but this would be at the expense of losing something of the character of the trial. We are now at the beginning of the third day of the hearing proper. At 10 a.m. the Magistrate took his seat in the schoolhouse and the Defence found themselves ready to cross-examine Jomo Kenyatta's neighbour Muthondu who, it will be remembered, kept a bicycle repair shop, an eating-house and fowls.

"You will remember," Mr Pritt addressed the court, "that this witness began giving evidence of a meeting at a market at Gathundu. We agree that meeting took place and we agree Jomo Kenyatta was present. . . . I think I can pass over the rather long story about his getting home to his chickens because I agree he went.

PRITT: I suggest to you that it is something like one and a half miles from Kenyatta's house to your eating-house.
MUTHONDU: No, between where my house is and his house it is only a small hollow and you can call across quite easily.
Q: It is not possible, is it, from your eating-house itself to see the house of Jomo Kenyatta at all because of the hedge?
A: From my eating-house you can easily see his house and you can see a lamp when it is shining on the veranda at night.
Q: You say that the songs you heard were new.
A: Yes.
Q: Do you mean new to you?
A: I had not heard them before.

Q: What was the name of them?
A: I heard the words of one of them and it was that we should
     unite to get together so that we can get self-government and
     get our lands given back to us.
Q: Who told you that was the song?
A: I heard it.
Q: I suggest to you that it is absolutely ridiculous and you could
     not hear a word of it.
A: I did hear it.
Q: When forty people came to your eating-house in the morning,
     were they people you knew?
A: Yes, some were my own relations—wives of my brothers and
     cousins.
Q: They were all people who if they wanted a cup of tea could
     get it in their own homes.
A: No, they could not have done so because they had spent the
     night at Kenyatta's house.
Q: Is it possible to boil water in Africa?
A: I say they came to get tea from me because sugar was scarce
     at the time.
Q: Can you give me the names of any one of those forty people?
A: One was Elephas Mutheki. I can remember ten more names
     at least.

The Defence were keen on getting names, as the Prosecution
were quick to observe, since every name could mean a fresh witness. As indeed it turned out, for ten of the people named by this
witness were later called by the Defence. Crown Counsel's
re-examination of Muthondu was confined to the question, "Did
any of these you have mentioned have cuts on their hands?"
Defence objected to the question and the objection was sustained.
   And now it was time to cross-examine Ephraim, the Limuru
secretary.

PRITT: How many members do you say there were in what you
   call the Limuru branch at the time of these meetings that you
   give evidence about, in March 1952?
EPHRAIM: I cannot give the exact number but something over
   fifty.
Q: Were there many members of KAU in Limuru itself who
   were not members of your so-called branch?
A.   Yes, there were a lot who were KAU (but also Mau Mau)
   who were not in our branch.

Q: Why do you volunteer the assertion that there were Mau Mau?

A: Because of their deeds.

Q: Are you desirous of getting your neighbours in Limuru prosecuted for being members of Mau Mau?

A: I cannot cover up someone who is doing wrong things.

Q: Then you are desirous for your neighbours to be prosecuted?

A: If they are Mau Mau, yes.

Q: How many members of KAU were there in the Chura branch?

A: I do not know, I did not go to their meetings.

[The Chura branch was in a neighbouring district and its secretary was the accused Karumba.]

Q: Do you know there were at least 6,000 or 7,000?

A: I have said I do not know anything about that branch.

Q: You are very ready to say they were all members of Mau Mau and now you say you know nothing about them?

A: I said there were many Mau Mau people. I did not say how many there were but I could say there were certain people at certain places who were Mau Mau.

Q: I am sure you could say anything. I suggest that your so-called branch was not a branch at all.

A: It was a branch.

Q: I suggest to you that it was a small group of dissident quarrelsome persons.

A: No.

Q: Do you know that it was never registered or recorded in the books of KAU as a branch?

A: If anyone says that they are lying.

Q: Do you know that a decision was arrived at by the Executive Committee of KAU that all requests and negotiations for permits to hold meetings should be managed from the centre?

A: I do know that.

Q: I suggest to you that the result of your interference was that instead of 120,000 people getting nine meetings 120,000 people got six meetings and the fifty people of your branch got three.

A: Our meetings were location meetings for our branch.

Q: About the third meeting—was the meeting a small one?

A: No, not very small, getting on for 400 people.

Q: I suggest to you about 100.

A: That is not true.

Q: No KAU meeting at that time when Jomo Kenyatta was

announced to address them consisted of less than anything from 5,000 to 10,000?

A: I do not know, I have not been to such meetings.

Q: Did Kenyatta say: "If you know who is Mau Mau do not just grumble, report it"?

A: He said it was the affair of detectives to report it.

Q: I ask you again, did he say "If you know who is Mau Mau do not just grumble, report it"?

A: He did not say that. He said, "If there is Mau Mau it is the job of the detectives and Government to deal with it."

Q: Have you in fact reported people to the police as Mau Mau?

A: No.

Q: Was most of Jomo Kenyatta's speech devoted to rebuking the branch for incessant internal quarrels?

A: He did speak saying our branch was not following what the other people were doing.

Q: I wish you would answer my question. Was he mainly devoting his speech to rebuking you for internal quarrels?

A: He did that at the head office but not so much at the meeting.

Q: When he was rebuking you for not following what other branches did, was he rebuking you for not understanding the principles and constitution of KAU?

A: Yes, he did rebuke us.

Q: Before I leave that meeting I would like to ask one question about it. Can you explain why it is that at the time you got a permit for three meetings all other meetings for the time being were refused or were banned?

A: Yes.

Q: Why did you have that good fortune?

A: We wrote a letter to ask the DC and told him the reason why we wanted the meetings. The first reason was that we wanted to tell people not to have anything more to do with Mau Mau and we wanted people who were willing to come into KAU and it was because of those reasons that we were given the meetings.

Q: Was this the reason: that by making an utterly false and dangerous accusation against KAU being mixed up with Mau Mau you played into the hands of the authorities and they gave permission for three meetings?

A: It was not like that.

Q: Had not the fact that KAU and Mau Mau had nothing to do with each other been expressed at many large meetings by Jomo Kenyatta and many other leaders?

A: I do not know.

Q: In other words you know nothing, only what can damage KAU?

A: I know nothing about damaging KAU, I want it to be clean and free from Mau Mau.

Q: And your method of doing that is to suggest that it is mixed up with Mau Mau when you know perfectly well it is not.

A: It is mixed up in some cases.

Q: Are you still a member of KAU?

A: Yes.

Q: Are you not ashamed of yourself?

A: Why should I be?

Q: For doing KAU more damage than fifty detectives can ever do, by making false allegations about it?

A: I think you are making a mistake because I want KAU to be clean.

Q: And your method of wanting KAU to be clean is to call it dirty when you know it is clean?

A: You are saying that.

Ephraim's two colleagues, Johana and Stephano corroborated his story in detail.

Crown Counsel's re-examination of Ephraim produced an interesting result.

SOMERHOUGH: Will you look at this book.

EPHRAIM: It is the book.

Q: That is the book to which you made reference?

A: Yes, it is the ledger.

Q: Would you read the last entry in the book.

A: We went to head office at Nairobi and used for expenses Shs.15/95.

Q: Is that the book you took to head office?

A: Yes.

Q: What was done to it at head office?

A: There was a transfer on that date to head office of Shs.100/- and a balance due of Shs.68/- and an allowance of Shs.15/95 which we had used in travelling to head office, and the stamp.

Q: Would you explain what the hieroglyphic against the addition column on page nine stands for?

A: The initial of the secretary and the same appears on page ten.

Q: What secretary?

A: Joseph Otiendi.

Q: You referred my learned friend to a receipt which you obtained on that date.

A: Yes.
Q: Would you look at that receipt.
A: I see it.
Q: What can you tell us about it?
A: This was given us by the General Secretary because of the Shs.100/- we took and handed over.
Q: What is the date on that receipt?
A: 17.4.52.

The next witness was the District Commissioner himself, the first European to give evidence in the case. As it turned out he did not make a good impression on the court, and in his judgment the Magistrate described the DC as "somewhat vague ... did not give evidence as satisfactorily as one would have wished", adding, "nevertheless I believe him to be an honest witness".

DC Noel Frederick Kennaway told the Court how he had given the Limuru branch permits for their meetings. Later Kenyatta came to see him and "wanted a rather large number of meetings which I thought excessive", but they settled for six, and he told Kenyatta that the enterprising Limuru branch had already booked three for itself. Mr Kennaway went on to ask that denunciation of Mau Mau should be on the agenda of the meetings but Kenyatta replied, "Well, people know about Mau Mau, but these things on the agenda they don't know about, and we want to talk about that."

A passage in the evidence was later brought into prominence.

SOMERHOUGH: Do you know the accused Karumba in this case?
KENNAWAY: Yes.
Q: Did he make any applications to you in 1950 to hold meetings of KAU?
A: No.
Q: Do you know of any meetings large or small organised by him of KAU in 1950?
A: I have no recollection of any such meetings.

The week-end intervened. Monday's session began with a welcome and a protest.

6

A Defence protest and
a DC cross-examined

THE welcome was for the arrival among Defence Counsel of Mr
Chaman Lall, a member of the Bar of Great Britain, the Supreme
Court of Delhi and the High Court of the Punjab. The protest was
that another Indian Counsel, Mr Sethi, advocate of the Supreme
Court of India, had been stopped at the Nairobi Airport, but was
later admitted to the Colony on condition he took no part in the
case. Defence Counsel went on, "The matter will not rest there,
and for the moment therefore Mr Sethi is remaining in the
Colony, not for the pleasure of having a holiday but in the hope
that some touch of common decency, and a desire for once not to
interfere with the course of justice will affect the authorities in
Nairobi." (This prayer was not granted. Mr Sethi never reached
Kapenguria.) Mr Pritt added, "I have been deprived of the assistance of an advocate from the Gold Coast. I do not know anything
about the assistance of advocates from the Sudan—and that is
the existing and thoroughly disgraceful state of affairs on this
point."

Defence turned to the cross-examination of Noel T. Kennaway,
DC Kiambu.

PRITT: Have there been any prosecutions in your Kiambu dis-
trict of anyone for being a member of the Mau Mau?
KENNAWAY: Several.
Q: How many?
A: I cannot say.
Q: Half a dozen?
A: More.
Q: A dozen?

58

A: More.

Q: If you are so confident that there are more, can't you make an effort and tell us how many?

A: I am sorry I cannot.

Q: More than thirteen?

A: Yes.

Q: More than fourteeen?

A: I just do not know.

Q: So you do not know whether it is more than twelve?

A: I should say yes.

Q: Do you know the membership of Chura branch of KAU?

A: No.

Q: Would you accept the suggestion that it is between six and 7,000.

A: That might be so.

Q: Do you remember telling us on Friday that so far as you knew the suggestion that Kungu Karumba addressed some ten meetings in 1950 to denounce Mau Mau was incorrect?

A: To the best of my recollection that is correct.

Q: I suggest to you that during that period, by permission of someone in your office, ten large meetings fully publicised and reported in the press, were in fact held.

A: I remember that there were some four small meetings in the latter half of 1950 and there were two larger ones in the Uplands area.

Q: Many more do you remember?

A: No.

Q: Six is a considerable improvement on your flat denial of last Friday isn't it?

A: I said that I did not give permission to Karumba to hold these meetings.

Q: Were you swearing by the card then?

A: Yes.

Q: When you were asked on Friday whether there were any meetings of KAU organised by Karumba in 1950 you replied that you knew of none. Was the state of your knowledge this—that a number of such meetings had been held but you thought they were not organised by Karumba?

A: Yes. The question was—Had I granted permission for meetings in 1950.

Q: You have since improved on your recollection by checking up on your records?

A: Yes.

Q: In other words it would not be surprising if last Friday

you swore on oath something that you did not know and is not true?

A: I said I did not give Karumba permission for meetings in 1950 as such.

Q: What is "as such"?

A: Karumba.

Q: You swore also that he made no application in 1950.

A: No. I did not.

Q: I wrote it down as you said it—"There were no applications in 1950 by Karumba."

A: As such. It is possible that I did not know. If he is secretary of one of the branches it is possible that he applied as secretary.

Q: Signing his name as Karumba, but not "as such", is that right?

A: Yes.

Counsel went through a list of ten meetings putting them one by one to the DC. A meeting at Limuru itself, a meeting at Waithaka, a meeting at Riu, meetings at Kukatano, Karengo Market, Mguga, Dagoretti Corner, Kahoho, Wangigi Market, Mgechia Market. To each question the DC replied: "There may have been a meeting, there may have been permission." "It would be a criminal offence to hold meetings without permission?"— "Yes, it would be a criminal offence."

PRITT: My instructions are that I can put to this witness in due course the written permission for these ten meetings, the existence of which he denied on Friday.

KENNAWAY: I did not deny on Friday.

Q: If you deny, how could you say you gave written permission for something he never asked for? This is what you said: "He never applied for any" and you know of none being held.

A: Meetings.

Q: I really do not understand such nonsense and I do not believe you do.

A: Sometimes I sign myself Kennaway personally and at other times as District Commissioner.

Q: Let us have it clear—when you swore on Friday that Karumba had made no applications, were you keeping back in your mind the fact that he had made no application as such, but had made applications as nonsuch. Is that what you had in your mind?

A: I was asked the question ...

Cross-examination went on to the DC's discussion with Kenyatta about the agenda for his meetings:

PRITT: Did he say—"We have no doubt about condemning Mau Mau in the course of the meeting but we do not want to have it made a condition"?

KENNAWAY: No.

Q: Do you know that in fact when he spoke at each of the six meetings he did in fact denounce Mau Mau?

A: On the contrary I had cause to talk to Mr Kenyatta at a later date when I was seeing him in connection with a proposed meeting in August this year when he intended to denounce Mau Mau. I told Jomo Kenyatta that his alleged previous denunciation of Mau Mau were not in fact denunciations to the members of Mau Mau, that the Kikuyu knew he was the President of KAU and the leader of Mau Mau, and that therefore when he made the alleged denunciation such as "I do not know Mau Mau" everybody present or every Kikuyu did know that that was not true and concluded that he had his tongue in his cheek. I further informed him that following such so-called denunciations to use an expression "let us now take a little tobacco" was the equivalent of the English "take that with a pinch of salt". Jomo Kenyatta made no direct reply, he said he did not know the expression "Let us take a little tobacco". I also told him that I hoped that in the forthcoming meeting which was to be on the 24th August that he would clearly from his heart denounce Mau Mau and not be evasive and make remarks like "I do not know Mau Mau".

Q: And you were in effect telling a Kikuyu how best to address a number of other Kikuyus in order to convey to them the meaning he desired to convey?

A: Not necessarily the meaning he desired to convey but the meaning I hoped he would try to convey.

Q: It is a fact, is it not, that on the 24th August there was a very big meeting held in the Kiambu Town Hall?

A: Yes, outside the town on the sports ground.

Q: Held for the purpose of denouncing Mau Mau?

A. Yes, organised by Senior Chief Wahuiri.

Q: Addressed by Kenyatta?

A: Yes.

Q: Who denounced Mau Mau?

A: By word of mouth, and in that connection when Senior Chief Wahuiri saw me after the meeting I asked . . .

Q: You will not tell us any conversation you had with him whatever. Did you see reports of that meeting in the press?

A: Yes.

Q: And photographs in the press?

A: Yes.

Q: Have you got them here?

A: No.

Q: Kaloleni Social Hall in Nairobi is not under your jurisdiction?

A: No.

Q: Did you hear of a speech made to denounce Mau Mau held by Mr Kenyatta there?

A: There have been so many meetings there.

Q: I did not ask you that. I asked if you knew about that meeting?

A: I believe when I was on leave I heard that he had had a meeting there.

Q: This is the letter of the 12th March which you received formally for permission for the six meetings which have been discussed. The agenda includes introductory remarks by branch officers of KAU—you would have no objection to that of course?

A: No.

Q: Report from the Delegate to the UK—that would be a very important matter to discuss?

A: Yes.

Q: Constitutional changes—would that be important?

A: Yes.

Q: Organisation of the union—would that be important?

A: Not so important.

Q: The African press or Sauti ya Mwafrika—that might be important to discuss?

A: What importance is there about that?

Q: Did you realise that if you can persuade a political party to spend the whole of its time repudiating charges against it you can gradually reduce it to impotence?

A: Most of the time . . .

Q: I asked a question and I want yes or no.

A: That may be so.

There was a small but pointed episode to end the morning. Rawson Macharia was recalled for cross-examination on the recollection of an intelligent schoolboy of thirteen.

PRITT: Do you remember saying that Mr Kenyatta had given evidence before the Land Commission both in this country and in England?

MACHURIA: Yes.

Q: Do you still say that it is true?

A: I should think so.

Q: Let us be quite frank. You say that Mr Kenyatta was here in 1932.

A: I had said so, but I said it is too long for me to remember.

Q: You said nothing of the sort. Are you still saying that Mr Kenyatta was here in 1932?

A: I am more or less certain that he was here in 1932.

Q: Are you still saying that he gave evidence before the Land Commission in Kenya in 1932?

A: Yes.

Q: Just take that report of the Commission and show me his evidence given in Kenya. I can tell you in advance that you will never find it because he was not here.

A: You must remember that the time is almost twenty years ago.

Q: What I remember is that you swore half a dozen times in answer to lots of questions and without a moment's hesitation that Mr Kenyatta was here in 1932 and that he gave evidence. Do you want to say now that you did not know whether he was here or not?

A: No; I am still maintaining that he was here. It must be noted that during that time he was not called Jomo Kenyatta but Johnson Kenyatta.

Rawson Macharia was not re-examined.

After lunch the compliments of the season. Christmas was coming, the DPP had had a word with his learned friend and proposed adjourning at four o'clock on the afternoon of December 23rd, "the reason being that a great many people are involved in a sort of minor attendance capacity in this trial and they would probably like Christmas Eve with their families, and my learned friend agrees with me that this is a consideration which could be attached." Attached it was, the Court decided to adjourn early on the afternoon before Christmas Eve. And, fanning itself in the afternoon heat, the Court waited for the evidence of Tabitha Mumbi who deserves a chapter to herself.

Tabitha

TABITHA MUMBI was a witness whose personality told. A Kikuyu girl of twenty-five, she had been interested in Jomo Kenyatta since she first saw him when she was "a fairly big girl" at Githunguri: and this interest was strong enough to carry her in a bus to remote Ol Kalou for one of his big meetings. She stayed at the meeting "right from the start to the end". Then she "went home to her aunt", who had a house there.

The attractions of her aunt's house held her only till about half past seven in the evening. The meeting and its excitement were long over, but the main speakers were still at hand. Jomo Kenyatta, for example, was staying in a shop not far away. And, at 7.30 Tabitha "first went to the lavatory and then went to get my coat, my overcoat which was with a girl called Wambui. But when I was there, outside, I heard some children saying they were going to see Jomo." So Tabitha too "went to see Jomo".

They all went "to a shop that belongs to Daniel Mbugwa"—and then "they ran round to the back". The door was closed but Tabitha heard Jomo speaking. He was saying, "Those of you who have been using force to make people take the oath, I do not want you in future to use so much force because if you use force they will go and report to the police, and it will be dangerous". And then he said, "I am remembering that many of our people are now in gaol, and we cannot waste our strength in that way, because if all our people are arrested in that way there will not be anybody left to take charge of administering the oath".

It was at this moment, according to Tabitha's story, that Wambui made her main entrance: she came out of the shop, Wambui who had borrowed Tabitha's coat: but Wambui's thoughts were not on coats just now. She pushed open the door

of the shop and pushed Tabitha in. Here, said Tabitha, they
found Jomo Kenyatta, Fred Kubai and several other recognisable
faces. "They were eating, some little things like little scones, little
breads." But the conversation was disappointing. "After we went
in they did not speak at all." At the end of fifteen minutes Jomo
Kenyatta rose and they all went out to the car.

SOMERHOUGH: I just want to ask you a couple of other questions.
You told us how you heard a voice from inside when you were
outside the door. What I want to know is—try to tell us if
you can—how long it was you were outside after you heard
the voice before you went in? How long could you have
counted—I will put it that way.

TABITHA: It might be up to ten minutes.

Q: Ten minutes or ten counts?

A: I do not know minutes.

PRITT: But she said it might be ten minutes. She said it.

There ensued a discussion, which became embittered, on
Tabitha's sense of time. It was in fact one of the more pyrotechnic
exchanges between Counsel which from time to time illuminate
the case, the Defence arguing that Crown Counsel in a criminal
case "says he is entitled to try to make a witness say what she had
not said before", Crown Counsel replying in kind: then a general
loss of temper. It was a hot afternoon. And, to add fuel to the
flames, it now turned out that Crown Counsel proposed to follow
up Tabitha's evidence with evidence from Acting Assistant Superintendent Edward Hugh Massey Alleyne, the officer in charge of
the Special Branch of the Rift Valley, who in the course of his
duties had taken a statement from Tabitha. "How can it be relevant", Defence asked, "to prove that the police officer took a
statement from the witness?"

MAGISTRATE: I think it is a question of credibility . . . It is common practice, or at least I believe it is, to call for evidence from
the Police as to a statement made by a witness if the credibility
of the witness is challenged.

PRITT: I have challenged the credibility of every Prosecution
witness before now, and they have not been followed by the
evidence of a police officer.

But "to save time" the Defence objection was waived, though
objection was made again when Crown Counsel appeared to

C

be "leading" the police officer, which again led to argument, prolonged, erudite, heated, on the nature of evidence and the nature of leading questions; on the Indian Evidence Act which governs procedure in the Kenya Courts—and then it extended to the practice the Defence was still driven to, of reserving cross-examination of Crown witness till the day after the evidence-in-chief had been given.

MAGISTRATE: I was hoping—Mr Pritt will forgive me for saying so, I am quite sure—I was hoping you would by now have ceased to ask for reservation of cross-examination. You do not want to put your clients to any prejudice, of course, but I at the same time wish—you would appreciate my task is a most difficult task, and with all these reservations of cross-examination they do not make my task any easier.

PRITT: May I say this. I have reserved no witness's cross examination longer than overnight. This is the only case I have ever heard of in my life in which the defendants on charges—serious charges—to which they might be sentenced to a sentence of seven years' imprisonment—very serious charges—it is the only case I have ever heard of in my life in which they have been prosecuted with no particulars of any description being given—particulars even being refused; and as each thing comes up, as each new incident comes up, I hear a completely new story, that I have never heard in my life, I do not know until four o'clock in the afternoon whether my clients have ever heard of it in their lives. I do not know whether they are going to tell me it is true, or a distortion, or a complete invention; and until four o'clock every afternoon, sir, I am as ignorant of it as any beggar in the streets of Nairobi—perhaps more ignorant. Therefore, it is utterly—and, of course, the moment they tell me "Well, such and such a witness can put this right" I have set in train a series of efforts to get this witness from three hundred miles away. Consequently, sir, whilst anybody regrets any inconvenience to a Court, the gross, cruel, deliberate injustices worked upon me by the Government of Kenya in insisting on having this trial up here, and the most unfortunate procedure, whereby we are put in complete ignorance of the thing we have to answer until half a day before we have to answer it, makes it, of course, quite impossible for me to do any more than I am doing.

MAGISTRATE: There are many cases—of course, your experience of cases in England is much wider and greater than mine—but there must of course be many cases where charges are made where the Defence do not know the details of the allegation. They know the nature of the charge, but not the details—dates, meetings, names and places. They do not know that until the evidence comes out.

PRITT: But since we have had applause from the back of the superiority of Kenya over England, let me say that never has any man in the whole course of history stood his trial in England in a single criminal court on a charge involving a sentence of seven years penal servitude, without every line and tittle of the evidence that is to be given against him on his trial being given beforehand in committal proceedings in police courts, with the express intention that he shall know, as the Government of Kenya is determined I shall not know, that he shall know the case before him in time for him to answer.

MAGISTRATE: I think the answer to that is that Kenya is unfortunately suffering at the present time from an Emergency.

PRITT: I know, sir, it is because of that; and the Emergency is being taken advantage of by the Government of Kenya to give my clients the minimum chance to defend themselves. I am employed by my clients to see that they shall get as much, and I have your co-operation with me in that, sir, I am happy to say.

It had seemed a long hot day and when it was over the Court reporters wrote in a slightly longer form than usual: "Court adjourned at 3.45 on the 8th December, 1952."

8

An African Policeman and
Tabitha are Cross-examined

AN African Senior Inspector of Police George Kipture Arap Kitur
had been to the shop on the afternoon of Tabitha's story. He had
been "covering" Jomo Kenyatta's meeting in plain clothes. It was
raining, and he followed the speakers and some of the crowd after
the meeting. There was some dispute about whether the speakers
went on foot or by car—the witness seemed a little confused in
his story—but he watched them all go into the shop and he
waited outside. Earlier in the day he had been told that this was
the room arranged for Kenyatta's entertainment, and this interested him and he had a look inside. It was just an empty store-
room next to the shop—a room without windows in a stone
building with a corrugated-iron roof. He was cross-examined
on this.

PRITT: The back door was an ordinary wooden door was it not?
KIPTURE: Yes.
Q: Do you know a girl called Wambui?
A: There are many Wambuis.
Q: That is what I thought you would say. Did you take any part
     in preparing the statement or taking the evidence of Tabitha?
A: No, sir.
Q: I did not ask you at the moment whether you knew her. I
     asked you whether you knew of her in any way being in touch
     with a girl called Wambui?
A: That I do not know, sir.
Q: I asked you whether you had ever heard of it?
A: No, sir.

When he stood down from the improvised witness box Senior
Inspector George Kipture must have been perturbed. Defence did

not know at the time, but they found out later, that, while it is true there are many Wambuis, the one that mattered was very well known to Senior Inspector Kipture. In fact she was his mistress.

But now it was Tabitha's turn to be cross-examined. The Court heard about her life. From five to nine years old she went to a mission school and this was all her schooling. She had been living with a man "but he has not married me"; previously she had been "doing trade" at Nakuru, but six months ago she became a bar-maid in the Municipal Club at Nakuru not far from Kambui where she lived, and from here she travelled the 27 or 28 miles to Kenyatta's meeting at Ol Kalou.

PRITT: How did you travel?

TABITHA: In a taxi.

DR LEAKEY (interpreter):   They call it a taxi—it is not a taxi. A taxi—a taxiringi—is a real taxi, but a taxi is a native bus.

PRITT: How long did you travel in the bus?

A: We left in the morning about six and we got there about eight.

Q: When did you first think of attending a KAU meeting?

A: On the 27th.

Q: What made you think of it?

A: I wanted to go. I had heard there was a meeting of KAU and I wanted to go and see my aunt.

Q: Did you have to ask anybody's permission to leave your work to go from Nakuru to Ol Kalou?

A: I told a policeman I was going.

Q: Had you got an employer at that time?

A: No. I was working on trade.

Q: Why did you tell the policeman you were going?

A: When I was working in the market I had been told, I am a Christian and I had been told if I heard anything about Mau Mau and would like to report it, I should go and do so.

Q: Did the policeman suggest to you that you should come back and tell him what happened?

A: He told me that if I heard anything bad I was to come and tell him.

Q: Was it the policeman who suggested that you should go?

A: When I was in the market, I had heard about things, and I went to tell him, because I had been told that if there were people dealing with Mau Mau I should go and give him infor-mation about it, and I thought as I was going to Ol Kalou I thought I would tell him that I was going, so that if there was anything about Mau Mau in Nakuru when I was not there— so that if there was anything to do with Mau Mau in Nakuru when I was away he would know I was not in Nakuru.

Q: The question I asked was very simple. I am going to ask it again, and I want yes or no. Was it the policeman who suggested that you should go to Ol Kalou and see if you could find out something to report?

A: No, I went to the policeman and told him I was going.

Q: What is the name of the police officer you spoke to in Nakuru?

A: Bwana Lane.

INTERPRETER (Leakey):   She says Lane.

PRITT: What is the name of the police officer in Nakuru—could she spell it? We had better not have any false points about this. I think we had better ask the gentleman in question to come in and for the witness to say whether that is the man or not. It is, after all, a criminal case.

(Mr. Alleyne was called for.)

PRITT: Is the gentleman you see standing in the doorway the gentleman whom you call Lane?

A: Yes.

Q: Would you please tell the Court your name?

ALLEYNE: Alleyne, sir.

PRITT: And you are in fact a prosecution witness? Thank you very much.

PRITT (to Tabitha):   How long have you known Alleyne?

A: From the first to the sixth month.

Q: How did you come to know him?

A: He had sent to find somebody who could listen to things and tell him.

Q: Is he stationed in Nakuru?

A: Yes.

Q: Do you know George Kipture son of Kitur?

A: No, I did not know him before I saw him here.

Tabitha went on to tell how she went to see her aunt Muthoni, a woman "without occupation" and at her aunt's she met the girl called Wambui, a slight acquaintance whom she had met only once or twice before, and "because it was very cold", Tabitha, who had a jersey as well as an overcoat, lent Wambui her coat. She arrived at her aunt's on the night of the 27th. At

2 o'clock next day she went to the meeting and heard several speakers, last Kenyatta. At the end "when everybody scattered I saw Kenyatta and Kubai walking towards a motor-car".

PRITT: You had had enough of the meeting by then and wanted to go home?

TABITHA: If there had been a taxi-bus there I should have gone home in it.

Q: Now we know what our audiences think of us! Without your overcoat?

A: No, I would not have left that.

Q: How did you hope to get the overcoat back?

A: If there had been a taxi-bus ready to go I would have gone and got my coat from Wambui.

Q: How would you have done it if you did not know what her name was or where she lived?

A: She had pointed it out to me.

Q: And then, about half-past seven you went to the lavatory. You intended then to fetch your overcoat?

A: Yes.

Q: How would you know that Wambui would be back home then?

A: When she took away my coat she said to me, if I wanted to go, I was to go to her place about half-past seven.

Q: So you went out intending to go to her house?

A: Yes, that was what I wanted to do.

Q: Why did you not?

A: Because that was when I heard the children say they were going to listen to Jomo.

Q: Was it dark?

A: Not very dark.

Q: And you followed the children to this building? Had you ever seen the building before?

A: No.

Q: You went to the back door hoping to listen to Kenyatta?

A: Yes.

Q: You had never spoken to Kenyatta in your life?

A: No.

Q: And he has never, apart from public meetings, spoken to you?

A: No.

Q: And you had not heard him speak very often, had you?

A: Yes, I had heard him speak often.

Q: You said that you had heard him at the children's sports at Githunguri? Is Githunguri near to where you were at school?

A: Not very far.

Q: And did you go to those sports when you were at school?
A: No.
Q: When was it you went there?
A: I think it was in 1947. All the sports in that period, around 1947, I went to.
Q: Just only in 1947?
A: And in other years.
Q: What other years?
A: And 1948.
Q: So you can remember two years in which you heard Kenyatta speak, five years before this meeting at Ol Kalou?
A: Yes.
Q: I suggest to you that you could not tell his voice from anybody else's behind a wall?
A: No, that is not right, I do know his voice.
Q: Why did you not open the door and walk in?
A: I thought the children belonged to that place, and when they ran away then I heard voices so I stopped and listened.
Q: There were people going in and out all the time, were there not?
A: No.
Q: How long in all were you standing outside that building before you did go in?
A: I said I think it was about ten minutes. I said so.
Q: When you were standing there for that ten minutes, how far from the door were you?
A: Right close to the door.
Q: Remembering what the Police Officer Alleyne had asked you to do?
A: I did remember what he had told me, but I was feeling afraid.
Q: What were you afraid of?
A: Because I was a stranger.
Q: What were you afraid of doing because you were a stranger?
A: I was afraid of going in there alone, I wanted to see if somebody would come in or go out so that we could go in together.
INTERPRETER: I think what she means is if somebody came out temporarily to the lavatory she could have gone in with somebody else.
PRITT: How many feet from the door were you standing?
A: Very close.
Q: So that if anybody had opened the door, they would have hit you in the face?
A: I was like that, and the door was here.

Q: Can we say that was two yards from the door? I am going to ask you, sir, to direct in due course that a test should be made in a room which has been kindly allotted to us in this building, which seems to me to present a very fair parallel, and get somebody to say something in that room, to say it as loud as you direct, and I do not think you will ever hear a word.

MAGISTRATE: I do not think I can allow that, because I do not know what the doors are like. They are very different; African doors may be made in a very "shenzy" fashion, or they may be very good.

PRITT: What was the door like?

A: It was a wooden one.

Q: Was it like the door over there?

A: Yes.

Q: Was it like that?

(The Clerk opens the door).

A: Yes, but its pieces of wood were not narrow ones like that. It was not made of narrow slats like that.

Q: She will understand thickness—was it thicker than that?

A: The other was a bit thicker than that.

Q: Just at the very moment you arrived, Kenyatta suddenly began to make this speech, did he?

A: No. I arrived—he was in the middle of speaking.

Q: Why did you not arrive earlier?

A: I did not know about it.

Q: Had not Mr Alleyne told you what time to arrive?

A. No.

Q: I put it to you quite bluntly you never heard a single word spoken by Jomo Kenyatta in that building.

A: He did speak and I did hear him.

Q: How long after that did you wait before Wambui came out?

A: Just when he had finished speaking, Wambui came out.

Q: Was it a complete surprise to you that it was Wambui who came out?

A: Yes.

Q: Had she got your overcoat on?

A: No, she had not got it.

Q: And then you were taken into the room?

A: We went in together.

Q: What did Wambui come out for?

A: She said she told me she was coming out to go and look for me.

Q: And then you went in with her?

A: Yes.

c*

Q: A complete stranger?

A: I had known her in Nakuru and she had come down twice.

Q: It is my fault, for putting the question wrong. You were a complete stranger and were taken into this room where such terrible things were being said—is that your story?

A: When I was taken in nothing more was said. Things had been said.

Q: What was Kenyatta doing when you went into the room?

A: He was drinking beer. I saw a bottle. I do not know just what kind of a bottle it was.

Q: How many other people were in the room?

A: I cannot give you an exact number, I did not count, but about ten.

Q: About ten others?

A: No, ten altogether.

Q: Did you not try to find out who they were in order to tell Alleyne?

A: No.

PRITT: Not a very good spy yet, is she!

SOMERHOUGH: She is new to it.

PRITT: Had Wambui been there all the time that Kenyatta was saying the words that you say you heard?

A: Yes.

Q: Where is she now?

A: I do not know where she is at present.

Q: And you say they remained silent whilst you were there, for fifteen minutes?

A: I did not hear anybody talking.

Q: You just sat there like a dumb stranger for fifteen minutes?

A: Yes.

Q: Why did you leave?

A: Everybody went out of the room. I went out too.

Q: What did Jomo Kenyatta do?

A: He came out.

Q: Did you say yesterday that he went towards his car?

A: Yes.

Q: Do you know that everybody knows perfectly well that so far from getting up and going out, Jomo Kenyatta spent the night in the store and it was because he was spending the night in the store that the police had inspected the store earlier in the day? Do you know, as a fact that Kenyatta spent the night in that room?

A: No.

Q: Did you ever get your overcoat?

A: No.

Q: Where is it now?

A: I still have not got it.

Q: When you went out of the place, what did you in fact do?

A: Wambui told me to go to her place, because I had not been there before, and she would go and give me some beer. We went to her place and she bought three beers and we drank them, and I then said to her, "I must go back to my aunt's place to sleep".

Q: Why did you not get the overcoat?

A: I asked her, and she said "Let me keep it until the morrow."

Q: What did she want to use an overcoat at night in the house for?

A: She was wearing it; I do not know where she was going to go to.

Q: Did you sleep the night at your aunt's house?

A: Yes.

Q: When did you go back to Nakuru?

A: On the Sunday.

Q: Was it the next day?

A: Yes.

Q: And did you go straight to Alleyne?

A: No.

Q: When did you go to Alleyne?

A: On the Monday morning.

Q: Why did you not collect the overcoat in the morning before you went?

A: I got up in the morning and my aunt told me to get some tea from the eating-house, and I met Wambui also at the eating-house getting tea, and she told me that Kubai had spent the night at her place and she was going with Kubai to Thomson's Falls. I then felt very angry with her. I did not even think of asking for my coat then. I did not feel I wanted to talk to her at all.

Q: Because she had gone after the gentleman? I suggest to you you never saw Kubai that night, either in the shop room or when you went home.

A: I saw him at the shop, in the room at the shop.

Q: Now, sir, perhaps I might just make my application now. I think I have finished my cross-examination. Just tell me. You heard Jomo Kenyatta speak in the afternoon at the meeting?

A: Yes.

Q: Tell us everything you remember that he said.

A: When he stood up he first of all said to everybody, "Greetings", and that when the Europeans came here they told us they come here as our guests. When we lived side by side with them——

MAGISTRATE: You are going on cross-examining for some time?

SOMERHOUGH: Can we get it as far as we have got? If it is near the end I should have thought it better to have gone on.

MAGISTRATE: I would rather not. I am not criticising in the least, I am merely saying my hand is getting very tired.

PRITT: Perhaps I might ask you if I may, when we come back, to direct that in the room which we have got, that this lady should station somebody, not Kenyatta, at a point which she says corresponds roughly to where he was, then she should station herself roughly two yards outside the door, and that a person should speak, in varying tones of voice, words pre-arranged—not with her of course, and then she should tell us whether she had heard a single word or not.

MAGISTRATE: I do not like it. First of all, we have not got the same room, the same door, the same person talking inside the room. All we have got similar to what she relates is that she was standing outside the door. I do not like parallels which are merely parallels and not a reproduction of the actual thing.

PRITT: Then I shall have to ask at some stage to have Kenyatta taken to Ol Kalou so that we can have a test in the actual building.

MAGISTRATE: That is what I should prefer, although it may be difficult.

PRITT: Justice is sometimes difficult to do, but it is worth the difficulty.

(Later, in his speech submitting there was no case to be answered, it was alleged by Defence Counsel that Prosecution carried out these tests, and then refrained from calling evidence on the result, from which he drew the natural conclusion: see page 140.)

After luncheon interval cross-examination of Tabitha was resumed.

PRITT: Please continue your story and tell us what Jomo Kenyatta said at the public meeting.

TABITHA: He said that the Europeans told us to shut our eyes and pray and to say Amen when our eyes were shut, and while our eyes were shut, they took our land. And then he went on by saying, "I know there is no God, and Jesus Christ they talk about, is an Englishman". When he got as far as that I could not listen any more—I was so upset. I just could not understand any more, because in my mind Jesus Christ is the Son of

God, and right to the end of the meeting I had no joy in my heart because of it. That is all.

Q: Let me put it to you that Kenyatta did not speak in Kikuyu at all, but in Swahili?

A: He spoke Kikuyu.

Q: Do you remember an incident when he had finished speaking in Swahili somebody asked for it to be translated into Kikuyu and said they did not want to do so?

A: He spoke in Kikuyu first, but afterwards for a bit he spoke in Swahili.

Q: I suggest that his observation about Jesus Christ being an Englishman was never said at all in any language?

A: I think, in fact, I know, that he did say it.

Q: If you were so shocked and upset by him, why did you want to go and hear him again in the evening?

A: To hear what else he would say.

Q: Did the meeting begin with a Christian prayer?

A: No, there was a joyful sound and hand clapping.

Q: Did you hear Achieng speak?

A: Yes.

Q: What language did he speak?

A: He spoke in Swahili and it was translated into Kikuyu.

Q: You have told us that you were living with a man for some time. Where did you live with him?

A: He took me from my home and he hopes to marry me.

Q: When and where did you live with him?

A: I went and lived with him where he worked—at Naivasha.

Q: When did you begin to live with him?

A: Nineteen forty-nine—fifth month.

Q: Are you still living with him?

A: I separated from him in 1950; he was arrested.

Q: Where are you living in Nakuru?

A: In the native quarters of Nakuru.

Q: What furniture was in the room you went to at night in the shop?

A: There was a table shorter than that one (indicating Counsel's table about five feet long). There were benches—that is all. No bed.

Q: Although Kenyatta was going to sleep there?

A: I did not see a bed there.

Q: When you went to see Wambui why were you angry with her?

A: She told me Kubai had spent the night there.

Q: Why should that make you angry?

A: Because I had found her with Kubai and I was angry with her because she was turning Mau Mau.
Q: And you think as lightly as that of your friends?
A: I do not know.

Tabitha was not re-examined by Crown Counsel.

Later this afternoon Defence cross-examined Acting Assistant Superintendent Alleyne, who said Tabitha had been brought to him as someone who might give the police useful information. "So you thought the first thing you would try her out on was the Ol Kalou meeting?" Superintendent Alleyne said no, he was interested primarily in Tabitha's beer-hall.

PRITT: So that from your point of view her first job was to act as an informer of anything she could pick up in the beer-hall.
ALLEYNE: More as an agent than an informer.
Q: What is the difference between an agent and an informer?
A: An informer is someone who does it for his own gain. An agent is someone who works for you for the good of the cause.
Q: The agent is the amateur and the informer is the professional?
A: Yes, if you put it that way.
Q: She was working there as your agent from early in June up to at any rate the 27th or 28th.
A: Yes.
Q: How often would she report to you in that approximate three weeks?
A: Two or three times.

By now the Crown case had almost reached the end of what was called "the first block of evidence involving all the accused": that is to say Rawson Macharia and his story of oath-taking; Muthondu and his story of his fowls and his tea-house; the three gentlemen from Limuru; DC Kennaway and his interviews with Kenyatta; and last, Tabitha the "agent" with the heart of gold. All that remained to hear of the so-called "first block" was a piece of supporting evidence about what was said in the summer campaign of public meetings (the DPP's "stump campaign") and an attempt, which was soon dropped, to show that there was an increase of crime following the meetings.

First there was evidence about one of the comparatively few occurrences of the words Mau Mau. The story was told by a clerk from Thomson's Falls, Japeth Godfrey Agutu who had been listening to a Kenyatta speech.

SOMERHOUGH: What did he say, what can you remember?

A: He said that he was in Europe for very many years and he never took even a piece of land of table size.

Q: He did not take a piece of land the size of a table. Then what?

A: The Europeans came to this country and took very big land ... And when they demanded it back ...

Q: Who are they?

A: When they—Jomo Kenyatta—demanded it back, they were called Mau Mau Mau Mau—four times.

And later there was an eloquent sidelight in the witness's account of Fred Kubai's speech at the same meeting. "One of the topics was Africans wearing hats and women wearing handkerchiefs. The other topic spoken about which had already been emphasised by previous speakers was Africans drinking English beer."

The incidence of crime and the Kenyatta meeting at Thomson's Falls had been linked in the opening speech for the Crown. When the appropriate District Commissioner William Niel Brown Loudon was called he was at once asked:

SOMERHOUGH: And during the year 1952, in relation to crimes related to Mau Mau, what was the position as regards your district?

PRITT: Sir, I must obviously object to this. The charge against my clients is that they manage, assist in the management, or are members of Mau Mau. Mau Mau is a proscribed organisation and if they manage or assist in the management of it, they are guilty of a crime. But how can it be part of the proof of their being officials of Mau Mau just to give general evidence that somebody is alleged at some time in the year 1952, both before and after that meeting in a district, to have committed some kind of crime which is alleged to be connected with Mau Mau? In my humble submisssion, it would be really a grave departure from the rules of evidence and incidentally a substantial waste of time to have crime statistics or criminal reports from this district and, I might suppose, from every other district in the country.

Crown withdrew the question, and reached the end of "the first block". The second block began with evidence against only one of the accused, Paul Ngei.

9

Mr Pedraza

A DISTRICT OFFICER Geoffrey Pedraza came to tell the story of how he was cursed by Paul Ngei in words which Crown argued admitted membership of Mau Mau. He began his evidence rather unhappily, for no sooner was it established by Crown that as DO he was *ex officio* a magistrate, first-class, than Mr Pedraza embarked on what was apparently going to be a piece of hearsay evidence and had to be stopped, and this caused a momentary inhibition which at first rather confused his story. Crown Counsel excused him: "He has never given evidence before", and Mr Pedraza went on to tell how he was called from his bed at eleven o'clock at night, picked up four askaris and drove in his car to an alley beside a shop, pushed at an unlocked door, and, entering, found Paul Ngei and two other men. He at once arrested Paul Ngei and had him marched off between two askaris to the local gaol. Then Mr Pedraza drove home to bed, but he was roused again at 2.30 a.m., went to his office, saw his askaris and drove off again to Paul Ngei's house and knocked at the door. For about ten minutes there was no answer, and then a woman put her head out of the window and talked to the askaris. Mr Pedraza's knowledge of African languages was not sufficient to enable him to follow. After a few minutes Paul Ngei came out.

MAGISTRATE: But I thought he had been arrested.
PRITT: Some way or other he had ceased to be under arrest.

In fact it now appeared that everybody had become so wary about giving hearsay evidence that it had become quite difficult to tell the Magistrate that the askari standing by the DO's bed at 2.30 in the morning had reported that his prisoner got away. So Mr Pedraza went to catch his escaped prisoner, but when the

police party came to his house Paul Ngei appeared in the doorway and addressed Mr Pedraza in English, saying it was "scan-
dalous or something like that, that his house should be searched
without a warrant." Mr Pedraza's reply was to give orders for him
to be handcuffed; whereupon Ngei became abusive. Pressed for
the exact words Mr Pedraza hesitated to offend the ears of the
Court but in the end quoted a sentence which ran, "Pedraza, you
bloody cunt, I hate you".

INTERPRETER (Dr Leakey): I cannot do that in Kikuyu, I am afraid,
   sir.
SOMERHOUGH: Oh, dear, it is a more refined language than I
   thought.
PEDRAZA: He said: "You f—— English, I hate you all."
PRITT: I suggest, as possibly a short cut, that miscellaneous
   abuse is not——
SOMERHOUGH: I do not want to take this out of its context.
PRITT: I do not mind travelling through mud if it is necessary
   but possibly we might avoid this.
SOMERHOUGH: I do not like to cut bits out of the conversations.
PEDRAZA: He also said: "You, Pedraza, you had better get out
   quickly before the Europeans are all killed."
PRITT: I think, sir, I ought to record my objection now. I assumed
   there was something relevant in this conversation. Now, we have
   just had a plain, ugly bad-language row between two people,
   absolutely nothing whatever to do, up to this point, with any
   sort or kind of the offence with which this man is charged, and
   I ask you, sir, to strike the whole thing out of your notes. I press
   the objection, with the greatest respect. It is utterly irrelevant—
   we might have had a slanging match the week before——
MAGISTRATE: It is more than a slanging match, it identifies the
   accused with a desire to drive out of Kenya all the English.
PRITT: Then that, sir, makes it additionally objectionable. It is
   either a slanging match and no more, or it is an accusation
   against this man of a criminal offence with which he is not
   charged. It is quite possible to want to be rid of the English
   without being Mau Mau. For all I know, it is quite possible to
   be Mau Mau without wanting to get rid of the English. But if you
   are going to rule this admissible evidence, because it shows an
   objection to the English, or rather say, if you are considering
   the possibility of ruling it to be admissible because it is an
   objection to the English, in my humble submission, it becomes
   graver and more objectionable.

Crown Counsel suggested that the proper course was to wait to hear the rest of the witness's story and then see, the Magistrate agreed and examination continued.

SOMERHOUGH: Did you travel any distance with them towards the gaol?

PEDRAZA: I walked just behind them, or really level with them for about 200 yards.

Q: And was there any conversation at this stage?

A: There was.

Q: Who by?

A: By Paul Ngei.

PRITT: I rather think this comes under—in the Criminal Procedure Code—this is after all a statement made to a police officer.

MAGISTRATE: It may not be a confession.

PRITT: If the evidence that my friend is seeking to adduce is a statement which is a confession, that is to say, not "I confess" or "Yes, I am guilty" or anything of that kind but "I did X" or "I am Y", or whatever it may be, which constitutes a statement of a man's guilt, a statement of an offence committed by the man, then Section 25 of the Evidence Act does in my humble submission rule it out ... What I was thinking, and I believe my friend understands the position very well, as one would expect him to, I expect he is pretty confident in his own mind that what the witness is likely to say is in one of two categories, or partly in one: either something that does not matter tuppence or something that will have to be struck out.

As the argument developed it became a question: Was Mr Pedraza acting as a police officer when he arrested a prisoner and ordered him to be handcuffed? And if so, did the fact that Mr Pedraza was also *ex officio* a magistrate, make sense of an argument that *ex officio* Police Officer Pedraza took a statement from a prisoner in the presence of Magistrate (first-class) Pedraza, and that therefore the usual safeguards were observed? The Court ruled that "Since there was no risk of a jury having heard something and being unable to divorce it from their minds" the evidence should be heard first and legal argument could follow.

SOMERHOUGH: I think you answered that there was further conversation?

A: Yes.

Q: And on whose part?

A: Paul Ngei.

Q: And to whom was it addressed?

A: Presumably it was addressed to me because the askaris do not understand English.

Q: Was it in English?

A: In English, Yes.

Q: Right. Now, would you take it very slowly, what was in English?

A: He said, "To hell with the British Empire."

PRITT: That might have to be struck out with the rest, but we will not worry at the moment.

Q: Go on, Mr Pedraza. Sentence by sentence, if you can.

A: He then said: "Mau Mau is going to drive you out of the country, the same as you were driven out of India and the Gold Coast."

Q: Was anything else said?

A: Yes.

Q: In what language?

A: In English:

Q: More or less at the same time or after an interval of time?

A: Practically following directly afterwards.

Q: Is all the conversation in this 200 yards' walk?

A: Yes.

Q: Yes. What else was said?

A: He then said: "All you bloody Europeans will very soon be killed by Mau Mau."

Q: Yes, and what happened then? What happened then?

A: Then he said: "We will drive you out of the country. I am Mau Mau."

PRITT: That is the kernel of my objection.

SOMERHOUGH: Did you, when you were arresting him, that is to say, at either of these interviews, the 11.30 o'clock or the 3 o'clock in the morning one, say something to him to indicate the capacity in which you were arresting him?

A: During the first meeting, the 11.30 one, when he kept on demanding a warrant of arrest, I explained to him at least three times that as a magistrate I had no need of a warrant of arrest under the law.

MAGISTRATE: During the first 11.30 meeting, then, he kept on asking for a warrant of arrest at the first meeting, as well as at the second?

A: That is so. I informed him that under the law as a magistrate I had no need of a warrant of arrest.

PRITT: I was suggesting to my learned friend that this is such an important point that we ought to argue it today or tomorrow when we have had time——

MAGISTRATE: I think so, because, let me be quite frank, I have not said much yet while the trial was proceeding, that statement "We shall drive you out of the country, I am Mau Mau" is certainly a confession to the charge of being a member of Mau Mau.

PRITT: That is why I was trying to be a little bit firm before. I am not thinking of the difficulties as to whether it is a confession but rather what is the true position of an admission when you get the odd position that one of the people present happens to be a magistrate. We have all got it in mind—it is very different to a couple of buildings in India in one of which there is a whip and in the other a magistrate——

MAGISTRATE: I agree; this most important and vital point regarding Ngei should be argued at length, when you are ready to argue it. There is one other point which I have been thinking about. I do not say it causes me anxiety, but it has been passing through my mind. I should like the benefit of your views on it. How far can I, as a magistrate, take notice of the fact of what I think Mau Mau stands for?

SOMERHOUGH: Only, I think, within the limitations of the evidence you have before you, Your Honour, and we have had some evidence as to the terms of an oath administered.

MAGISTRATE: I cannot take into account what I read in the newspapers?

SOMERHOUGH: I think no, Your Honour, the only thing as far as I know—subject to my learned friend's correction—the only things as far as I know you are permitted to bring into the court-room with you are general common sense, knowledge of the world in general and such matters upon which you are permitted, expressly by statute and in your express knowledge.

PRITT: Of the world but not the underworld. (Laughter.) I had to investigate very closely, for an American case I was doing, the limitations of judicial knowledge and the furthest I discovered any Court to go beyond the law, and a state of war, and the signature of a judge, and all that sort of thing, was that the Court had gone so far as to say that the Court could take judicial notice of the fact that whisky was intoxicating. That is as far as they go.

MAGISTRATE: I cannot take any account of what I have read or

what I have in my mind what I think that the society known as
Mau Mau stands for other than what appears in the note?
SOMERHOUGH: What appears in the note, yes, sir.

The next "block of evidence" was still concerned with Paul
Ngei, and concerned a letter alleged to be his, which had been
intercepted.

10

A Song and Hymn Books

THE Crown case had arrived at "Bless 'em all". Counsel addressed the Court, "Your Honour, the next evidence that is going to be called concerns a letter which was, according to the Crown, written by the accused Paul Ngei ... It was intercepted under a Governor's order in Tanganyika, read, copied, and retransmitted".

Henry Nzioka Muli was called, an assistant chemist in the Government Laboratories in Dar-es-Salaam, and a relative of Ngei. He had a letter from Paul Ngei in 1952, though by now it was lost or destroyed.

SOMERHOUGH: You read the letter?

MULI: I looked through the letter. I looked, mark, looked, I say looked through the letter.

MAGISTRATE: What is the difference between looking and reading through the letter?

MULI: My difference is this, that looking through a letter is looking through, say, the first two lines and then the other paragraph and then, perhaps see from whom it comes and then put it away to read it later on.

SOMERHOUGH: Did you read it—that is my question?

A: Unfortunately, I did not have time to read it.

Q: Did you notice in what language it was written?

A: It was written in English.

Q: Did you recognise the writing?

A: No, because it was written in something which I cannot know whether it is a pencil or, I mean, charcoal, or anything of that nature. It was very roughly written, and that is why at the first I did not have time to scrutinise it. At that time I was very busy in the laboratory.

Q: I am going to ask you about the contents of this letter. From where was it written.

A: Care of a certain Ngei, His Majesty's Prison, Nairobi. That was the address at the top of the paper.

Q: Tell us what you remember of the contents of the letter?

A.   Ngei was just telling me about his family at home.

Q: Who was?

A: I think it might have been Ngei.

Q: Did you look at the writing?

A: Yes, but the writing could not tell me anything.

Q: Did you recognise the writing?

A: No; it was written very badly.

Q: What else did he say?

A: He talked at length about his family—his wife especially; she was in hospital; she gave birth to a baby. He also told me about my own home. He told me that my people were all right, and he mentioned something else about some money I had borrowed from him. He then mentioned about several other people who were arrested.

Q: Who were they?

A: As far as I can remember, he mentioned Mr Kenyatta and Mr Oneke. I do not know the other names.

Q: Anything else?

A: I do not remember anything else that he mentioned.

Q: If you saw a copy of the letter and read it, do you think you would recognise it as a copy of the original letter?

A: I cannot say yes, nor can I say no, because when I saw that letter I did not have time to read it, and what I have said in the way of remembering is what I remember.

Q: Have you made a statement before in this matter?

A: Yes.

Q: Long ago?

A: Oh, yes, a long time ago.

Q: How long?

A: It may be a month or more.

(He was questioned on his statement.)

Q: "The writer Paul Ngei was in prison." Did you say that?

A: Yes.

Q: "As far as I can remember he sends me greetings and said he was in prison in connection with Jesse Kariuki"?

A: I remember that.

Q: He said how many people had been arrested; he mentioned Jomo Kenyatta and Oneke?

A: Yes. I said that.

Q: Did you say "I only read the letter once"?

A: Yes.
Q: "It was here in the laboratory. I took it home and put it on
    one of my shelves. Three or four days later I looked for it but
    could not find it"?
A: Yes.

A Tanganyika Assistant Superintendent of Police told how the
letter was brought to him. He opened it, and his secretary a Miss
Lewis made a copy. He was cross-examined by Defence.

PRITT: Did you check this copy over very carefully.
SUPERINTENDENT: Yes, I did.
Q: I see for example about half-way down the first page there
    is a word which has been written in pencil and then struck out
    and then written again. Did you think that was a proper copy
    to make of the document of some importance?
A: No. Kangundo was written in the original and the other ver-
    sions of the word were made by Miss Lewis.
Q: And Miss Lewis first wrote Karghudo?
A: Yes, she always finds difficulty with African names.
Q: You see this thing, "Praise Mau Mau", a four-line verse to
    George Formby's tune. Did you know that was a joke in the
    prison at Nairobi?
A: No.
Q: Did you know that the author, composer, and constant singer
    of it was a South African European prisoner who was singing it
    all the time in the prison?
A: No, I know nothing about it.

From the song the Crown case moved on to a new block of
evidence to which the DPP attached a good deal of weight, this was
the evidence about the so-called hymn books, which later came
to be known by the Kikuyu word for hymn book, Nyimbo.

One of the hymn books—the pale blue ones—had been bought
from accused Kaggia by a Police Inspector and the Court heard
the translation of "Hymn Number Nine".

PRITT: These really ought to be called songs—not that I have
    any religious squeamishness.
SOMERHOUGH: They are sung as hymns. What is the title of
    Number Nine?
INTERPRETER (Dr Leakey): "On the night Dedan Mugo was being
    arrested."

Bit by bit the whole poem came out. The first verse runs:

On the night Dedan Mugo was being arrested
In order that he might be given sorrow or
      oppression by his enemies
He was not afraid.

SOMERHOUGH: Could we have the second verse?

Dr Leakey stumbled over the first line "*Anene*—here is a word sometimes used for chiefs, sometimes used for important people".

PRITT: VIP's?

DR LEAKEY: Yes, that is a very good word.

A number of VIP's had gone to his place with the
      Europeans
Many police askaris carried guns but Mugo was not
      afraid
And he said to them: "It is my body which I give over
      freely to be oppressed or to be made sad because
      of *ruriri.* . . .

"*Ruriri*"—that is a Kikuyu word which is very hard to put exactly into English—"because of the race", "because of our people" might possibly be equal translations. There is no exact equivalent of *ruriri* that I can find in English. "Because of the people" would probably be as good as anything.

Then there is a last line. "And in order that you should remember continually and do the same until my return."

Q: That was verse three?

A: "And Mugo said to them" was the beginning of verse three.

So verse three became:

And he said to them "It is my body
Which I give over freely to be oppressed or to be
      made sad because of the people
And in order that you should remember continually
And do the same until my return."

The poem continued:

When Dedan Mugo came into the courtyard he asked
      the VIP's to agree that he should return into the
      house to don his clothes.
When Mugo came out with the others,
He had no sorrow but only joy
He asked them, "Into which vehicle shall we enter
      that we may go?"
And he told us Kikuyu, told us in our Kikuyu country
'Even if I am imprisoned there should be unity
For God is great.'

DR LEAKEY: At the end there are the common Kikuyu words of praise and worship: Thai-tha-thai Ngai thai"—prayer and praise to God—prayer".

MAGISTRATE: What God does this refer to?

DR LEAKEY: The word Ngai is the word used by Christians for God in our sense, but also it is the supreme god of the Kikuyu.... Very often the Kikuyu word is qualified by the word Ngai Mwene Nyaga, as the "Owner of Mount Kenya" but more often as "the owner of brightness".

Hymn No. 5 was translated, in verse three:

> The friend of the black people, Dedan Mugo, was
> blessed in respect of Kenya because of the black
> people.

Dr Leakey stumbled over the phrase "blessed in respect of Kenya" and then, putting on his glasses, he saw differently.

DR LEAKEY: Yes—I beg your pardon, I should have been wearing my glasses, I am entirely wrong. I have misread the whole word. I beg your pardon, Your Honour. It is "Athamirio"—I had not put my glasses on, it is entirely different. "Athamirio" —"he was removed from Kenya—or deported from Kenya— because of the black people".

SOMERHOUGH: Verse four?

Verse four was translated:

> Dedan said to the house of Mumbi
> Do as I do until my return.

SOMERHOUGH: Right. That is all, thank you.

Now the DPP explained the relevance of the poems. This would depend upon evidence he propsed to call, that Dedan Mugo, treasurer of KAU was convicted of Mau Mau activities in 1950, in connection with oath-taking. If this was proved then it could be said that here was a book which in adulatory terms dealt with a person convicted of Mau Mau activities.

The Defence protested that it was an attempt to import gross prejudice into the case. Mau Mau was not an unlawful body till August 1950. When the point was pressed it appeared that Dedan Mugo was convicted in March 1950 six months before the proscription of Mau Mau, and in fact, when later evidence was called of his conviction, it came out that the charge had no reference to Mau Mau but was one of imposing an oath which bound members to an unlawful society, to wit the Kenya Central Association proscribed in 1940. Then, argued the Defence, in order to make sense of the evidence, "You get the following hopelessly tenuous argument, that because you have a song praising Dedan Mugo and because, in the course of x years of his life during which he may have done hundreds of virtuous, and for all I know hundreds of unvirtuous things, because he was convicted about March 1950 of taking an unlawful oath—and this is where it really becomes cloud Kikuyuland—therefore anybody who ever praises him thereafter must be a member of Mau Mau! And to that utter nonsense, utter tenuous nonsense, we are brought in a case in which the Government of a great Colony is prosecuting six people for serious offences!"

The Magistrate deferred his consideration of the admissibility of the evidence from "the hymn books" and meanwhile listened to one more translation. This was a poem which bore the title *False Allegation,* and it has the importance of being one of the only two or three pieces of evidence in which Mau Mau is mentioned by name.

In the box Dr Leakey produced his translation of Hymn 27. "The heading is *Kigenyo* which is usually translated 'False Witness or False Allegation'. Verse 1 reads:

> I go to Nairobi and I find haste
> When I return to Kikuyu I am of Mau Mau.
> *Chorus:* What shall I do, what shall I do
>   to be freed of my sorrows?

Verse 2:

> I will give money to search for light
> And when it is found I shall be like a
>   big beer gourd.
> *Chorus:* What shall I do, what shall I do
>   to be freed of my sorrows?

Verse 3:

> Let us all work hard together, we of
>   the house of Mumbi
> And hold ourselves together like the
>   corner stone

MAGISTRATE: What is Mumbi?

DR LEAKEY: Mumbi is the Eve of the Kikuyu as distinct from Adam. Gikuyu was the Adam and Mumbi the Eve of Kikuyu.

Dr Leakey was cross-examined by Defence.

PRITT: The heading means false allegation or false story?

DR LEAKEY: False witness.

Q: The first few words say: "I go to Nairobi" and the second words are: "I find there that all is haste". Do you know the slang meaning of the word "Haraka"?

A: No.

Q: May I suggest to you that the activities of the police in Nairobi recently of herding people wholesale into lorries and carting them away and saying to them "Haraka" to make them hurry up has led to the police being called in Kikuyu slang "Haraka"?

A: I have not come across that.

Q: May I suggest that if that is right the translation of the first line is "When I go to Nairobi I come into contact with the police", or the English equivalent "When I go to London all I get is 'Move on there'"?

A: I do not think that is the interpretation.

Q: The second line—"When I go back to Kikuyu"—what is the word "ndi"?

A: I am.

Q: Having regard to the title and to what I suggest, isn't the probable, at any rate the possible, meaning of the last part of the second line "I am alleged to be of Mau Mau"?

A: It says "I am of Mau Mau".

Q: Some people when I get in front of the police say I am a thief?

A: I have no knowledge of that.

Q: Having made that strong complaint of how they treat me in the town, when I get back to the country I say, "What shall I do to be freed of my sorrows"?

A: That is a common interpretation of the words.

Q: Isn't the objection that it is a true meaning of the first verse?

A: I do not think I can say that. I am on oath as an interpreter.

Q: Could you say it could mean that?

A: I have never heard the word "Haraka" used by the police.

Q: You could not say the interpretation as suggested to you is impossible. It would then be possible to have the interpretation "I go to Nairobi, I find the police, I go back to Kikuyu, I am of Mau Mau". It may mean not that I am in fact Mau Mau, but that is what they call me?

A: Yes, but that is a matter of opinion.

From songs and hymn books the Crown case moved to the customs of the Kikuyu tribe.

11

Superintendent Henderson

POLICE Superintendent Ian Henderson was born in Kenya and speaks Kikuyu, a combination rare enough to make him something of an expert witness—indeed he was one of the only three European speakers of Kikuyu to appear in the case, the other two being interpreters. He had attended one of the 1952 summer campaign meetings, the one at Nyeri, where he said Kenyatta addressed a crowd of 25,000. In the course of the meeting Kenyatta was questioned by an African District Officer, one of the few African DO's in Kenya. The questioner wanted to know "what he was going to do in the way of stopping Mau Mau in the district". Kenyatta's answer to this question was subsequently given by the Crown a significance so heavily underlined that the rest of this part of Mr Henderson's examination is given verbatim.

SOMERHOUGH: Was there any reply to that.

HENDERSON: There was. Mr. Kenyatta replied to that. He said amongst other things: "I do not know what this thing Mau Mau is—Kikuyu elders do not know it." He went on to say: "If a person is hit with a stick he will come back, but if one is hit with justice he will never come back" and he decried those people who he alleged were going about the country accusing the Kikuyu generally of being Mau Mau.

Q: Did he say anything else in that particular speech about it?

A: Yes. He also criticised very bitterly people who he alleged were going about the country accusing every person who committed some small infringement of the law of being a Mau Mau. He said that beer—European liquor—was harmful to the African and that those who drank it were doing wrong and that they may be the so-called Mau Mau.

MAGISTRATE: Was all this in English?

A: No, Kikuyu.

Q: What was done about the Swahili language at the meeting?
A: It was interpreted into Swahili by Jesse Kariuki.
Q: What else was said?
A: In the same speech of Jomo Kenyatta he said that those who
     call the KAU the Mau Mau are not truthful, but he said he did
     not know what this thing Mau Mau was—he repeated that a
     number of times.
Q: What was the popular reaction to that, if any?
PRITT: I must object to that. The crowd are not charged with
     Mau Mau, it is only my clients.
MAGISTRATE: Surely it is admissible to know what, if anything,
     the crowd said.
SOMERHOUGH: What was the effect or apparent effect?
A: On that occasion and also whenever there was any vagueness
     as to what Mau Mau meant the reaction was one of applause.
Q: How long did the meeting last?
A: The meeting lasted from 1 p.m. until 3 p.m. They were
     formed up ready at 11 a.m.

Superintendent Henderson's evidence began in the afternoon
and was interrupted by an adjournment. Next morning began
with the usual discussion of small administration details between
Magistrate and Council. Defence announced that they found
themselves unable to pay for the four copies of the transcript,
which had been ordered, and proposed to renounce all but one
extra copy which they would pay for. The Court made an order
for four copies to be supplied free of charge. Defence asked for a
copy of the Governor's formal "consent to the trial"—this became
important in legal argument later. And finally:

PRITT: I think that is all, sir, but in order that we should have a
     little light relief occasionally, perhaps I might mention——
MAGISTRATE: I could not agree more.
PRITT: Perhaps I might mention that the Right Honourable
     Gentleman, the Secretary of State, has informed the House that
     I have made no protests up to date! (Laughter.)
MAGISTRATE: I had better not say anything I think.

Defence Counsel's reference was to a statement by Mr Lyttleton in the House of Commons, news of which had just reached
Kenya. Now the Crown proposed to move from evidence, by
Superintendent Henderson, on the meeting he had attended, to
more general evidence from him as expert on the Kikuyu, and on

Mau Mau—for it turned out he was also the police expert on Mau Mau ceremonies. This produced argument between Counsel, Defence objecting that to have evidence of Kikuyu customs was irrelevant, and, since Mau Mau was proscribed, evidence of Mau Mau customs was unnecessary. The objection was overruled and witness told the Court that the passing of the calabash seven times round the head and the seven small incisions on the arms "are in my opinion very characteristic of Mau Mau".

Q: And the wiping of blood off with a certain type of leaf, does that strike any chord of significance or not?

A: No, sir.

Q: And the putting of blood to the lips, that is in various evidence? That is characteristic of Mau Mau?

A: Characteristic of Mau Mau and it is also done in Kikuyu custom in various ceremonies.

MAGISTRATE: And what?

HENDERSON: It is also carried out in ordinary Kikuyu custom in various types of ceremonies.

SOMERHOUGH: Has it any particular significance?

A: Licking of blood, sir?

Q: Yes.

A: Yes, it is symbolic of the adoption of one person by another, and even blood brotherhood.

Q: We had evidence from a witness in this case, at what I will call a ceremony, if I may use that word without objection——

PRITT: Without prejudice.

SOMERHOUGH: Without prejudice—that a goat's head was present, that certain bones, the atlas and the axis at the back, had been removed. Has that any significance?

A: It could have, sir. The atlas bone is often used in oaths, some legitimate oaths.

MAGISTRATE: Sometimes used in legitimate oaths?

SOMERHOUGH: Yes. And we also have evidence—I am reading now from page thirteen [of the transcript] the eyes were taken out of the head, that is, the goat's head, and these eyes were placed on the side of the calabash and were stuck on thorns. Has that got any significance of any society or body of men?

A: Yes, it is significant in the Mau Mau and it is also—the eyes of goats, sheep are also used in ordinary Kikuyu ceremonies relating to land.

Q: The same witness described a ceremony, he described a calabash mixed with earth and stomach contents and later I think he said earth and blood. Has the use of earth in the sort of way any significance in your experience?

A: In Mau Mau, yes, sir. And also earth and blood mixed up together is, like the eyes of sheep, used in land cases.

SOMERHOUGH: Legitimate land grievances?

MAGISTRATE: Earth and blood mixed have a significance in Mau Mau and——

A: And are also significant in legitimate Kikuyu ceremonies concerning land.

SOMERHOUGH: We also had evidence from the same witness about the existence of an arch in the house made of grass and banana leaves and sugar cane leaves about four feet high. What can you tell us?

A: That is very significant, not only to the Mau Mau, but also to all ceremonies connected with the *rites de passage* of the Kikuyu.

MAGISTRATE: You have both used some expression which sounded to me vaguely like French.

SOMERHOUGH: *Rites de passage*—rites of passage—it is very common, I believe, in anthropological circles. It is a common— it is a generic name for things like birth, death, marriage, circumcision, they are generically known as *rites de passage*.

MAGISTRATE: All ceremonies relating to *rites de passage*.

PRITT: If the witness would perhaps give that explanation?

SOMERHOUGH: Would you explain what is meant by *rites de passage*?

A: Ceremonies which take place, sir, as the life of an individual progresses. Where the individual is passing to another stage of life. In Kikuyu an example would be in circumcision, or in re-birth.

The evidence which might be dubbed anthropological ended here. Defence, having discussed his evidence with those concerned, were now in a position to go back to District Officer Pedraza and his shouting row with Paul Ngei.

12

DO Pedraza cross-examined

THE cross-examination of District Officer Pedraza involved a much fuller analysis of the legal problems of "confession" to a policeman and before a magistrate. Crown Counsel had argued that Mr Pedraza had acted simply as a magistrate, and that a confession like Ngei's "I am of Mau Mau", even though it was mixed with drunken abuse in a two-o'clock-in-the-morning scuffle, was admissible as being made before a magistrate. The Defence replied that as a District Officer is in effect in control of police in his district, Mr Pedraza, arresting and handcuffing a prisoner was acting strictly in his role as a policeman, and all the safeguards the law attaches to this situation must be applied.

Here perhaps a word of explanation might be helpful. In Indian law, and therefore in Kenya, the provisions of the Indian Evidence Act take special care of the circumstances in which confessions might be obtained in order to circumvent as far as possible police habits of beating either accused, a potential accused, or mere witnesses, into making confessions. The first of the Indian provisions simply makes all confessions to police officers inadmissible; but this has been amended in Kenya so as to make confessions admissible if the police officer were of a certain height of rank—which Mr Pedraza was. The second provides that no confession is admissible when the confessor is in police custody, unless it is made "in the immediate presence of a magistrate".

Thus, the Defence arguments were: (1) Ngei was in police custody, Mr Pedraza was acting as a police officer and not as a magistrate; (2) that the section of the Indian Evidence Act, having regard to the purposes for which it was enacted, contemplated three participants, the accused, the police, and a magistrate. Consequently Mr Pedraza could not double the roles and say, "I am the police, and I hold him in custody; he has confessed in the presence of a magistrate, to wit myself".

As to being a policeman, Mr Pedraza now admitted, "I have powers of arrest but I seldom exercise them". This time he had exercised them twice in one night, and each time he had arrested Paul Ngei for resisting arrest by askaris who had originally tried to arrest him for "breaking a chief's order about drinking after hours".

PRITT: You will excuse my ignorance, I am sure, but as a District Officer, do you administer some district or sub-district?

PEDRAZA: I administer what is actually called an area, which is a sub-district.

Q: In that area how many police are there normally stationed?

A: What sort of police do you mean?

Q: Well, let us start with the Kenya Police.

A: Six.

Q: Kenya Police Reserve at the time in question?

A: None.

Q: And Tribal Police?

A: Seven.

Q: Under whose orders were those—firstly, the Kenya Police?

A: They are under the orders of the Assistant Superintendent of Police at Machakos.

Q: And how far away is he?

A: Twenty-five miles.

The District Officer admitted that "as such" (apparently a favourite phrase with District Officers) he was entitled to give orders to the police. "In certain circumstances the law allows me to, yes."

Q: You are in charge of law and order in your district?

A: I am responsible for it.

This was the foundation of the argument that he was acting as a policeman making arrest. There were a few more details to be added.

Q: May I suggest to you you did not in fact arrest Ngei at all, either by word of mouth or otherwise.

A: That is quite untrue.

Q: Did you demand from him and receive from him a quantity of property that he had?

A: I searched him and removed from him certain items.

Q: Yes, on a charge of resisting arrest you deprived him of practically everything he had got on him?

A: Of the things in his pockets, yes.

Q: Let us see. His brief case?

A: Yes.

Q: Was that in his pocket?

A: He was holding it in his hand.

Q: So that a moment ago when you said you took from him the things that were in his pocket, you were not telling the whole truth? Is that right?

A: You could put it that way, but it is splitting hairs. What I meant was that I did not remove his clothes, when you said "you took everything off".

Q: You give that as a serious answer as a responsible officer?

A: Of course.

Q: Well, please, a little more intelligence the rest of the time. Did you take his savings bank book off him?

A: Yes, I am almost certain there was a savings bank book.

Q: Did you take a hundred and thirty shillings from him?

A: Yes.

Q: Did you take an American book on propaganda from him?

A: I do not remember that at the moment.

Q: Did you take a couple of fountain pens from him?

A: Yes.

Q: And left him with the clothes he stood up in, as you kindly reminded us, and nothing else?

A: Nothing else that I remember, no.

Q: On a charge of resisting arrest. Were you acting as a police officer or a magistrate or a brigand, when you did that?

A: As a magistrate.

Q: I suggest to you that you were acting unlawfully as an administrative officer grossly abusing his power.

A: That is quite untrue.

Q: Under what power did you take everything he possessed away from him?

A: I do not know what the section of the penal code or whatever it is. The normal power of searching a man when you arrest him and of putting him in gaol.

It appeared later that there was more in the story than drinking after hours. Asked if Paul Ngei had told him the chief had arrested him and others for holding a meeting without permit Mr Pedraza answered: "It is possible."

PRITT: Did he tell you he had committed no crime and held no meetings?

PEDRAZA: I do not remember him actually saying that. It is quite possible.

Q: Did he demand of you to tell him what he was alleged to have done?

A: Again it is possible. What I do remember is that he kept on demanding the warrant of arrest.

Q: Not at all a bad idea, either, was it?

A: It is quite unnecessary to have one.

Q: If I lent you the criminal code do you think you could find the section under which you have power to search?

A: I could not guarantee it.

Q: Well, have a try.

Mr Pedraza had a try. He thought it would be Section 24 (b). At once it became clear he had chosen a section that gives the right of search only to police officers.

PRITT: Thank you very much. Just listen, will you, to the section you have drawn my attention to. I will miss out the irrelevant words and my friend will follow me in case I am missing out something which is relevant. "Whenever a person is arrested (*a*) by a police officer under a warrant, or (*b*) without a warrant by a private person under a warrant, the police officer making the arrest, or, when the arrest is made by a private person, the police officer to whom he makes over the person arrested, may search the person and place in safe custody all other articles than necessary wearing apparel." That is the section under which you acted? . . . Did you give Ngei a receipt for the stuff?

A: No. This search took place during the first arrest at 11 p.m.

Defence Counsel put the case that Ngei did not at first know he was supposed to be arrested. He was told by the askaris to go to the District Officer's office, took a short cut, arrived there before the askaris, waited some time in vain, but there was no District Officer—as we know Mr Pedraza had gone home in bed—and presently Paul Ngei went home himself. To all this Mr Pedraza could say only: "I don't know, I wasn't there." A little later, how-ever, witness and Defence were more or less on common ground. Some time between 3 and 4.30 a.m. Mr Pedraza and his men knocked up the sleeping African household saying they were looking for an escaped prisoner. It was some time before the people in the house opened the door.

PRITT: They thought you were thieves?

PEDRAZA: I don't know, they were talking in Kikamba.

Q: What right had you to enter the house?

A: I was looking for an escaped prisoner. I did not enter the house myself.

Q: But you entered by your askaris?

A: Yes. Paul Ngei asked to be shown a search warrant and a warrant for his arrest.

Q: When he asked for these things did you tell him to shut up and that he was Mau Mau?

A: Certainly not.

Q: And did you and he, at various stages, have a good deal of hand to hand fighting?

A: No, we did not.

Q: Did you have some?

A: Very little.

Q: Did you push his wife some six feet across the room?

A: I never went into the house and therefore I did not push her across the room, or push her six feet at any time.

Q: How far did you push her?

A: I did not push her at all in the sense that you mean.

Q: In what sense did you mean?

A: She and some other women were getting in the way of the askaris and I went to these women and asked them to move away from the fight. They took no notice and went on shouting and screaming and trying to interfere, and finally with the gentlest possible touch under her left elbow I said: "Now come on, you must get out of this."

Q: And was his mother pushed and beaten by askaris?

A: Not at all.

Q: Your car was 300 to 400 yards away?

A: About 200 yards.

Q: And was he marched there in handcuffs?

A: No, he was not.

Q: He was not handcuffed?

A: Yes, he was.

Q: Did he tell you that the askaris had accused him of being Mau Mau.

A: No.

Q: Did he complain that you were arresting him for nothing?

A: I do not remember those actual words.

Q: Did he complain to you that you had assaulted his wife and mother?

A: He kept on saying, "If you touch my wife, you bugger, I will kill you".

Q: That could fairly be interpreted as a complaint. And did he accuse you of calling him Mau Mau?

A: No.

Q: And did he threaten you with legal proceedings?

A: Earlier, yes.

The legal argument about the status of Mr Pedraza in three persons, magistrate, policeman and administrative officer, was now developed thoroughly, a complex argument involving the Indian Evidence Act, Kenya Emergency Regulations and legal definitions of several kinds. It was of legal importance, and the Magistrate reserved his ruling. The rest of the afternoon of 12th December was taken up with routine evidence which need not be summarised here.

Then, next session, out of an apparently clear sky, a storm blew up.

13

Contempt?

THE morning of Monday 15th December had begun quietly enough. Defence Counsel told the Court that there would later be an application for the recall of Ephraim, the Branch Secretary from Limuru. Defence had had a stroke of luck and the article in *Munyenyeri*, the journal which the Limuru branch had been complaining about in their famous meeting with the Executive, could now be produced. There were still one or two things to clear up about translation—the newspaper article about Limuru had been translated in two versions, one by the Defence, and the other by Dr Leakey. "It will take a little time to get that straightened out" Defence Counsel said. "I only mention it as a warning." But the Magistrate turned aside from this and with some solemnity addressed Defence Counsel.

MAGISTRATE: Mr Pritt, I now have something to say to you which gives me the greatest regret, seeing that it has to be said to one so distinguished in our profession of Law, but your attitude towards this trial and this court makes it now necessary to say it. My attention has been drawn to a paragraph in the *East African Standard* of the 15th December——

PRITT: Fifteenth of December?

MAGISTRATE: Sorry, the thirteenth.

The news item ran as follows:

NEW PROTEST BY MR PRITT
Answer to cable from MP's
Standard Staff Reporter—KAPENGURIA

The conditions under which the trial of Jomo Kenyatta and five other Africans is being held at Kapenguria are such as to amount to a denial of justice Mr D. N. Pritt, Q.C., leading Defence Counsel has declared in a cable which he sent yesterday to four Labour Members of Parliament—Sir Richard Acland, Miss Jenny Lee, Mr George Wigg, and Mr A. Wedgwood-Benn.

At Kapenguria on Thursday, Mr Pritt received a cable from the MP's claiming that the Colonial Secretary, Mr Oliver Lyttleton, had said that apart from the application about the venue of the hearing "Mr Pritt made only one protest about facilities and said he was satisfied with the arrangements made as a result".

The MP's wanted the Colonial Secretary's statement confirmed.

In his cable yesterday Mr Pritt said that the statement was unfounded and had "caused much amusement".

The cable added: "I am protesting continuously, first against the inconvenience of holding the hearing in a remote region where one must send 280 miles to Nairobi to look up authorities on the frequently arising points of law, or get documents or witnesses.

"There are no facilities for research or study nearer than Nairobi and no means even of eating nearer than Kitale, 24 miles away.

"Secondly, against the trial being in a closed district, virtually causing the exclusion of the public from the court.

"Thirdly, against the inexcusable exclusion of some counsel from the Colony and others from the district where the trial is being held, although the accused have asked for them.

"In ALL—

"All this makes the proper preparation of the Defence case almost impossible, greatly increases expenses and wastes time. It amounts in all to a denial of justice.

"I feel so strongly on this that I have undertaken to remain without further fee, however many weeks the case lasts.

"The only point upon which I have expressed satisfaction is that the District Commissioner provided better facilities for interviewing the accused and secured the services of a Kenya African Union official which were essential to the Defence by granting him an Entry Permit which had previously been refused by the authorities in Nairobi.

"My accommodation in Kitale is good and my colleagues are being accommodated by friendly private citizens, but under conditions making the work difficult. But they refuse to complain."

The original application to the Supreme Court covered not only the venue but also the circumstances in which the Magistrate was appointed.

When the hearing was resumed at Kapenguria yesterday Mr Pritt referred to the news in the telegram he had received from the MP's.

What Defence Counsel had referred to on Thursday as "a little light relief" now became rather heavy weather. The Magistrate was hurt. "If you are correctly reported in this cable," he said, "you have stated that what amounts to a denial of justice is taking place. No such charge has ever been made against me in the course of my judicial career of over twenty-one years, and I take the gravest exception to it." He complained that no mention had been made of the concessions—the free transcripts—and facilities the Court had granted to the Defence. In his opinion the cable made an improper comment on a case *sub judice*, and raised matters which would more properly come before a Court of Appeal. The trial was being made into a political issue both in Kenya and in Britain.

Defence Counsel made haste to explain that his criticism was in no sense directed against the Magistrate but entirely against the Government of Kenya. He read out the cable he had received from the four MP's, and described how he had studied the matter very carefully for some hours and, "after a good many drafts", sent a telegram which was certainly intended to be a "strong attack upon the authorities—not the judicial authorities—but the authorities responsible for the inconvenience" of a trial in Kapenguria. As this cable was plainly going to be a document which would be made public in the middle of a trial, he had had to be careful what he said in the way even of appreciation of what the Magistrate had done. He had mentioned gratefully the facilities given for interviewing the prisoners. He had not mentioned the offer of free transcripts—that would scarcely have been proper to mention, and in any case it happened twenty-four hours after the cable had been sent. If the case was being made to assume a political aspect in England, which the Magistrate complained of, that was hardly the responsibility of Counsel in Kapenguria. As for its being made to assume a political aspect in Kapenguria, Counsel humbly submitted "that I have been pretty careful up to now not to make any general political observations although there has been considerable ground for doing so. But, sir, whatever is the precise definition of a political case—it is never very easy to define—this case, if not a political case before, became a political

D*

case on 3rd December when my learned friend announced that he proposed to establish that Mau Mau was the militant wing of KAU." Counsel went on he might have complained "but as a matter of fact I actually welcome it". And he illustrated the situation, as he saw it, with an English parallel. "If six people in England were prosecuted for conspiracy to murder, that might well be a non-political case. But the moment the Counsel for the Prosecution, opening the case at the Old Bailey, announced that he proposed to establish that these six gentlemen whom he charged with murder, were, in fact, acting as the militant wing of a political party X, well known in London, whose address could be found in such and such a street, it would be a political case."

Counsel added that he was quite content to face an accusation of contempt of Court. "I have faced one before; I daresay I shall face one again; I have never lost one yet. I am not worried about it in the least, but I naturally do not want to put anybody to inconvenience or trouble." So he searched for a form of words that would remove the Magistrate's feeling that he had been personally attacked. "There has been no sort or kind of charge in my mind—or in my words—against you, sir, of having been a party to a denial of justice, which in my cable I alleged to be in existence, and to be caused by the Government.

"Let me see if I can go as far as this: that if it could be thought by anybody, Your Honour or anybody else, either on a complete report or an incomplete report, reasonably or unreasonably, that I had made any accusation against Your Honour of being party in any shape or form to the denial of justice of which I have complained, I would unreservedly withdraw any allegation which in that connection would be thought by anybody to have been made."

It did not suffice. There was an atmosphere of crisis in the court and the Magistrate at last declared more in sorrow than in anger: "In my present frame of mind I am quite unable to continue the hearing of this trial today." He felt his honour had been touched. He hoped to have very soon a shorthand note of what Mr Pritt had said, and the most he was prepared to do was to study this carefully. "If at the end of that time I find that I can with honour proceed with this trial, I will do so. But I still feel I cannot and the matter must take the course I suggested. I will give my decision at ten o'clock tomorrow morning."

Next morning the Court re-assembled to hear His Honour rule that although Defence Counsel had argued that no reflection on the Magistrate was intended, "that, in my opinion, is not the view that any reasonable person would take . . . I therefore decline to proceed with the hearing of this trial until the question is settled one way or the other, namely that I am wrong or Mr Pritt is wrong, and accordingly this trial stands adjourned *sine die*."

It had to be pointed out to him that to adjourn *sine die* was outside his powers. Defence Counsel argued that the case for contempt need not interrupt hearings—except that, when the time came, he personally could take a day off to go to Nairobi—but it was of no avail.

His Honour said he was only too well aware of the inconvenience of adjournment, and went on: "That, however, is not all that matters in this important trial. A high question of principle has developed. Greatly as I deplore the adjournment, the order which I delivered earlier this morning must stand, with the exception that the order for the adjournment *sine die* is amended to read one of an adjournment to the 30th December. In this way we shall lose about a week."

14

Wambui found, and a newspaper for Ephraim

In FACT the adjournment was till Friday, 2nd January 1953. The Supreme Court sat to hear the case for contempt in Nairobi on 29th December and on 31st December acquitted Denis Nowell Pritt, q.c. from the charge. Next day, Thursday, all Kenya knew the result, but since no official communication had been made to him the Magistrate opened on Friday by declaring that he was still "in the dark" about the case. Perhaps it was a case of judicial ignorance since he had presumably read the newspapers. Perhaps he noticed in the movements of the leading Counsel for the Defence indefinable signs of shock?

The adjournment had given the police time to find Wambui: it had also given time for the Court to consider the arguments on the status of Mr Pedraza. The Magistrate now found that, although Mr Pedraza had made the arrest, he "had not the status of a police officer", whereas he did possess the status of a magistrate (first-class). Accordingly the self-inculpatory statements of Paul Ngei were admissible.

Superintendent Alleyne returned with plans of the shop and store-room where Tabitha had listened outside the door. Tabitha's story was weakening as time went on. The premises consisted of a concrete block, divided into two rooms of equal size designed for use as shops. It was common ground that on the evening in question Kenyatta had been in the room on the right as seen from the front, and this room was not a shop, nor fitted as a shop in any way, but was vacant, having in it for the moment no more than a few pieces of furniture. The other, or left-hand room, was fully fitted as a shop, with a counter, stocked with goods, and in use as a shop. When Tabitha gave her evidence her description was quite plainly of the fitted shop; she called it a shop and said it had a division in it which might be a counter. And, sure enough, when she came to show the place to her employer Superintendent Alleyne she took him to the wrong room. When, under other guidance, the police got their plan straight, they found a number of cracks in the door of the room where Kenyatta slept, but the wood was poor and might well have shrunk in the strong sunlight of the many months that had passed since the Ol Kalou meeting.

As well as being Tabitha's employer, Superintendent Alleyne also knew Wambui. Now, in the box, he was asked:

PRITT: Have you had anything to do with a girl called Wambui?
ALLEYNE: Yes.
Q: When did you see her?
A: On the 30th December.
Q: Is she now in police protection and available to give evidence?
A: Yes.

The next witness to be recalled for further cross-examination, was Inspector George Kipture himself.

PRITT: You remember when I was cross-examining you before I asked you if you knew a girl named Wambui.
KIPTURE: I do remember.
Q: What did you answer?
A: The answer was, There are many Wambuis.
Q: When you gave that answer, did you know that there was one Wambui whom you knew very well?
A: There are several of them whom I know.
Q: Is there one with whom you have been on very intimate terms for a good long time?
A: Yes.
Q: Were you trying in your previous evidence to give the Court the impression that you did not know anyone called Wambui?
A: No, I meant that I knew many Wambuis.
Q: But there is only one with whom you have been on very intimate terms?
A: Yes, that is correct.
Q: Did you know perfectly well that that was the one we were asking about?

A: No, sir.

Q: Do you remember the night of the meeting in Ol Kalou?

A: Yes.

Q: Did you know where Kubai slept that night?

A: No.

Q: Did you sleep with Wambui that night?

A: I cannot remember.

Q: Do you remember fetching her from a house that night?

A: I cannot definitely remember.

Q: You often did fetch her?

A: Yes.

Q: Now, let me suggest this to you, that on the night she was called in by somebody in the house where Kubai was going to sleep she made up the bed for Kubai to sleep in. And I suggest that soon after she had finished making the bed you called for her and took her off.

A: I cannot remember.

Q: Do you know where she is now?

A: At Ol Kalou; the last time I saw her was on the 21st November.

Q: And she had been there pretty continuously from this occasion from June until November?

A: Yes.

Q: And she was a girl who was said to have been in the storeroom of the African shop when Kenyatta is said to have made this statement that Tabitha claims to have heard?

A: That I do not know.

Q: If the Prosecution had wanted to find her at any time from June to November, they would have asked you and you would have found her in five minutes?

A: Yes, if her name was given to me.

The rest of the day was mostly devoted to formal evidence of one sort or another such as evidence of the searching of Kenyatta's house where a police pick-up van was filled with papers. It was a quiet afternoon for a reason that did not come out till Monday morning after the week-end recess, when the Magistrate opened as follows:

MAGISTRATE: Mr Pritt, before we begin this morning I would like to say how sorry I was to hear about the motor-car accident in which you have been involved.

PRITT: It is very kind of Your Honour. By, perhaps, an undeserved miracle, I came out with nothing but bruises.

MAGISTRATE: I am very glad to hear there was nothing serious.

It is not a pleasant matter, to put it no higher than that, to be involved in an accident in which a car overturned. Had I known, I would have, of course, offered you an adjournment.

PRITT: We, my friend and I, had a conspiracy, we brought up nothing on Friday which involved very hard brain-work.

MAGISTRATE: I hope it is nothing serious.

PRITT: No, no, the doctor is quite satisfied.

The Supreme Court in Nairobi had dismissed the case for contempt of Court and Defence Counsel's car had overturned on the way back.

The next thing that happened this morning was a reminder of the day the storm burst. It may be recalled that on that morning before Christmas Defence Counsel had asked that Ephraim, the Secretary of the now famous branch at Limuru might be recalled to be cross-examined about the newspaper report he and his branch had complained of to KAU headquarters. Now after this delay Ephraim Gichereri reappeared and a copy of the Kikuyu newspaper *Mumenyereri* was put into his hand. He admitted this was the issue which he went to head office to complain about. Counsel read a translation. There was a long headline:

YOU DO NOT KNOW ANYTHING ABOUT KAU

You ought to have fetched the KAU Constitution and read it to this gathering.

This is what Kenyatta told the meeting which was held at Limuru on Sunday.

It was clear that Kikuyu journalists had picked up a bright newspaper style. Counsel continued with his translation, while Ephraim read the original.

If you ask Limuru people why they do not attend that meeting which is of KAU they answer you that the followers of the association do not belong to KAU but have applied for permission to hold the meetings in the name of KAU even if they held no KAU receipts, and that before this, this particular association was known as the *Association of Those Who Wait*—those who are waiting to see what will happen in future: if the black people get the land back to side with them, and, if not, to side with the Europeans. Further, they say that the followers of this group administer an oath on a fowl and when a person takes this oath he says that he will never agitate for the land, that he will never enter into association with Mau Mau. These are the things that people in that small area of Limuru say, where it appears that there is a great dissension among people according to the speeches made by the leaders of the Association.

The reporter's journalistic style had slipped but his meaning was not too obscure. (The Defence, as it came out later, had found the precious copy of the newspaper to all intents and purposes by accident. Kenyatta's papers were with the police and there were no files in Kapenguria.) Ephraim admitted that this was the passage they had complained about at head office. He added, curiously, that the report "has nothing to do with what happened at the meeting itself, it is something that happened at a subsequent meeting of the Mau Mau after the main meeting was over". Pressed for explanation he said: "They went off to another meeting in the house of a Mau Mau man", "they" being among others Kenyatta and Kubai.

PRITT: You have got an obsession about Mau Mau have you not?
EPHRAIM: I was only thinking about the case and the things I know.
Q: Do you always think that everybody who does not agree with you is Mau Mau?
A: Nobody could think that everybody was Mau Mau.
Q: I did not ask you about everybody, unless you mean that everybody disagrees with you. I asked you the question, do you think that everybody who disagrees with you is Mau Mau?
A: Nothing would make me think somebody was Mau Mau if he was not Mau Mau.
Q: Do you think I am Mau Mau?
A: I do not know—you come from Europe.

There was laughter in court and Ephraim was examined about the *Association of Those Who Wait*. It took some time to get from him the simple answer "yes" to the question did he know of the Association.

PRITT: Are you a member of that Association?
EPHRAIM: Yes.
Q: He is a member of the Association though he could not tell us whether he knew of it or not. Is that Association correctly described in this article?
A: No.
MAGISTRATE: You mean by its title?
PRITT: No, I meant the description which follows in the words,

sir. Do the followers of that Association administer the oath on fowls?

A: Nothing like that; that is just Mau Mau saying things about us. If there was anything like that we should have been arrested by the police.

Counsel returned to the newspaper report of what Kenyatta said at the meeting.

PRITT: Did he say to you: "I have been to Nyanza Province and I find the people there understand better what KAU is than you people here"?

EPHRAIM: Yes, he did.

Q: Did he say: "Somebody has already asked me to speak about Mau Mau"?

A: At the meeting?

Q: Did he go on to say: "I reply I do not know what it is"?

A: Yes, he did.

Q: Did he say: "As for you who say that you have investigated you had better tell us what it is like"?

A: Yes, he did say that. He was trying to please the Mau Mau people who were present.

Q: How do you know what was in his mind?

A: I know because he was saying that we were spies, like the Fort Hall people.

Q: Well, you were, were you not?

To the last question witness seemed to say "Yes" or "Yes but——" which he later altered to "No".

Q: Now, coming back to Kenyatta's speech, did he say this: "What I do know is that KAU demands self-government and speaks in the day".

A: Yes, he did say that.

Q: And is it common to say, and correct to say, that Mau Mau speaks in the night?

A: Yes, and in the day.

Q: Did Kenyatta go on to say that KAU works for our country?

A: Yes.

Q: And did he go on to say: "If anyone tries to take our country even if it be that animal called Mau Mau, we shall put a rope round its neck"?

A: He never spoke the word about the rope.

Q: What was he going to put—what did he tell you to put round the neck of Mau Mau?

A: I did not hear him say anything—he said it should be hit.

Q: Did he say: "This dissension you have got amongst yourselves does no good to the country at all"?
A: Yes.
Q: Did he go on to say: "You say you have seen where Mau Mau is. I say to you find an axe handle and hit it on the neck"?
A: Yes.

Defence Counsel was to refer later to this piece of evidence in a phrase: "The three tailors came to complain that Kenyatta did not denounce Mau Mau: we have the master tailor's evidence that he did."

15

Last Witnesses

Now Wambui had been found it was logical that Tabitha should be recalled and the Court learned a little more of her private life.

PRITT: What is the name of the man you told us you lived with for some months?
TABITHA: Zacharie Kihata.
Q: What did he go to prison for?
A: His mistakes.
Q: Mistakes in being found out for what?
A: He was a clerk to a judge but I do not know what he did.
Q: That is not an offence in itself. Do you still say you never made any other statement to the police?
A: No.

From this point Tabitha's confusion became worse confounded. She had in fact given two written and signed statements to the police, one at Nakuru on 25th October 1952 and one at Nyeri on 13th November 1952. According to the police officers who took the statements, each of them was read over to her at the time it was taken, was acknowledged by her to be correct, and was then and there signed by her. The two statements were very different from each other, and the first of them mentioned neither Wambui nor Kubai. Now in cross-examination Tabitha was foolish enough to swear she had given one written statement only, and that she did not sign it, but put her thumb mark on it. The statement was produced and found to bear a signature but no thumb mark. Then she swore repeatedly that she had made only one statement to the police—perhaps she was remembering the significant omission of Wambui and Kubai from her first statement, for the one she was willing to admit was the second of the two, the fuller one. Defence threatened her with prosecution for perjury, and then she admitted she had made the two statements which were then produced, and it was noted they were both signed, and were "as different as they could possibly be". Presently it appeared she had made at least four statements to the police. In re-examination Mr Somerhough produced a garment which Tabitha declared was her long-lost coat.

When the coat was produced Tabitha tried it on in court.

PRITT: When you went to Ol Kalou were you wearing a jersey under that coat?

TABITHA: Yes.

Q: I suggest to you that when you have a jersey under that coat, the coat is much too small for you?

A: No.

Tabitha was then re-examined by Crown Counsel.

SOMERHOUGH: Are you in figure now the same size as you were six months ago?

A: I am fatter.

Q: Why are you fatter?

A: I have a baby coming.

Defence were of the opinion that the coat had been given by the police to Tabitha's aunt, for it had turned up in the aunt's house. And Defence Counsel added: "The allegation that the evidence about the coat is a concoction from beginning to end is not withdrawn. And if, as a natural assumption it is said by anybody, 'Then the police must be in it', certainly I am not going to say the police are not in it. But I am not making a specific allegation, because at present I cannot prove it, that the police actually carried the coat to the aunt's house and gave it to her."

When Tabitha's aunt came to be cross-examined the Defence set out to overturn both Tabitha and the aunt. Certainly this turned out to be an employed aunt whereas Tabitha had described her as "without occupation". But Tabitha's aunt made herself famous in the case history by becoming the occasion for the boiling up of an objection that had been simmering for some time against Dr Leakey.

Dr Leakey had just translated one of Tabitha's aunt's remarks. There was a reaction in the dock, as had frequently happened before, whispered consultation took place between Counsel and clients, and Counsel turned to the Interpreter to say: "My clients

say she never said that. You are not interpreting, but just giving
your own opinion." The remark was resented. Counsel insisted.
"I have been pressed for five weeks now by all my clients and
colleagues. They do not trust this interpreter."

MAGISTRATE: I assure you and your learned colleagues and the
accused that they will not get an interpreter in Kikuyu anything like as good as Dr Leakey.

PRITT: They may get a Kikuyu who understands English, they
mistrust this interpreter.

MAGISTRATE: I repeat that I have had Kikuyu interpreters in
front of me in the Supreme Court for fourteen years and the
standard with one or two exceptions is extraordinarily low.

PRITT: Here we have an interpreter who is biased and has
written a book against my clients ... He puts things in and he
puts things out. He is a partial interpreter.

The outcome was that Dr Leakey walked out of the court and
refused to come back, and the case was adjourned over the week-
end till a new interpreter could be found. When the new one
arrived on Monday he turned out to be a Kikuyu provided by the
Supreme Court—an outcome which apparently distressed the
Crown Counsel who made it clear that "he would not be happy
with a Kikuyu interpreter". The Magistrate hastened to excuse
himself. It was not his doing, he explained: the Supreme Court
had sent the man. There was an atmosphere of alarm and despon-
dency.

The first thing the new man had to translate produced a small
legal victory for the defence on a point of procedure. To understand this it is better to break continuity and bring together evidence heard some days ago and its continuation now.

In his evidence-in-chief, a Prosecution witness John Gichungwa,
a Kikuyu, told how he met Kenyatta in Paris about 1929 and had
from time to time seen him since in Kenya. He described how
Kenyatta came to him one day at Githunguri in 1949 and asked
"why I did not enter into his association". Naturally Gichungwa
asked: "Which association are you talking about?" and he said
that Kenyatta replied: "The Mau Mau association." But so far
as was known the words *Mau Mau* had not been heard of quite as
early as this. The point was put to witness in cross-examination.

PRITT: I suggest to you that the word Mau Mau was in 1949
not even known?

GICHUNGWA: Even if Mau Mau was not talked about, the plan was known.

Cross-examination brought out more details of the story. Gichungwa had a stock of second-hand corrugated iron for sale. All over Africa of course corrugated iron or aluminium, for "pan roofs" as West Africans call them, is a highly treasured commodity. John Gichungwa dealt in this and he was carrying through a deal with Kenyatta for pan roofs for the teachers' training college at Githunguri. There was a big campaign going on at the time to raise money for schools. As several witnesses had already mentioned, the Kikuyu age groups were active in this money-raising campaign. And it was put to the witness that this was surely what Kenyatta was talking about—not Mau Mau, but school building and money raising. Witness resisted this suggestion and at this point Defence asked to examine the statement the corrugated-iron merchant had made to the police. The request was refused on the strength of a ruling by the Kenya Attorney General about two years previously that police statements need not be handed to Defence.

This cross-examination had taken place on Friday, 2nd January. It so happened in the course of his researches for the Defence that next day, Saturday, Mr Kapila, one of the Defence Counsel, was in Nairobi. He got the local paper to see what was going on in Kapenguria in his absence and there he read that the question of police statements being accessible to Defence had cropped up. Something reminded him that an earlier case he had been in, had some bearing. His memory was vague about the details but he went across to the East Africa Court of Appeal and asked the clerk to hunt up the judgment in the earlier case which for some reason had not been reported. By an odd coincidence that same Saturday the leading Defence Counsel in his hotel at Kitale reading another set of papers altogether, came on a cross-reference to the same case. So the case had been named and its number noted, and now Crown Counsel had to announce that the judgment had been found and it gave the Defence precisely what they asked for. To the surprise of both Crown Counsel and Magistrate the unpublished judgment of the East African Court of Appeal gave Defence the right to demand any statement any witness had made to the police and cross-examine on it. "If the Crown case were composed of police statements they could call for the whole of my brief" said Crown Counsel.

"In those circumstances, Your Honour, that being the law it is no longer incumbent on me to decide whether or not the Defence ought to see a particular statement" Crown Counsel concluded. "They have a right established, as I understand that judgment, to call for the statement. They can exert it in any and every case.

MAGISTRATE: You must not take it from me that I agree with what you say. I should like to study the judgment. There seems to be some preamble which you have not read out. If I had to rule—I do not, you have handed over the documents and there it is—my interest now is purely academic, but I would like to see it because it goes very much further than I expected, further than I expected the practice was. I would not disagree with them, if that was the decision, so be it.

SOMERHOUGH: It was a surprise to me. It is even more of a surprise that a judgment of such a very wide importance and of enormous interest to the Prosecution and the Defence equally, was never reported, but I am indebted entirely to my learned friend, to Mr Kapila, who was here in 1945 and made a note of it at the time and has put us on to it.

MAGISTRATE: There is nothing to prevent now, if the judgment means what you say it does, nothing to prevent the Defence saying to the Prosecution Counsel in any case, as each witness comes into the box: Produce anything that he has said to the police before."

(Inaudible comment by Mr Pritt sitting down.)

The point had been raised about one witness, but—a trial is a kaleidoscopic pattern—it was applied in the case of another. This was Njui, son of Gitau, who was afterwards given by Defence Counsel a nickname easy to remember: the Season Ticket Witness.

Njui had a shop and a car-hire business. He told how one day in March 1950, after the school sports, Kenyatta and a number of others called at his shop and they all drank beer. Later, at night, they drove off "to the house where food had been prepared". He had some food and waited. Kenyatta and some of the others had gone to another room. Presently one of them came to fetch Njui.

NJUI: The lamp was burning low when I went in, it was turned right low, practically out, and I was asked, "Are you Njui?" I felt myself having my hands seized. I was told, "Take off your boots, and if you have any money take it out". And I resisted. Then I felt somebody give me a blow on the back of my neck between the shoulder-blades. Then there was a disturbance

and I bolted out and met a man called Dedan Mugo in the doorway. Next I saw Jomo Kenyatta and Koinange. Jomo Kenyatta
came in and said, "What is all this noise about?" And he said,
"You have to go in". He took me by the arm and Dedan Mugo
by the other hand, and they pushed me in. As they were taking
me in they tried to calm me down. "It is not a bad business,
stop, stop, it is nothing bad." I was taken back into the room.
There were a lot of people there in a big line, and there was an
arch. Jomo took hold of me and passed me with him through
the arch. When I felt it as I passed it had banana leaves and
other things. There was only a small light which every now and
again was turned very low, and then turned on again, turned
up and down. The arch was about five feet high, we had to
bend down to get under it. Kenyatta was holding my arm. We
stood side by side together on the far side of the arch. I heard
the murmur of voices saying, "Eat this meat, and if you ever
sell our country or our people may this meat destroy you". And
I was told again, "Eat this meat. If you sell our land to the
Europeans you will die". And again, "Eat this meat and you
will have to pay 62 shillings and 50 cents. And you must say,
'Unless I do this the meat will hate me and I will die' ".

A second witness Kimani Muiriri told a similar story of the
same evening after the sports. He was in the next room when Njui
was being persuaded to take the oath and could hear through the
partition what was said by Kenyatta. Later they all sat outside and
sang a hymn beginning:

> Let all the Europeans go home
> Let Kenyatta be in charge of bananas.

It was on this evidence that Njui was now cross-examined and
now the Defence had before it a copy of the statement he had
made to the police. First he was asked about the date of the sports
meeting. March 25th, 1950. How could he be sure it was the 25th
and not the 24th or the 26th? "I remember it because there was a
sports meeting, and I noticed that a spectacular thing was done
which I will never forget until I die." What this variant of the
four-minute mile amounted to the Court never learned, for witness
was now asked:

PRITT: Is your memory good or hazy of this event?
NJUI: It is not hazy.
Q: Just listen to what you swore to: "The ceremony occurred a

long time ago and my memory is a little hazy on detail." Did you say that?

A: Yes.

Q: Did the police arrest you two or three days after this alleged oath-taking?

A: No, I was not arrested. I went of my own accord.

Q: Were you arrested and taken to the police station?

A: After I made a report, it was then two policemen came to my house.

Q: You were taken before the DC?

A: Yes.

Q: Did you tell the DC that there had never been any oath-taking at all, but only feasting with much meat?

A: I told the DC that an oath was administered and there was meat and people eating the meat.

Q: Was William Karuki afterwards arrested?

A: Yes.

Q: And he was arrested because you told the DC that it was Karuki who did the oath-taking?

A: He was arrested because it was his house where the oath was administered to us.

Q: Was he afterwards released because the police and the DC thought that nobody on earth would ever believe your evidence?

A: That I do not know, but later I gave information to the effect that Dedan Mugo was also present.

Q: So you are a police informer?

A: No, I am not. I have my own private business.

Q: In addition to being a police informer?

A: No, I only made a report of the oath that had been administered to me.

Q: And nobody believed you?

A: I was later told that if I mentioned Kenyatta's name to the DC it did not matter whether I went to live with the Governor —I would be got hold of and I would be killed.

MAGISTRATE: Who said all that?

A: Many people said it.

PRITT: Any of the accused?

A: No, none of the accused.

MAGISTRATE: This is inadmissible evidence.

PRITT: Is it a fact that you never suggested to the police or to the DC at Kiambu that either Kenyatta or Mbiu had anything to do with the transaction?

A: I said they were at William's house; it was later that I

was informed that, should I mention his name, I would be killed.

Q: So that at the time you were before the DC at Kiambu, a day or two after the oath-taking, nobody had yet threatened you?

A: I was threatened.

SOMERHOUGH: I am instructed that his answer was "I had been threatened". That is the impression I have had the whole time. Now he says, "I was threatened".

Later Njui added: "I did not give evidence at Dedan Mugo's trial. I only made a report."

At this point Crown objections to the Kikuyu interpreter, which had been boiling up for some time, flowed over. "There is always trouble with this particular tribe", cried the DPP, urging, "there is all the difference in the world between 'I had been threatened' and 'I was threatened'."

The witness was being evasive, seven or eight repetitions being sometimes required to obtain answers to simple questions. Under pressure, he admitted that he had had a law-suit with Karuki—the man who was first arrested after his report to the police—because one of Njui's drivers had backed into Karuki whose bicycle was damaged and the driver had to pay. Njui admitted, after more questions, that the other man he reported to the police in the oath-taking story was an ancient clan enemy, and admitted later that the quarrel between his clan and the other man's was the occasion of a current law-suit. At the end of the day Defence Counsel remarked: "I think that is all the questions I have to ask, unless I can just play the old campaigner's trick of keeping the cross-examination open until the morning, so that I can look at the statement at greater length." When next morning came, it appeared that Defence Counsel had indeed had a second thought. Njui was put in the box again.

PRITT: When you went before the District Commissioner shortly after the alleged oath-taking in 1950 did you make any statement that was taken down in writing either to the police or to the District Commissioner?

NJUI: Yes, I gave my statement to the DC.

Q: Is it possible to supply a copy of that to me, Mr Somerhough?

Certain copies were produced. Witness took so long to reply to the question how many statements he had in fact made to the police that the Magistrate had to intervene, saying, "Either you are being very stupid or you are refusing to answer the question", and, even so, got no very clear answer. Finally Njui was cross-examined on two of his statements.

PRITT: You remember saying, giving an account, last week of being told to take off your shoes and to give money and being told that it was a simple matter and you were not to make a fuss?

NJUI: Yes.

Q: Did you say last week that it was Jomo Kenyatta who said that?

A: Yes.

Q: Did you say in your statement which you signed in May 1950 that the person who said it was Dedan Mugo?

A: I said that because I had been threatened before I went to make that report.

Q: Are you a person who would tell any lie on oath if you were frightened of anybody?

A: I wanted to save my life, that is why I said so.

Q: If your life was worth saving would it not be in as much danger if you falsely denounced Dedan Mugo as it would if you falsely denounced Jomo Kenyatta?

A: I omitted Kenyatta's name because I had been frightened. I had been told that even if I sought shelter at Government House I would be killed.

Q: Did you not think you would be killed, if your statement is to be believed, did you not think you would be killed if you mentioned Dedan Mugo?

A: Yes, I thought I would be killed but at that time there was not much protection.

Q: Is it correct that you never told, in writing, the story of being frightened to give Jomo Kenyatta's name until the statement you made at Nyeri on 17th November last year?

A: I do not give this statement, I gave the statement at Nyeri.

The two statements were put into his hand. Njui identified his own signature.

The Njui episode had a certain bearing on relations between the Crown and the Defence generally. Njui had been brought to Kapenguria some time before the trial began, presumably as a witness. As we have seen he was not mentioned in Crown Counsel's opening—perhaps because, as the Defence put it later, "at that stage the Prosecution had arrived at a wise and honourable decision that it would not call Njui". Then came the adjournment while the contempt case was heard, and presently in came Njui.

At this stage of the trial the Prosecution had been generally following the practice of handing to the defence, of its own motion, copies of any previous written statements made by any Prosecution witness whenever these appeared to be inconsistent with the evidence the witness was now giving in court. Njui's previous police statements went a long way to destroy what he was going to say in court: but in this instance Prosecution showed Defence none of the previous statements and if they had not been elicited in course of cross-examination their existence would never have been disclosed. The Prosecution gave Defence no information and just tacitly put forward Njui as a witness of the truth. Defence felt strongly, and later made this a point in their petition to the Privy Council, that the Magistrate ought to have reproved the Prosecution for not handing the statements to the Defence, and indeed for calling Njui as a witness at all.

(It should be added that when the file was examined of the Prosecution, which had been started and then abandoned after Njui's first statement to the police, it was found to contain no mention either of Kenyatta or of Mau Mau.)

Crown Counsel now, without re-examining Njui, moved to Incident Number 13 which was in effect two stories by a certain Munyi, one of an oath-taking in Nairobi, another of a series of a sort of Mau Mau study-circle meetings in Nairobi every Saturday night in September 1952 as a regular thing, the supposed leaders being the accused Kubai and one Willie George. Defence proved later that Willie George and Fred Kubai had quarrelled some time before and were not on speaking terms in autumn 1952—indeed according to the evidence of the accused, several Executive Committee members tried hard to patch up the quarrel but in vain. Prosecution witness Munyi, son of Daniel Gatabai, stuck to his story.

The witness was a smith by trade, and his story was that one Saturday afternoon in September 1952 he went to a tea-party in Pumwani Hall, Nairobi, as a send-off to three men who were going to England. At this tea-party Kubai and another arrived "in a real taxi". Later all the party-goers went to a house in the Burma Market and took the Mau Mau oath. From this time on Kubai and

Willie George administered the oath every Saturday night in Willie George's house. "People were told when there were enough the horn would be sounded."

Today the DPP had lost his voice. Examination was conducted by his assistant.

WEBBER: Did you say what is to happen when the horn is sounded?

MUNYI: That when we had enough, when the horn was blown, all the Europeans in Embu were to be driven out by us or killed.

MAGISTRATE: He talks about the horn being blown—does he understand that literally when a horn is blown—or is that a figure of speech?

WEBBER: You say the horn is blown. Is literally a horn to be blown or is that merely a figure of speech?

MUNYI: When the time came, I do not know what horn was to be blown.

Q: What part do you play at these meetings?
A: We go to hear the orders we are to be given.
Q: Who gives you those orders?
A: Willie and Kubai.

MAGISTRATE: I take it this gentleman is a member of the Mau Mau?

WEBBER: That is my next question.

Q: Are you a member of Mau Mau?
A: I am, and I have taken the oath.
Q: You have told us about everyone—men, women and children taking the oath; what other instructions, if any, do you receive?
A: That if a person reveals the secrets of the Kikuyu he is to be killed because he despises his country.
Q: What secrets are those?
A: About the way the oath is given at night. If I should be called out by the people of that Association I must not refuse.
Q: Who told you that?
A: Willie George, Kubai, the leaders of Mau Mau.
Q: When did that meeting start?
A: From seven o'clock until nine o'clock in the evening.
Q: Where was that?
A: Majengo.
Q: Whereabouts in Majengo?—Whose quarters?
A: Willie's house.

Subsequently in cross-examination it was elicited witness had been what he called "an oath askari", that is to say his function was "to keep cave" at oath-taking ceremonies. Asked "Are you hoping by your evidence to buy off a prosecution of yourself for being a member of Mau Mau?" He replied: "I do not know whether I shall be forgiven."

Apart from the documents such as "hymn books", which were still to take time and trouble, only two witnesses remained for the Prosecution. They can be taken together. The first of these gave his evidence-in-chief before Christmas and before the adjournment. He was Waweru Kunu, a non-Christian, who affirmed that in June 1952 he was fetched from his home and taken to another man's house.

Waweru said: "I had barely got inside when I felt myself seized by the back of my neck, and then I was seized here and here on the arms by three different people. The fire was made up and by its light I saw people sitting all round like that"—and he made a circle with his hands. "They had knives, and Kungu Karumba was sitting near the door. He is the one in the dock on the extreme right. And Kungu said, 'It is I who have ordered you to be seized, because we want you to take the oath'. I said, 'Oath? What for?' He said, 'It is for the Kiama Kiabururi Association of the Country which has been organised to drive out the Europeans and it is secret. That is why we have seized you because you are a very bad man; you belong to the Government and you go about and about. I do not in future want you to reveal our association because you are a Government man'. And I said, 'Well, that is so; I will not disclose it because I am afraid of being killed'. And he said, 'You will have to pay sixty-two shillings fifty cents in order to become a member—and a ram'. I said, 'I have not got these things now'. I was then asked, 'When could you bring them?' and I said, 'I might bring them the day after tomorrow'. He said, 'The sixty-two shillings fifty cents cannot wait, but must be paid here and now'. Then he said to the man who brought me, 'That is for you to deal with because you brought him here'. After the oath had been administered to me, he said I could go.

"I went out of there and went away. I left them there, all of them. When I got outside I did not even go by the path, I went through the garden in great haste. I went right to my home. The money I did not pay. I went next day to find the white magic man called Ngungiri. I found him with another man who died recently.

After I had done all these things I went to the Chief to make a report."

SOMERHOUGH: What is your job?
A: I am in the Kenya Police Reserve.
Q: And before that?
A: I was before that in the Kenya Police.

The adjournment delayed his cross-examination and witness had a fortnight to think things over. Cross-examination began early with the direct question:

PRITT: Are you acting now as a police informer?
KUNU: Yes.
Q: Do you remember, towards the end of 1950 you had a land dispute with some of your relatives?
A: Yes.
Q: Was Karumba one of the elders who settled that dispute?
A: Yes, he was a good man at that time.
Q: Was it at about that same time when you were visiting Karumba's shop and you complained that he was not giving your family a proper sugar ration?
A: No, I do not remember anything about that sugar.
Q: Did you about that time try to borrow money from him to buy wattle-trees?
A: I have never borrowed money from him.
Q: Is he in partnership with your younger brother?
A: Yes.
Q: Did you try to borrow money from that brother and from Karumba to buy wattle-trees?
A: I do not know anything about that.
Q: Were you very angry and determined to have vengeance on Karumba because he would not lend you the money?
A: No. I do not know anything about it.
Q: I suggest to you that there is no truth whatsoever in the story that he administered the oath to you?
A: He did. He did give it to me. He is the leader of the big organisation of Mau Mau.
PRITT (to Magistrate): I ought to object firmly to that statement by a dirty little police informer.
MAGISTRATE: You may object Mr Pritt but it is nevertheless an answer to your question in the first part.
PRITT: On what day of the week did all this oath-taking happen?
A: I think it was a Sunday, the 24th June, 1951.

Q: Do you remember saying you went to see a white magic man
and you found him with another man who recently died?

A: Yes, a man called Kimani Wa Kahiu, and he died on the 1st
January 1952.

In his examination-in-chief the witness had put the oath-taking
not in June 1951 but in June 1952, when Kimani Wa Kahiu was
already dead. Defence was later to claim that his quick switch of
the date of the oath-taking from 1952 to 1951 was the fruit of his
fortnight's consideration, during the long adjournment for the
hearing of the case of contempt.

The other witness was concerned with one more Kenyatta meeting. He was Mwangi, son of Njonogi who affirmed that his occupation was that of police informer, that he went to a meeting at
Thika in July 1952 where Kenyatta spoke in Swahili. Kenyatta
said he wanted the people to be given self-government. Kenyatta
went on to say that he heard people saying that there was something called Mau Mau and he did not know what Mau Mau was;
and when he spoke in that way he spoke in Swahili. Then he
changed over to Kikuyu and said, "Let the people take a little
snuff".

SOMERHOUGH: What, if anything, happened when Kenyatta used
that expression?

MWANGI: The women trilled, and the men clapped their hands.

16

The Black Exercise Book

On 14th January Crown Counsel asked for an adjournment while the "hymn books" were translated. Evidently Crown had been so certain the Magistrate would grant the request that they had turned up at Kapenguria without witnesses. In the hotel at Kitale it had been common gossip that there would be no hearing today. The Magistrate expressed surprise, saying, "I have even brought my lunch with me". Defence strenuously objected—both at the way the Crown had taken things for granted, and at the delay—arguing that in any case all the evidence on the "hymn books" was irrelevant since "It is an indisputable fact that in all the hundreds if not thousands of folios of printed matter involved, the word 'Mau Mau' appears only once". Under very strong protest the adjournment was granted, and everyone went back to Kitale, having travelled 24 miles for a ten-minute argument.

Next day the translator, the Rev Robert Philp, a missionary of the Church of Scotland, Kenya born and the son of a missionary, took his place in the box. But what Crown Counsel now began to read through to him—though too quickly for the Court or the shorthand writers to follow—was the beginning of his translation, not from the "hymn books" at all but from the Black Exercise Book. Now the Black Exercise Book was said to have been found in Kenyatta's house when the police seized a truckful of his papers. It was never proved to have been in his possession; it bore the name of another person as its owner; and it did not contain a word in his handwriting. Most of the entries in it—which were in the handwriting of a large number of people—had no bearing on the case, but it did contain the text of some songs which also appeared in some of the song books. Defence had taken the attitude from the start that the book was plainly inadmissible. Now Crown Counsel seemed to be trying to get it into the record, reading the translation so fast that his very speed defeated the object—if object there was. Whereupon Defence Counsel jumped to his feet with a passionate appeal. He said to his colleague, "If you have a shadow of regard for your professional reputation don't put this document in". Crown Counsel replied that these protests "are made for the gallery—what you call 'The Continent of Europe' whenever you want to make some grossly improper observation". The fat was in the fire, old resentments revived, and Crown Counsel declared, "because you have come to Kenya you think you can do as you like!" Defence Counsel answered: "I conduct myself here as in any other court. The accusation that I treat my friend in any way differently is utterly false. I have praised him on several counts if I thought he ought to be praised. Now I feel he ought to be reproached and I do reproach him. He can talk Billingsgate to me if he likes, but that is a little unkind to Billingsgate; but if even he can produce the faintest justification for having put this altogether irrelevant document into this case I will apologise to him for not having understood the incomprehensible."

It turned out the Magistrate was almost as aggrieved as Counsel. "One officer of the court"—Dr Leakey—"has retired because he says he was insulted by learned Counsel for the Defence. I am beginning to think the object of the Defence is to drive me from the court too"—to which Defence Counsel replied that Dr Leakey retired because he was challenged and added, "The last thing I desire, sir, is to cause you trouble. My friend and I have been on good terms most of the time, and have been a little cross at times. I did warn him in a friendly way that if he insisted on putting in all these documents he would earn a very strong measure of my indignation".

The Magistrate adjourned till tomorrow to calm down. Next morning there was still a ground-swell. Crown Counsel it appeared had been brooding on the word "Billingsgate" and asked for it to be withdrawn. It was withdrawn. The Magistrate added a word or two on the Kenya Bar and how "We here in this Colony have as much pride in our professional reputations as anybody who comes from England". The Black Exercise Book made its second entrance in an uneasy atmosphere. Court Clerk and Crown Counsel numbered its pages, page 6 the diary entry, page 7 the continuation, page 8 the first of the three pay-day pages, pages 11 and 12 blank, 13 blank, 14 a folk tale of the Hyena and the Squirrel, and, at last, the manuscript texts of two of the hymns. Copies or originals? That was one of the questions. The first hymn dealt with was the one entitled *False Allegation*, which Dr Leakey had translated in his evidence on page 91. Now the Rev. Robert Philp was cross-examined on the verse in this song in which the words "Mau Mau" occur.

PRITT: You start with the heading "allegation" with perhaps a tinge of falsity. The first chorus indicates that the singer is in trouble, and the trouble which may be caused by the allegation is, I suggest to you, this: "If I go into town I am harried by the police; if I go into the country somebody calls me Mau Mau." Do you think that is a fair effect of the meaning?

The answer came in preacher's language; for the Rev Philp replied:

If one were asked to expound this rather difficult composition that is one possible expounding. I would not like to hazard an opinion. I would draw attention to this: that the chorus itself is not an original composition, it is a chorus copied from one of our well-known hymns.

There was also cross-examination about the translation of a "hymn" entitled "One day the leaders of KAU met at Kaloleni". The translation contained a phrase hinting at secrecy: Defence argued the reference was simply to a committee meeting.

PRITT: You know the Social Hall at Kaloleni? About as good a place to have a secret meeting as the Albert Hall in London or the Usher Hall in Edinburgh?
PHILP: It would depend on the conditions which you would get. You might hire it and apply it to your own particular group of people.
Q: With regard to the Black Book—I will take them in the order in which they came in the evidence. Mr Philp, with regard to the Black Book, which you must remember fairly well. You don't know, of course, anything about its origin or who wrote any of the things in it?
A: Apart from what I have heard in the court and from what I have seen in the book.
Q: The book does not tell you who wrote the things, does it,

except in one instance, on the last page, where I see Wanjiko is said to be the writer?

A: The book contains on its fly-leaf a name, Mwango, son of Jomo Kenyatta, which indicates something to do with the book, and then there is that name at the end—the name of another person. As for all the stuff in between, there is no clue.

Q: You don't know, of course, how an entry appears to have been made in it by somebody three days after the police say they took control of the book?

A: I have no idea.

In later argument the Defence put forward a theory. The position was curious, but it was a fact that a number of police officers, who had been described by Mr Somerhough as "rather slovenly", had produced the book, and a police officer had stated that he had spent some three weeks examining the seized books and papers. The Black Exercise Book seized by the police on the 21st October, continued Mr Pritt, had in fact got a diary entry in it of 24th October, and if one were allowed to guess one would guess that the person who was actually keeping the diary was arrested with the book in his possession. Could it be, asked Counsel expanding his theory, that when the book was subsequently examined, somebody, without realising what he was doing, had probably said: "This book does not belong to this fellow: it belongs to Kenyatta", and the book was then transferred from one bundle of documents to another? This was theorising, but what was certain, was that internal evidence raised a question whether the book could possibly have been taken by the police on 21st October. "If", said Mr Pritt, "it was not taken on 21st October, then there is no evidence that it was ever in Kenyatta's house." In those circumstances, Mr Pritt suggested that His Honour ought to say that he was completely satisfied that there was no evidence that it was ever in Kenyatta's house, and in any case the mere discovery of a document in Kenyatta's house was no evidence that he had ever had anything to do with it. The book was obviously a book which had been kept by half a dozen people. There was somebody's name at the beginning of the book, and there was another person's name, as the author of a hymn, at the end; and there was a diary kept by this person. The one person who had never touched the book with a pen was Kenyatta. Lastly, he would ask His Honour to say that, having seen the whole of the translations, there was not a line in the book which could help in the decision of this case, and that therefore His Honour should rule out the Grey Book, the Blue Book, Black Notebook and all.

The Magistrate ruled in favour of all the books—Black, Blue, Yellow, Grey. People make mistakes about dates and the entry in the Black Book had in any case said: *Tuesday 24th October*, whereas Tuesday in that week was 21st October.

Some of the remainder of the ruling is worth quoting:

I now turn (said the learned Magistrate) to the Grey Hymn or Song Book. Verses three and four of the first hymn in the book surely suggest Mau Mau policy according to the evidence. These hymns deal with KAU to a large extent and it is one of the Prosecution's submissions that the leaders of KAU are in fact the leaders of Mau Mau. If this be true, then verse six of the 9th hymn in the Grey Book has some significance. This verse reads as follows:

"The day that the white people go home those who associate with them will have their necks wrung like chickens in distress."

There is nothing in the Defence so far as I have heard that this threat of violence is part of the KAU method or policy and yet, as I have tried to remark, the Grey Book sets out, or seems to set out the policy of KAU and dwells on benefits to be derived from membership of KAU.

Verse six rather suggests, *prima facie*, that KAU is getting somewhat close to Mau Mau in its tenets or policy or methods, also verse three of the hymn or song Number 29 is as follows:

"I am helped by the oath, this oath of the Children of Mumbi that I will not sell this land but will remain on it forever."

There is no evidence before me yet that it is part of KAU to administer an oath or to take an oath. There is evidence that the administration and taking of an oath is part of the Mau Mau ceremony. It therefore seems, at first sight, that this hymn Number 29 may be concerned with the Mau Mau Society and that KAU may have some connection with the Mau Mau Society. In these circumstances in my opinion, the Grey Book is also relevant and is therefore admissible in evidence. It has been said that there is no evidence that any of the accused has ever known of the existence of these Hymn or Song Books. I should find it somewhat difficult to believe, especially since there is so much in the books about Kenyatta, that he at least is not well aware of their existence, however, he will be able to say so if that be true—yes, Mr Somerhough?

SOMERHOUGH: That is the end of the Prosecution case.

MAGISTRATE: The Prosecution case is closed.

17

Submission of no case by Defence Counsel

DEFENCE had now important submissions to make on the case as a whole.

These began with a somewhat technical claim that the proper consent for the trial had not been given: which led to argument taken at some length not only in this court of the first instance, but later in the Supreme Court of Kenya, and again before the Privy Council. The argument concerned jurisdiction: and, behind the lawyers' care for forms thus displayed, there is perhaps something more substantial than at first appears. In this case it was a question of whether the true intention of the law had been observed. The law says that before a prosecution of this kind can be launched in Kenya the consent of the Governor must be obtained, and the question that arose was, Can the Governor delegate this power? Can he, as in this case, leave the decision to the Member for Law and Order? If he does so, again as in this case, what it comes to is that the Member for Law and Order gives permission to himself—wearing so to speak another wig—to prosecute as Attorney General. And Defence argued that this absurdity showed that the obvious intention of the law had not been observed. The law intended that the Governor should bring to the question of whether to prosecute or not, the common sense —not the legal knowledge—of the Queen's representative in the Colony. If the Governor delegated this power to his law officers, he defeated what was the express intention of the law. The question invited and received subtle legal argument. In the result all courts, the Magistrate, the Supreme Court, and the Privy Council decided that the Governor could delegate his powers, and the consent of the Member for Law and Order in Kenya to himself as Attorney General in Kenya to prosecute Kenyatta and five others was a valid consent and should stand.

The rest of Defence Counsel's speech took the form of a destructive analysis of the Crown case in such detail that when the time came for the final speech of Defence many of its points had already been made. A thorough analysis at this stage contributed to the clarity with which the case could be viewed and it is useful to reproduce several passages of the speech.

Defence Counsel asked: "What does the Crown case add up to? What do we get?" He answered his own question: "A certain number of police officers who proved very little, a certain number of confessed informers, a certain number of accomplices, and of all these forty-four witnesses "there was not a single one except Waweru who claimed to have attended a Mau Mau meeting since the middle of 1950." There was in fact another exception and Counsel thought of him a moment later—"the little accomplice Munyi from the Burma Market who was called in at the last moment". Apart from these small exceptions in respect of the whole period of the charge, namely August 1950 to September 1952, "there is not a tittle of evidence of any Mau Mau transaction of any description that ever took place over the two years' period mentioned in the charge sheets—not a meeting, not a photo, not a microphone, not a report from police watchers—there is hardly an individual who could be named as having anything to do with it except for Munyi". There was not a building in the world which had been proved to have anything to do with Mau Mau, not a single letter produced by or from Mau Mau, not as much as a ten-cent piece of Mau Mau money. "There is not even a mark on the body of any single one of the accused or anybody else involved." The whole resources of the Government had been bent to prove that "these six somewhat important gentlemen" were involved, "in an organisation which is denounced by the powerful voice of KAU and which surely the vast majority of people of all races in Kenya must be opposed to". And in the outcome there was so little proved that ought to have been proved Counsel found it significant—and puzzling. There were only two possible explanations, one of which he rejected out of hand, that was incompetence in the Kenya police. This he rejected not out of courtesy but sincere conviction. The other conclusion from "the extraordinary

absence of any real evidence at all" was that the accused were
innocent.

Counsel had sorted the case into incidents and this led eventually to a much-mentioned chart of the case prepared by Defence
which appears at the end of this book. At first there were 17
incidents—later they were counted as 21—beginning with Rawson
Macharia's story, going on to Muthondu's and ending with the
meeting at Kiambu.

"I have two comments to make. The first is that practically all
the evidence seems to be on the extreme edge or periphery of the
case. If you ever find a witness who says he was present at a Mau
Mau ceremony you discover that it happened some months before
the period covered by the charge sheets. . . . Everything is on the
extreme edge and nothing from the centre ever really appears." In
incident after incident the names cropped up of potential witness
after potential witness. One might have thought the Prosecution
would be glad to call them. Yet in practice "almost every incident in
the case from beginning to end rests substantially on the evidence
of one witness". The first incident was typical. It rested on the evidence of Rawson Macharia, "a witness so utterly untrustworthy
that he should be disregarded". In his story he mentioned at least
ten people who were, according to him, present at various stages.
Not one of them had been called by Crown.

Macharia was obviously consumed with self-importance. "One
wonders whether he wanted to show off by giving his evidence in
English out of incurable vanity or whether it was because he made
his police statement in English. He began by saying he was quite
willing to have his name published and then, when the evidence
was read over to him, he said most emphatically that he did not
want his name given and that he had never said he did. He gave
me at any rate, the impression at several stages that he had learned
his evidence by heart because he kept missing out words, which
people often do when they have learned evidence by heart, and
words slip out. You will remember that quite unnecessarily he told
us a whole lot of stories about 1932 when he was a boy of thirteen
which served to show what an unreliable person he is." Counsel
said "almost the last straw" was Macharia's convivial picture of
Kenyatta sitting down to have drinking bouts "with this little
person who probably scarcely ever saw Kenyatta in his life".

The Muthondu story was briefly dealt with. "What does it prove at best? That five or six months before this society was proscribed, some people sang songs in Jomo Kenyatta's house, and the following day some people came to breakfast who might have come from Kenyatta's and who had marks on their hands, which, so far as evidence goes, is not a place for Mau Mau marks at all."

Then the third incident, Limuru. The essence of the case as developed could be put like this: "The three tailors of Tooley Street were the only God-fearing, honest, and anti-Mau Mau people for miles around.

"They gave me the strange impression of thoroughly enjoying the wickedness of other people and the righteousness of themselves, rather like the narrow-minded chapel deacon in a Welsh valley licking his lips over the wickedness of his neighbour's daughters." They did not attend the KAU meetings in their district though these were on a very large scale, they pretended to know nothing about them, they arranged meetings of their own without informing headquarters, and when Kenyatta turned up at one of their meetings their story was they tried to persuade him to denounce Mau Mau and he evaded the question. "To pay them out for their virtue they were hauled up to head office, had their branch dissolved and were told to leave Mau Mau alone because it was a *dini*.

"I would suggest to Your Honour that this little group of three people, very likely quite honest and sincere, and as it proved in the end, after very long cross-examination, were members of another organisation altogether called 'The Association of Those Who Wait', which might be put into good English slang as the Mug Wumps Union, sitting on the fence waiting to see what happens. Your Honour will remember the famous definition of a mug wump as a politician sitting on a fence with his mug on one side and his wump on the other. But there is this little bunch— and as I am hoping to demonstrate to you hereafter, they are unique, and the fact that there is nobody else to be found like them is the significant fact I want to develop. They are, obviously, obsessed with the belief that everything and everybody, except themselves, is Mau Mau."

Just as some people blamed the Jews for all they feared and disliked, Counsel went on, these blamed Mau Mau. And in their obsession they completely forgot the positive side of KAU policy. He contrasted two possible attitudes, one bad the other good. So

E*

far Prosecution evidence had shown KAU taking the good attitude. "And that attitude is: 'Keep clear of Mau Mau. Have nothing to do with Mau Mau. Explain publicly whenever you are allowed to hold a meeting, explain what KAU is, explain its policy and repudiate Mau Mau. But do not fall into the error of doing nothing but denounce Mau Mau. Do not be, as it were, 100 per cent negative. Understand, explain and expound the policies of KAU and work constructively for them.'" That was the good attitude. And Counsel recalled that one of the witnesses, Mr Kennaway, admitted that if you can coax or cajole KAU or any other organisation into spending most of its time in defensive repudiation of suspicion and criticism you can destroy its effectiveness.

The bad attitude, the converse of this, was that of the three tailors. "It is the old story, 'You are miserable sinners and you have gone whoring after strange gods, repent before it is too late'. This is the attitude of this branchlet and I am quite sure that if any other branchlet could have been found anywhere in Kenya prepared to take up the same attitude, the prosecution would have called them."

More serious, he thought, was Mr Ephraim's story of Kenyatta saying, 'Mau Mau is a *dini* you must leave it alone'. "Of course there may be an answer to that but at the moment we are not discussing answers and therefore I want to say a word about it on the footing that it was proved." Here again, Counsel said, whenever you get up to the point where it looks as if the Prosecution were about to prove something, you had to pause. Here was Kenyatta. Prosecution described him as an outstanding figure. He was alleged to be managing Mau Mau. "And what is the high-water mark of what is said against him? He said 'Leave Mau Mau alone, it is a religion'. It would be a serious thing to say, an unpleasant thing to hear, but it did not mean he had anything to do with Mau Mau. If a Labour leader in England said, 'Leave the Tory Party alone and talk about our own policy' would it prove he was a Tory?" The mountain was in labour but produced so little Counsel wanted to apologise to the mice.

Next, he went on, Ephraim had talked about the big neighbouring branch—the Chura branch of KAU—being riddled with Mau Mau. Yet what witnesses had the Prosecution brought about Chura? "If there were a word of truth in this it would be manna to a thirsty Prosecution and we would have had a mass of evidence about it." The other main thing in Ephraim's evidence-in-chief was an obsession that he had never heard of Kenyatta denouncing Mau Mau. Yet from the whole of the Prosecution evidence of any meeting addressed by Kenyatta "there has been express evidence that Kenyatta was denouncing Mau Mau."

Of Mr Kennaway, Counsel recalled that what he did was first quite plainly to tell the Court that he had never heard of a whole series of meetings denouncing Mau Mau, and finally he was driven to produce documents showing that he had given consent for every one of them.

Next Counsel came to the passage in which Ephraim was taken through the report in the journal *Mumenyereri* "with very remarkable results indeed". Now it could be seen "how the Limuru case stands—or in my submission, more accurately, falls.

> In my submission we have the position that the whole of the essence of this story from the beginning to the end—"We were begging and begging Kenyatta to denounce Mau Mau and he would not, and it was for that reason that we were dragged up to head office and debranched", the whole thing disappears completely, because the witness, whilst agreeing with practically every word of the report insofar as the report purports to be a report of what Kenyatta said at the meeting, includes in that agreement the fact that the real answer to the bleat that Kenyatta did not denounce Mau Mau, is that Kenyatta denounced Mau Mau in the plainest and most unequivocal terms that could be imagined.

Counsel came to incident four—Tabitha.

> She goes to Ol Kalou in June 1952 to hear a KAU meeting; she is not a KAU member, she has never been to a KAU meeting, she goes to greet her aunt and we shall see in a moment which aunt it really was, because in the end it became clear that she had two aunts. She listens to the meeting, she gets nothing out of the meeting, and then goes in the evening—this is the most fantastic story—she is at home with her aunt, she thinks she will go and fetch her coat, she goes out to fetch the coat—she hears some children say they are going to listen to Jomo, just at the very right moment she comes out of her aunt's house—she follows the children and they arrive at a building, she parts with them in some way, just at the right moment she arrives at just the right place, she hears through a stone wall and

door the man who she estimates as fourteen feet away from her with a stone wall and a door in between, she hears Jomo, she recognises his voice, she hears him talking in Kikuyu to people —whom I think he would be more likely to address in Swahili— at the right moment she gets there and he says something most useful to Mr Alleyne or Tabitha, he says it loud enough for her to hear, although if her story is correct and Jomo Kenyatta must be treated for the moment as a reasonably intelligent leader of a proscribed organisation, if he was really giving Mau Mau advice to a miscellaneous collection of people in the room at the time, you would think that if he was ever going to say any-thing so foolish he would have said it very quietly; whatever else Kenyatta would do, he would not say anything of the sort in the presence of the girl Wambui about whom we have heard so much.

It is too coincidental for anybody to accept. If anybody put it into a second-rate farce, no theatrical manager would put such an impossible thing on—here it is in a second-rate prosecu-tion, it is put into a prosecution for felony. What does it mean for the Prosecution? The Prosecution, accordingly put it to Tabitha alone, an unreliable informer, to depose to something through a stone wall——

MAGISTRATE: Are you quite right?

PRITT: It is a stone wall with a door.

MAGISTRATE: Which door has openings in it.

PRITT: Which door is proved by the Prosecution witness to have some interstices in it six months later, to have been at the time of the meeting a new door, and to have been a door in respect of which it would be right to assume from an ordinary know-ledge of timber, had no interstices at the time. There is also evidence before you that the Prosecution have made tests to see if you can hear and have not called evidence of the results of the test!

SOMERHOUGH: Your Honour has indicated quite clearly about parallels which are not parallels.

PRITT: There may be some good reason for the Prosecution not to call evidence—all I have to say is that they have not called it.

SOMERHOUGH: It is not evidence, that is why.

PRITT: I would say bluntly that if anybody had heard, the Prosecution would have had a couple of witnesses.

SOMERHOUGH: You would say it quite falsely.

Even so, said Counsel, what about Wambui? Surely she should have been called by the Prosecution? Whatever was said about walls and doors, did not get rid of the fact that Wambui was supposed to be inside all the time. If they believed Wambui was in the room "then either she heard it or she did not hear what Kenyatta had to say. If she had heard it and was not called the Prosecution had no right to proceed with this section of the case at all".

What the Crown had done was investigate the shop—with the help of Tabitha. Yet "the first thing she did in the way of identifying the shop" was to tell Mr Alleyne that the occupant was a man called Solomon, which turned out to be false. Then Mr Alleyne said "she took him to the shop and he then and there made a sketch of the shop. It proved almost immediately that Mr Alleyne was sketching the wrong shop, and he of course was just an ordinary honest police officer trying to do his job and she showed him the wrong one".

Counsel had finished with Tabitha. He went rapidly through the Ngei incidents, and came to the first hymn books.

Incident Seven on the chart was concerned with the pale blue hymn book bought from Kaggia in which Hymn Number 9 is "The night Dedan Mugo was arrested". Counsel thought it was probably "the high-water mark in Your Honour's mind against my client, Kaggia". And yet, "many people have committed crimes which incite general indignation yet they have displayed courage and people admired their courage. Many people have admired the wit of Oscar Wilde and sympathised with his sufferings yet nobody would say they approved of unnatural sexual practices."

Suppose "certain things happened which I trust will not happen. Suppose one had to write a report and answer objectively, 'What happened to Kaggia in this case?' This is the answer I hope will not be given. 'He was convicted of membership of Mau Mau'. Oh, was he? What was the evidence? 'Well, there was no evidence that he ever had anything to do with it?'—I am only dealing with this one incident—'no marks on his body, no evidence that he ever attended a meeting, but evidence that he was in a car in which there were some copies of a song book, and he sold a copy of the song book to a policeman. There was in the book a song in which praise was offered to the courageous demeanour of a man who had been arrested for taking an unlawful oath, not the unlawful oath of Mau Mau but of another organisation'. That is, in my submission, a fair and objective description of what the position would be if Kaggia was convicted on that evidence alone of membership of Mau Mau."

He went on to the yellow song book—it was found in Kenyatta's house among papers that took three weeks to sort, and it contained the song headed *False Allegation*. If the song were a confession of Mau Mau membership—suppose ten thousand people in a crowd sang it? Would they all be confessing membership of Mau Mau? "Then I want to reinforce all that by looking at the heading ... If this thing stood alone and Mr Kenyatta was convicted of being a member or indeed a manager of Mau Mau and somebody said, 'What was he convicted on?' one would report, 'Well he had never been seen with the yellow song book, there was no evidence he knew what was inside it, but among documents found in his house where he and six other people lived, there was a yellow song book, and in that book was this song, and on the basis of that Kenyatta has been convicted', and I think people would say, 'Surely that is impossible?' And that is all."

The next four incidents were quickly dealt with. The fourteenth is "the story of Mr Njui". This witness came as a person who was prepared to attribute to Jomo Kenyatta both a transaction and a particularly damning conversation which he had already attributed on oath to another—Dedan Mugo. "One would have thought no Prosecution would ever call such a witness and the Prosecution apparently took that view—though one can only assume this—right through December when they never called him. My learned friend in a reasonably full opening never mentioned this incident. ... I think it fair to say that if the Crown had closed its case without the accidental gift of a fortnight's adjournment it would probably never have called Njui at all. It is a pure speculation whether in the course of that fortnight the Prosecution thought over the possible nakedness of its case and decided to put into the box this gentleman who told about Jomo Kenyatta the story he previously told about Dedan Mugo. I leave the story to make its own comment. I wonder how many times he could be used—I wonder, if in some subsequent case against somebody else, this gentleman will turn up with a smile and say it was really some third person. 'I know I have sworn on oath that it was Kenyatta; I know I have sworn on oath that it was Dedan Mugo; but I was frightened, and it is Mr So-and-so'—a sort of season-ticket witness."

Counsel ran through the chart. The X's in the vertical columns show that a prisoner was implicated in an incident: the O's mean he was not mentioned. Adding them up we see one incident against Karumba, three against Paul Ngei, two against Kaggia. "Achieng, if I may put it that way, is involved in one and a half incidents: Fred Kubai is involved in four and a half incidents.

It is interesting then to look at Kenyatta, merely on the graph, and you see thirteen incidents in which he is said to be involved, and then consider soberly how terribly thin that is when you see what the actual incidents involving Kenyatta are. I want to say this about him. He is the leader of a very large political organisation representing the largest community in the Colony. He is charged with managing for a period of over two years beginning in August 1950—a subversive terrorist organisation. The charge is made by Government with all the investigation resources of a modern Government, with as many months as it likes to take for investigation before it made the charge, then two months after it made the charge in which to gather and adduce further evidence; and it is interesting to look first at what is proved, if all the evidence is true, that Kenyatta did in the period of the charge. I am leaving out for the moment the things that he is alleged to have done before the period August 1950 to October 1952. Brought here to meet this charge, you would have thought that at least in the course of that time we would have been told that he had attended a meeting of Mau Mau or addressed Mau Mau somehow, or been to the office, or signed a letter. One would have expected, when the Government, without warning to him, seized a good many thousands of his documents, that there would have been one document somewhere which suggested that he should do something about Mau Mau, or was doing something about Mau Mau, and the actual total of what the Government has proved of this gentleman's alleged Mau Mau activities in the course of the two and a bit years with which this charge is concerned are so utterly trivial and tiny that if I recited to you what he is actually said to have done in that time, I would submit that it is the most childishly weak case made against any man in any important trial in the history of the British Empire.

I take the incidents roughly in the order in which I have got them in the graph. I ought to mention eight, and the first one is

that at Limuru. In answer to a challenge that he should denounce Mau Mau, he denounced Mau Mau. That is the first
great crime he committed.

The second crime he committed, if the evidence can be
believed, is that he told three gentlemen, who were pretty near
paranoiac, that they were not to worry about Mau Mau.

The third great crime, if you could ever believe Tabitha's
story, is that in a back room in Ol Kalou, he told half a dozen
people not to use too much force when making some people
take some kind of an oath.

The fourth great crime is that when he disclaimed all knowledge of Mau Mau at a meeting in Nyeri it was applauded.

The fifth great crime is that he told a meeting somewhere
that it could take a pinch of snuff, which means, according to
the Prosecution, that it could take a pinch of snuff.

The sixth great crime is that there lay in his house—perhaps
belonging to him or perhaps belonging to somebody else—a
yellow song book which contained two hymns relating to Mau
Mau which is conclusively proved by the prosecution to have
no sinister meaning whatever.

The next great crime is that there also lay in a room in his
house a black exercise book belonging to somebody else.

I do not know whether the next crime should be treated as
coming within the period or not, but there also lay somewhere
in his house a letter not proved to be written by him, but bearing his name—harmless enough in itself—and written to somebody in 1948.

The last great crime attributed to him in the period is that
somebody found a grey hymn book containing praise of Kenyatta.

That is the whole of the case against Kenyatta of anything he
ever did in the period August 1950 onwards. If one then had to
look in addition to the obviously untrustworthy evidence given
by Macharia, Muthondu and Njui of things he is supposed to
have done before it was proscribed, the irresistible conclusion
would be that he took the course, when it was proscribed, of
not having anything to do with it at all. Sir, I am not sure that
it would be right and proper, after the great length of time I
have been addressing you, to draw any kind of conclusion and
therefore I leave it with those submissions, and suggest to you
that the case shoud be thrown out for lack of evidence and
want of jurisdiction.

MAGISTRATE (to Mr Somerhough):   I will call upon you to answer
these submissions that there is no case to answer.

18

The Crown's Reply

CROWN COUNSEL'S reply may be summarised briefly. The first point, made with some emphasis, was that despite all argument to the contrary, this was by no means a political case. "It is a criminal case, *Queen against Kenyatta and others,* for what is a crime." To call it a state trial conjures up visions of Westminster Hall and the Earl of Essex with the axe edge turned towards him, and Warren Hastings: but in these humdrum days there are no such things". The case would be the same if it were for felony or picking a pocket. "To describe it as a state trial is to invest it with a halo it does not really possess."

But the main argument was the Crown case did not rely on any of the incidents singly. Crown relied "on their cumulative effect". Crown by no means relied "on the weighing up of each incident with its explanation which taken by itself means nothing".

Crown Counsel went on to dispose of one or two difficulties. Rawson Macharia may have made a genuine mistake when he swore he saw Kenyatta giving evidence before the Carter Commission in Kiambu in 1932—the sort of mistake anybody might make. Muthondu, the eating-house proprietor, saw people "with incisions on the arm: the fact that they were in an unusual place is a small point". The Limuru branch officials charged Kenyatta with failing to denounce Mau Mau—and they were right. How could he be denouncing Mau Mau when he said "I do not know what it is"?

Later, according to the Limuru branch officials, Kenyatta described Mau Mau as a religion. "Now the Defence rather brushed that aside but the Crown attached a good deal of weight to it."

Incident Number Four: "The incident, as my learned friend says, depends entirely on the evidence of the witness Tabitha.

145

The supporting cast, the police, the aunt, the architect and so on, play a comparatively small part. The incident stands or falls by Tabitha." Crown Counsel thought it stood. Tabitha was cross-examined three times "and on the main part of her story, in my submission, was not shaken at all."

In Incident Five certainly there was a shouting match between Paul Ngei and Mr Pedraza, but Paul Ngei had declared "perhaps slightly in alcohol, 'I am Mau Mau'". And Crown added: "I revert to my previous argument that it is the cumulative effects of these incidents you have to consider."

So to the "hymn books".

> My friend says there may be lots of people besides Mau Mau who want the Europeans to go and wail in the sea. If I can establish that Mau Mau want that, and that there is a body of persons praising that particular course of action, then there at least to this extent is something which is characteristic of Mau Mau, as Mr Henderson puts it. It may be characteristic of other things, but it *is* characteristic of Mau Mau, and, of course, as you know, some of those hymns are found in the famous black manuscript book.

Finally Crown answered the peroration for Defence—first finding some significance in the fact that Defence Counsel now actually spoke of "Kenyatta's great crimes", a claim which naturally caused some surprise to be expressed by the Defence. Crown Counsel's last words were:

> "And as regards the general submission, the omnibus one, that there is no case to answer, the Crown say that the test to be applied at this stage, a well-established test is a question Your Honour has to ask yourself, "If I were to hear no more, is there evidence on which I could convict?" and the Crown say that looking at the evidence and the cross-examinations as a whole, the answer to that must be in the affirmative and they therefore ask that the case may go on and the accused be put upon their defence."

The Magistrate ruled that the proper consent to the trial had been obtained, there was a case to answer, and the Defence case opened.

19

Kenyatta's Evidence

JOMO KENYATTA was taken through his evidence-in-chief by Mr Chaman Lall. He spoke in English. "I do not know when I was born—what date, what month, or what year—but I think I am over fifty. I was educated first in the Church of Scotland Mission and after that I educated myself. I am a Christian."

He started political activity first as a sympathiser with the East African Association in 1922, then from 1928 as a full-time worker with the Kikuyu Central Association. The earlier body, the East African Association had been concerned to agitate about forced labour, wages, land and "what is known as the Kipande or Registration Certificate which was introduced in 1920". Then—"before I forget"—there was agitation about taxes. "We used to pay Poll Tax as well as hut tax which means that if a man had more than one wife, for example many Kikuyu people have one, ten or even fifteen wives so you might be subjected to paying sixteen taxes, including one for yourself." The methods employed in these agitations were always constitutional, "making representation to the Government in the most peaceful ways we possibly could". The Kikuyu Central Association had similar aims, but "as you will understand things grew, and in 1928, there were more grievances.

"By 1928 most of us had become aware of an Ordinance known as the Crown Lands Ordinance of 1915, according to which—but you have the relevant books, you can correct me—I think it says something like this, 'All land previously occupied by native people becomes the property of the Crown, and the Africans or natives living thereon become tenants at the will of the Crown'. Up to that time many Africans, including myself, were unaware of such an ordinance and therefore, when we came to know of it, we started a demand for its abolition." Another protest was "against the country being changed into the status of a Colony instead of a Protectorate, because in a Protectorate we were told that the British Government was protecting us until such a time as we were able to protect ourselves: then we could be left to do our own affairs; but under the Colony we were told—I don't know how true it is—that it becomes everybody's country, that is, Her Majesty's country, and anybody would have the right in it, and Africans would have less right in it."

Land was the main object for the KCA. "I think if you woke up one morning and you found that somebody had come to your house and had declared that house belonged to him, naturally you would be surprised and you would like to know by what arrangement." Kenyatta was working in the Nairobi Municipality when the Hilton Young Commission came to investigate the land problem in Kenya. "My people approached me saying they would like me to represent them." After some hesitation he left Government service and started a paper, "the first paper in this part of the world to be published by Africans". Then he became General Secretary of the KCA. In 1929 "I was approached by my people as a member of the organisation and they asked me if I could go to England to represent them".

By this time two new political problems had appeared. One was a new demand that the Africans should have direct representation on the Legislative Council: the other was a controversy with the Church of Scotland about female circumcision. "This custom which was and still is regarded as dear to the Kikuyu people, that is the circumcision of Kikuyu girls, was maintained by the missionaries as being cruel to the womenfolk, and we as Kikuyu maintained that it was a beautiful custom, and there was this disagreement." Those who followed the custom were now debarred from the Church Schools "which previously we had built jointly". These were among the grievances Kenyatta came to ventilate in England in 1929.

"We were told when we approached the Government, 'Well, you know we have no objection for you coming to Legislative Council or any other place of Government provided you have education'. Now, the question of education was occupying the minds of our people very, very strongly, because we wanted to educate our children, and that was another point why I went to Europe—to seek ways and means by which we could establish our schools." He went to England in March 1929, returning in September 1930. In May 1931 he went to Europe again and did not come back to Africa till 1946.

In England he entered into correspondence with the Secretary of State for the Colonies and the correspondence was afterwards published. He addressed meetings. He interviewed both the Archbishop of Canterbury and the Moderator of the Church of Scotland about female circumcision, and a Committee of the House of Commons was appointed to review the question. "After a long discussion it was decided by the Committee to recommend to the Government the abolition of such a custom, and to educate the Kikuyu so that they would be in a position to decide which of their customs were good and which were bad.

"Then I maintained myself that with education we, the Africans, did not want just to say that our customs are better than anyone else's, but my point was that we could take some of the good European customs, and Indian customs which are good and take our customs which are good and see how we could build a kind of decent society which would be embodied with good things. Mind you, there is not a society of angels anywhere—anybody is bound to make mistakes, but we were right to borrow other people's customs, provided they were suitable to our mode of life, and of course abolish some of our bad customs."

KCA agitation won an early concession—from 1930 Kikuyu were permitted to establish schools: "if we could find land to build on, money to build, and money to pay the teachers, then we could start our schools". Accordingly two new organisations were formed, the Kikuyu Independent School Association and the Karinga Independent School Association. "When I came back I found the two Associations between them had over 300 schools educating something over 60,000 children." Kenyatta also found KCA had been proscribed.

"I saw His Excellency the Governor about twice on the question. Sir Phillip Mitchell said he did not see any reason why the Association should not start functioning but he left the matter with his officials."

LALL: Were you hopeful about the negotiations?
KENYATTA: Yes.
Q: Have you seen a letter which has been put in by the Prosecution as an exhibit? [It is handed to the witness.]

A: Yes. I see my signature here. This, if I remember rightly is the letter which I asked my secretary to draft in order to inform the members of the Kikuyu Central Association of the negotiations that were going on, and I think that is why the writer says, "Members and those who call themselves members of KCA". Therefore at the beginning he wrote the word *antongoria* which means leaders, and I objected to the idea of using that word because I wanted to write the word *ariamani*—"those who were the leaders". But here, it is written as though the association was functioning, and after signing it in a hurry I refused to send it, and the letter as far as I remember was not sent.

In any case negotiations with the Government officials broke down soon afterwards and the whole matter was dropped.

The KAU had been formed in the meantime, but he did not enter into its activities at once. "When I came back I went to see His Excellency the Governor, and I was told, 'Now Mr Kenyatta you have been away so long you are almost like a foreigner; you have got to stay here for one or two years in order to adapt yourself again into the country'." At that time witness was busy with the independent schools, but in 1947 he joined KAU "and when the elections came I was nominated for the office of president". Before joining he had studied the aims and objects of KAU.

LALL: Would you kindly have a look at this and tell me if this is the constitution of the Kenya African Union?
KENYATTA: It is.
Q: Tell us what the aims and objects are, as specified in that document?
A: The aims of the Union are: (*a*) To unite the African people of Kenya; (*b*) To prepare the way for the introduction of democracy in Kenya; (*c*) To defend and promote the interests of the African people by organising, educating and leading them in the struggle for better working conditions, housing, etc., etc.; (*d*) To fight for equal rights for all Africans and to break down racial barriers; (*e*) To strive for the extension to all African adults of the right to vote and be elected to the East African Central Assembly, Kenya Legislative Council, Local Government, and other representative bodies; (*f*) To publish a political newspaper periodically; (*g*) To raise and administer the funds necessary to effect these objects; (*h*) To fight for freedom of assembly, press and movement.

Q: Have these always been the aims and objects of the KAU?

A: Yes; that is, from the time I have known the KAU when I started to lead it and even before that.

Q: If you look at (c) you will find that the word "struggle" for better working conditions appears; whilst in (d) the word "fight" for equal rights for all Africans appears. What do you understand by that?

A: To fight for equal rights does not mean to fight with fists or with a weapon, but to fight through constitutional means and negotiation.

Q: And "struggle"?

A: It almost means the same thing; it does not mean wrestling.

Q: Now look at (h) "To fight for freedom of press and assembly." What do you mean by that?

A: It means the same thing, that is to fight constitutionally—to negotiate for these things; in other words, to ask the Government that we should have the right of assembly—to meet—to be given our own press.

Q: Is it a fact that the KAU has struggled for better working conditions, for freedom of assembly, press and movement, and for equal rights for all Africans on constitutional lines?

A: Yes, that is so.

Q: Does the KAU believe in violence?

A: No; we do not believe in violence at all: we believe in negotiation, that is, we ask for our rights through constitutional means —through discussion and representation. We feel that the racial barrier is one of the most diabolical things that we have in this Colony, because we see no reason why all races in this country cannot work harmoniously together without any discrimination. That is one thing, together with many others, that we have been fighting, and we believe that if people of goodwill can work together they can eliminate that evil. We say that God did not discriminate when he put the people into the country. He put everybody into this world to live happily and to enjoy the gifts of nature that God has bestowed upon mankind.

MAGISTRATE: I think these answers are becoming too long; they are tending to be speeches.

LALL: Could you give us approximately the membership of KAU to date?

KENYATTA: I have forgotten exactly but I know it is over 100,000 members.

Q: Is there any other organisation of the Africans in this country?

A: No, not as far as I know.

Kenyatta went on to deny the whole of Rawson Macharia's story. On 15th and 16th March, the supposed date of the oath-taking, he was in Nairobi in a series of committee meetings where a controversy had arisen about political tactics, whether in fact KAU should participate in the Nairobi City anniversary celebrations or not. He had met Macharia only twice in his life. Once he gave him a lift in his car.

Next came the story of Muthondu, the eating-house proprietor. Muthondu's story began with a meeting in Gathundu Market of the Kikuyu Age Groups.

LALL: What are these Age Groups?

KENYATTA: The Age Group means persons, both men and women, who are circumcised in any particular year or season or period and all that group of people become known as an Age Group with a name attached to it. Shall I go on?

LALL: Yes please.

A: Every year, or two years, circumcision ceremonies are held in Kikuyu, which means there are many Age Groups in Kikuyu country. Now it becomes necessary for all these Age Groups to come together for the purpose of collecting money to build schools, the Independent Schools or Githunguri College and they came together, I think twenty-two Age Groups joined together, that is almost like joining the whole Kikuyu people together through Age Groups.

He told how the meeting began in the morning and went on till five or six in the evening. Afterwards Kenyatta was entertained by a local leader in a shop in the market, returning home about nine with some of the party who "just sat and talked". Muthondu's eating-house was over a mile away. The police station was much nearer.

The Ol Kalou meeting—Tabitha's meeting—was described. Koinange opened with prayer. Kenyatta "explained to the people the aims and objects of the KAU."

KENYATTA: I also told the people that the Kenya African Union had no connection with the Mau Mau, and we do not want any of our people, especially our members, to have anything at all to do with Mau Mau, and that if we want to advance our country we can only do it by being honest, speaking the truth, not engaging ourselves in any nefarious activities, such as hating other people, and I remember referring to the Ten Command-

ments which said—most of you know what they say and so I
need not repeat it. Thou shalt not steal, Thou shalt not commit
murder—and so on and so on. That is the point I stressed very
firmly because many of the people at the meeting were Christians.

Q: Did you say anything at this meeting derogatory to Jesus
Christ?

A: No.

Q: Or to the Christian religion?

A: No. I mean I have great respect to people's religion, not only
to Christian people's religion but also to religions such as
Mohammedism, Hinduism and others, many of which I have
studied from the scientific point of view and I have great respect
for—I mean adherence of any religion such as I have mentioned.

Q: You heard a witness Tabitha?

A: Yes.

Q: Tabitha said you referred to Jesus Christ as an English
gentleman and that it took the joy out of her heart.

A: That is utter nonsense.

Counsel had been taking witness through the several Prosecution narratives. Tabitha was soon dealt with: next was John
Gichungwa, the man who was selling second-hand corrugated
iron for the Independent Schools and "understood" that he was
being asked to join Mau Mau some time before the name had
been heard of.

LALL: Now when John Gichungwa was asked certain questions
and it was brought to his notice here that in 1949 Mau Mau was
not known, this is what he said: "Even if Mau Mau was not
talked about, its plan was known." Now can you tell me, was
any plan known to you concerning any organisation known as
Mau Mau?

KENYATTA: No. The best person to answer that question would
be John Gichungwa and his associates.

Q: When did you first hear about the word Mau Mau?

A: The word Mau Mau came into being in 1950, I think, where
we found the expression used in *The East African Standard*,
and everybody was surprised. What is this Mau Mau? The
word Mau Mau is not, as far as I know, and I claim to know
a few of our languages, it does not belong to any of the languages that I do know.

These he claimed as Kikuyu, "a bit of Masai", some Kiambi, a little bit of Buluria and Luganda, Swahili, "not to mention Meru and Biran".

So to Limuru. The first Kenyatta had ever heard of the Limuru branch was when DC Kennaway told him the branch had permits for three meetings. He "thought it his duty" to go and find out what this branch was. So with Kubai and Henry Mworia he went to Limuru market-place expecting to find the meeting there, but they found it was being held at a place called Kamirithu a little way off. They got there about eleven o'clock, nothing was happening "but the whisper went round that we were there and people started to come in", including local officials led by Ephraim Gichereri whom Kenyatta said he had met somewhere before. As the meeting proceeded "there were some questions put to branch officials". People were saying there were rumours of some connection between KAU and Mau Mau, and asked what was the difference between the two.

LALL: What did the local officials say?
KENYATTA: The local branch officials did not answer the question but said that that was not a proper place for those questions and perhaps they would be answered at some other time.
Q: What did you do?
A: When my time came to speak I first reprimanded the local officials for their ignorance in not being able to answer simple questions, and I told them it would be better for them to go to headquarters and get the constitution of the KAU. Then I went on to explain to the audience, first telling them that there was no connection whatsoever between the KAU and Mau Mau, and from that I explained to the audience the aims and objects of the KAU. I told the local leaders, who were saying that they knew some people who were Mau Mau, that it would be a better thing to report the names of those who they knew were Mau Mau, and then, speaking figuratively in the Kikuyu language, I told the people that the best thing to get rid of Mau Mau would be to look for it, put a rope round its neck; then find an axe handle, hit it on the head and finish with it for good.

In Kikuyu language, the heaviest weapon one could use to strike an enemy is an axe handle. In a fight you always reserve this handle to the end.
Q: You heard in evidence that was given here in this court when it was said you used the words "Ndui, ndui, Mau Mau". What does that mean exactly?

A: If at a meeting I say that there is nothing I myself know about Mau Mau, and I say "Ndui, ndui, Mau Mau"—equal to this— if you ask me if I am a friend of Judge Thacker and I tell you "Ndui Thacker" it means I could not have been his friend if I did not know him. Therefore it has a wider meaning than just saying "I do not know". It is an emphatic way of denying connection with something, but not just a mere "I do not know".

At the meeting at head office they heard among other things complaints from Ephraim and his colleagues that in Henry Mworia's newspaper it had been reported that their sect took oath on a dead chicken.

LALL: What sort of religion did they belong to?

KENYATTA: Dini ya Etereri.

Q: What does Dini ya Etereri mean, Mr Kenyatta?

A: That is a religious sect that waits for the Lord to come. They have got so many names. Sometimes they call themselves Dini ya Roho, the Holy Ghost or something religious, but this Etereri is as I have explained.

MAGISTRATE: Mr Chaman Lall, your question was, "What religion did they belong to". He has not said they belong to it.

KENYATTA: They belong. I have no—I cannot prove that they belong to it, but I think they themselves admitted that they belong to this religion and they must belong to it because they came to the office, they came to our office in connection with that Dini.

LALL: Is there any ceremony connected with this religious sect?

A: It is said that these Dini have a chicken oath or fowl oath, that is they kill a chicken, and they take oath from a chicken.

Q: I see. Then what happened?

A: Well, my colleagues, some of them, contributed in this talk about Dini or "Those who wait", and then finally we told these people at Limuru that this has nothing to do with the Kenya African Union and what they should do—they should write a letter to the Editor of *Mumenyereri*, pointing out that he has reported them wrongly and see what reply they get from Mworia. Actually they wanted Kenya African Union to institute a law-suit against Mworia. So we told them, "Well, we are not a court of law that we give you permission to prosecute. This is a dispute between a member of your religion and the editor of the paper".

Kenyatta described in detail the steps which led to the meeting arranged specially to denounce Mau Mau—the Kiambu meeting. There had been personal discussions between Kenyatta and his friend the late Senior Chief Wahuiri which led to a preparatory meeting.

LALL: Now, what was this meeting for?

KENYATTA: This meeting was also to discuss how we can speak to the general public, that is the Kikuyu people in the Kiambu district, to tell them about Mau Mau, or to denounce Mau Mau, but I think the best way is not simply denounce, but to try and give them guidance how they could stop Mau Mau or how they could eliminate Mau Mau from the Kikuyu people.

Accordingly an *ad hoc* committee was formed. Kenyatta described it as consisting of "five chiefs and four commoners" and this committee planned a public demonstration on a grand scale. There were to be loudspeakers, press photographers, news reels, a recording van for broadcasting and so on; Kenyatta was to be principal speaker, the Senior Chief to take the chair.

The meeting duly took place in August. The press reported an audience of 30,000. Kenyatta put it higher, 40 to 50,000. After explaining the aims of KAU he "called upon the audience for a public curse on Mau Mau".

LALL: Public curse on?

KENYATTA: Public curse on Mau Mau.

Q: I see.

A: And hear the strongest curse we could put in public in Kikuyu. I called on the people, and asked them to say in unison, that is in Kikuyu. I do not know how to say it in English, but I said, "All those people who want to get—who agree we should get rid of Mau Mau, put up your hands". Now all these people —I mean it is not in Barazi in this paper, but in some of the other papers, in the *East African Standard*—it shows the photograph while the people are holding up their hands.... Thousands of people holding up their hands. And after that I told them to repeat after me the Kikuyu curse: "Ngai Mau Mau, Irothie Na Miri Ya Mikongoe Yehere Bururi biui biui", which means to say, that is, "the Mau Mau may disappear in—abyss— or something—where you may not be recovered when you have gone, 'Irothie na miri ya Mikongoe', You can never be recovered again."

Questioned by the Magistrate he said this was a common curse in Kikuyu. The accursed object is sent to the roots of the Mikongoe tree.

LALL: Final, complete destruction. Is that what you mean?

KENYATTA: Yes, it is. "Mikongoe", there is no tree called Mikongoe, it is a saying.

MAGISTRATE: Well, well, it is very necessary I should know if it is a tree or not.

KENYATTA: It is not a tree.

MAGISTRATE: Does it mean "underneath the ground?"

KENYATTA: It means both and it goes down with the root of that which is not known—Mikongoe.

MAGISTRATE: I am going to speak quite frankly to you. What is passing through my mind—it is for you to clear it up, you are the witness—it may mean: "Let Mau Mau disappear, down to the roots underneath the ground."

KENNYATTA: Yes.

MAGISTRATE: That might not be a curse, that might be an exhortation to Mau Mau to disappear under the ground.

KENYATTA: No, no, no.

LALL: Could it possibly mean that the people could understand you to mean that the Mau Mau should go underground and work underground?

A: Nobody could understand that, because when I say "Irothie na miri ya Mikongoe" I say "You had better disappear, finish".

Q: Perish?

A: Yes, perish. Here "root" is not the root of a tree. I cannot translate these things.

MAGISTRATE: Now, Mr Interpreter, does this word mean as you said it meant, a tree or does it not?

INTERPRETER: I think I will accept Mr Kenyatta's explanation.

MAGISTRATE: You will not, you will interpret it to your own knowledge. That is what you are here for.

The interpreter, under heavy fire, seemed at a loss. Defence Counsel interposed.

PRITT: It may be an imaginary tree just as a unicorn is imaginary. If I was asked to say if a unicorn was an animal or not I would not know what to say.

MAGISTRATE: Is the suggestion of Mr. Pritt's correct? It might be an imaginary tree. Something which might be in fairyland, not on this earth?

INTERPRETER: I think it may be some mysterious type of tree which does not exist—it exists in the imagination of people.

MAGISTRATE: Have you ever seen one?

INTERPRETER: No, Your Honour.

MAGISTRATE: All I can say is it is not very satisfactory.

KENYATTA: I think, Your Honour, if you want to know the nearest meaning you can say "disappear with the roots of the unknown".

MAGISTRATE: Unknown what?

The examination concluded with a reference to Kenyatta's war record.

LALL: One last matter. You were in London during the war?

KENYATTA: Yes, throughout the war.

Q: Have you anything to say about that?

A: I was doing many things, but one of my jobs was to lecture to British soldiers. I lectured for, I think, over five years in different parts of England in various searchlight units as well as in barracks, from the south of England to the north, around Manchester and so on. I was sent north after "D" Day to lecture to sick soldiers in hospitals and rest homes. Before "D" Day I was lecturing on the south coast of England.

20

Kenyatta cross-examined

CROSS-EXAMINATION began with Kenyatta's early career. Crown Counsel worked from early jobs to universities, from universities to travel.

SOMERHOUGH: What about abroad?
KENYATTA: I travelled widely in various parts.
Q: Where?
A: Practically all over Europe.
Q: Where?
A: Belgium, Holland, Switzerland, Italy, France, Poland, Estonia, Bulgaria, Denmark, Sweden, Norway, and finally—what you have been wanting me to say—Russia.
Q: Did you attend any educational institute on the Continent?
A: A bit in Russia.
Q: What institution there did you attend?
A: Moscow University.
Q: How long were you there?
A: I think about two years.
Q: What years?
A: It must be between 1932 and 1934. I have been there twice.
Q: Twice to Russia or twice to the University?
A: Twice to Russia; once in 1929 and again in 1932.

Back in England he studied anthropology in London from 1935 to 1938 and wrote *Facing Mount Kenya* "a serious scientific study based on personal knowledge and observation".

Q: Looking back on it does it still represent your views on the Kikuyu tribe?
A: The book cannot necessarily be a guide during my whole life.
Q: Have you changed your opinions since then?

A: The book is not my opinion as such: but it represents the habits and customs of the Kikuyu people.

Q: You have described yourself as a Christian?

A: Yes.

Q: What church or denomination?

A: I do not believe in denominations. I am a true Christian believing in God.

Q: Do you practice polygamy?

[Counsel for Defence objects that polygamy is not one of the charges and is overruled.]

Q: Do you practice polygamy?

A: Yes, but I do not call it polygamy.

The question: "Do you swear that you have not stirred up racial enmity?" produce half a morning of legal argument. The effect was to high-light the answer Kenyatta had to make. He replied, "I will say no: but I would add that if things like asking for the abolition of the colour bar, proper distribution of land, wages for óur people, equal representation in Legislative Council —those are the things I have asked and I mean in a constitutional way——"

Q: Would you say that consistently to represent one section of the community as robbers and thieves is to stir up racial dislike?

A: I will not say that—if I represent African opinion no less than European leaders represent European opinion, I do represent African opinion.

The answer was declared irrelevant, Crown Counsel pressed, demanding a clear answer. Defence Counsel objected to the whole line of cross-examination and in particular to the form of a have-you-stopped-beating-your wife question. It was re-phrased.

SOMERHOUGH: I will put it the other way round. Have you represented consistently that the Europeans are robbers and thieves?

KENYATTA: No. But I have said in that connection, and I think I have been right in saying so, that Europeans have a better share in the land. They have better position. That is, if I am qualified in a certain thing, being an African—and this is why I attack the colour bar—no matter whatever qualifications an African may have he always has a lesser pay because of his colour, not according to his qualifications. That does not mean that I represent Europeans as wicked people, but I say there has been injustice, and as such I cannot be assumed to say that Europeans are bad. I say the law——

SOMERHOUGH: Your Honour, do you think there is anything I can do to limit this answer? The question is a fairly short one.

Witness was stopped at this point. It seemed this round had gone to Kenyatta.

Now he was questioned on his "undenominational form of Christianity". Did he regard the oath he had taken in court as valid, for instance?

A: Yes, otherwise I would not have taken it.

A passage was read from *Facing Mount Kenya* criticising European oath rituals such as "kissing the Bible and raising hands" as meaningless to Africans. The answer was he was writing of non-Christian Africans. He was questioned about the proscribing of the early *East African Association*; then about an interview he was said to have given to the *Sunday Worker* in 1929; and about the banning of the Kikuyu Central Association— KCA—during the war while he was in Europe. Kenyatta argued that a war-time ban by no means proved that the Association had adopted unconstitutional means. He was pressed about the draft found among his papers calling the former leaders of KCA to a meeting at his house. He repeated that on reading the draft he had changed his mind and had not sent out the circular.

SOMERHOUGH: I suggest to you that you know very well they (KCA) were banned because of the oath they took.

KENYATTA: I did not know—I did not know and even today I do not know the specific reasons why the KCA was banned apart from war conditions.

He had had consultations with the Governor of the Colony. "I explained to his Excellency, 'The war is now over and I can't see any reason why the ban should not be lifted'."

Q: Was it true that the negotiations broke down because KCA members had been misbehaving themselves and were in gaol?

A: He had already said as much.

Q: Was the annual income of the KAU 500,000 shillings—five shillings per member?

A: He could not give a figure. That was the treasurer's job.

Q: Rawson Macharia told of an oath administered to one

F

Solomon Memia. Did he know Solomon Memia?—Yes. He was a member of KAU. He did not know he had been sent to prison for unlawful oath activities, in April 1950. Did he feel no worry as president of KAU that a member should have been convicted on such a charge?

A: If I were to feel worry whenever a member of KAU dies I should be ill and dead myself.

Muthondu of the eating-house had told of a big gathering at Kenyatta's house. Kenyatta has said when he got home from the age group meeting he found only members of his household. How many would that be?—About twenty, including his brother and his brother's wife, their seven children, and four servants.

Mau Mau—he knew what everybody else knew of its activities. He did not know how many members of KAU had been convicted. To clarify this and similar questions was a main object of his summer campaign of meetings round the branches. "We wanted to visit these people and talk to them not just write letters."

Dedan Mugo—he knew as chairman of the Age Groups. He heard about his arrest, he did not go to his trial.

Limuru—the rule about head office permission being required before local branches sought permits for meetings was first a resolution at a committee meeting towards the end of 1951 which was circulated in the form of an open letter signed by Kenyatta and published in *Sauti ya Mwafrika* of 19th February 1952 (copy produced).

By this time, the late afternoon of the second day of cross-examination, tempers were short. Crown Counsel seemed to puzzle the witness by attaching an unexplained significance to a distinction Kenyatta did not seem to grasp.

SOMERHOUGH: We will now go back to the office of KAU of 21st April, you told us that the three office bearers from that branch came to the office?

KENYATTA: Yes.

Q: And you told us that they belong to a religion called Dini ya Etereri. How do you know that?

A: People say they belong to the Dini ya Etereri. They themselves have admitted that they belonged to that religious sect.

Q: What people said that?

A: It is a well-known fact that at that place there are these people. They are there. It is not a thing that came yesterday. It is there in that particular place.

Q: My question was, What people told you that they belonged to it?

A: No people told me as such but it is said or it is well known round Limuru that Dini does exist there. They themselves have agreed that they belong to it.

Q: Do you say that they agreed in this court that they belonged to it?

A: Yes. The man Gichereri was asked whether he belonged to the Association.

Q: The Association, but not Dini?

This led to a long but not particularly fruitful argument on the distinction between association and sect, kiama and dini. Then cross-examination went on:

SOMERHOUGH: It does not alter my point; it was never put to him under the description of Etereri.

PRITT: We now know the Prosecution's point, and if we had a millimetre gauge we might be able to measure it.

KENYATTA: I have said that such a Dini did exist in Limuru and some other parts.

SOMERHOUGH: I am asking you to answer a question. What is your authority for making this remark?

A: First, it is knowledge that there is Dini at Limuru and some other places; and secondly, the reason why the people came to the office to complain was because they objected that their Dini had been misreported in the newspaper *Mumenyereri* that Dini took a chicken oath. What they objected to was not Dini, but they objected that such a Dini should take the oath of a chicken.

Q: Would you look at *Mumenyereri*. How does *Mumenyereri* describe it?

A: It is simply reported and does not give facts.

Q: What name does it give it?

A: Kiama Etereri. That is the body which calls itself Etereri because the word Kiama can also mean a body of people.

Q: Is the word Dini there?

MAGISTRATE: Is it in print there, the word Dini?

A: No, it is not printed.

PRITT: The witness has already answered that question at least four times.

MAGISTRATE: I had to put the question myself in order that he should answer. The question was, "Is the word Dini printed there or the word Kiama?"

SOMERHOUGH: May the witness be asked to confine his answers to the questions.

PRITT: He has answered twice, and all I said in my observation was he made a perfectly true statement and that he had answered it four times. My submission is that he should be allowed to make a statement which can fairly be described as an answer.

MAGISTRATE: If the witness would only be intelligible then I could understand.

SOMERHOUGH: My request to you was, could he be limited to the answer.

PRITT: As my friend puts it, "I am up again"—I am up again with the humble submission that when my learned friend began to ask you to confine the witness to answer the questions he wasn't treating the witness fairly. I humbly protest against this conduct. The witness may take a long time to answer but he is on a serious charge and he is entitled to make his answer.

MAGISTRATE: The witness has been given, so far as I know, the utmost latitude in the manner of answering questions—the record will show, I hope. Many of the answers are unintelligible. Most of the answers of this witness are so long they are almost unprecedented. There are very few answers which the witness has given consisting of "yes" or "no". They are long answers. It is, therefore, unkind or discourteous to suggest to me that the witness should be allowed to answer the question.

PRITT: You have given the witness a lot of latitude which I shall have to make submissions about to you later. The witness has given long answers. There is not any part of the doctrine of English law to say that if a long answer is reasonably necessary a witness is not allowed to answer, and I humbly ask that this witness be allowed to answer.

SOMERHOUGH: The record will show whether that is true. One thing I am trying to make clear is that if my friend is going to interrupt I am going to sit down. I cannot carry on with this barracking which goes on.

Argument continued more heatedly. The Magistrate asked whether his own interjections were being objected to by the Defence, drawing the reply from Defence Counsel, "I shall submit to you when the case comes to an end that some of the comments made by the Court about the prisoners are such that I shall take objection to them".

Cross-examination continued for some time longer on the same point, establishing at last that a Sect can be called an Association, or an Association a Sect, in Kikuyu as in English and the difference can be ignored.

In the next phase of cross-examination Crown put the suggestion that Henry Mworia, the editor of *Mumenyereri* had served a sentence for sedition and "You were anxious I suppose that no action should be taken against him by Ephraim?" "No. I was not. I told Ephraim the proper thing to do was to write him a letter."

The week-end intervened. On the third day of cross-examination Crown put to witness the first of what became a very long series of newspaper reports of his meetings, the point being that the reports contained no mention of any denunciation of Mau Mau.

The witness replied: "Using common sense you will understand that I could not speak for half an hour and be reported accurately in just ten lines." When other newspaper reports were put, the Defence objected, the Magistrate ruled in favour of Crown Counsel, and then some sixteen newspaper reports were put in succession to the witness. Most of them Kenyatta found inadequate or inaccurate. He was asked had he complained of the inaccuracies, particularly since the two newspapers concerned were KAU journals, *Sauti ya Mwafrika* and *Mumenyereri*. He replied, "No. I rely more on meetings than the press because the majority of my audience cannot read or write". The point being made by the cross-examination of the scarcity of any reports of denunciation of Mau Mau was qualified by the fact that cross-examination now showed that even in their reports of the meeting at Thika, on which Crown witnesses had given evidence, and the meeting at Kiambu, both *Sauti ya Mwafrika* and *Mumenyereri* had devoted their reports almost exclusively to what Kenyatta had had to say about KAU, with very little mention of Mau Mau though all witnesses had made it plain that denunciation of Mau Mau, whether sincere or not, had been an important part of these two meetings. Cross-examination showed that the much discussed curse at Kiambu in which Kenyatta consigned Mau Mau to the roots of the Mikongoe tree, was not fully reported in either *Sauti ya Mwafrika* or *Mumenyereri*. Defence Counsel's offer to lend his friend a copy of the *East African Standard* in which a much fuller report was printed, was not well received.

The cross-examination on newspaper reports went on next day,

Tuesday, when one of the day's batch was a copy of *Mumenyereri* of 30th April 1952.

SOMERHOUGH: Does this carry any report of your speech at all?

KENYATTA: It just mentions that Mr Kenyatta, leader of the KAU did make a speech.

Q: Yes, and is there any mention of denunciation of Mau Mau by you?

A: Well, sir, if he has not even said what I talked about how could he put Mau Mau?

Q: The answer is no?

Some of the earlier newspaper reports were referred to and cross-examination was vigorously pressed.

SOMERHOUGH: The question is quite a simple one, you know. Do you call this, as reported, a denunciation?

KENYATTA: And I say the report is incomplete, it does not record all I said.

Q: May I have an answer to my question?

MAGISTRATE: Yes, if you can get it.

SOMERHOUGH: Do you call this, as reported, a denunciation—yes or no?

A: I have said—I told you that the report is not—the report is not complete.

Q: Do you call this, as reported, this page of your speech as reported, a denunciation of Mau Mau?

A: As part of it, yes.

Q: That is the answer you want taken, do you—this is part of a denunciation.

A: This is part of a denunciation.

Q: But by itself, is it a denunciation?

A: That is a matter of opinion.

Q: I will take that answer.

A newspaper report was produced of the meeting where an African District Officer asked about "the thing that was troubling them at Nyeri, that is the people of Mau Mau who were burning down houses and also saying they would murder some of the leaders in that area".

SOMERHOUGH: Mr Githe said that?

KENYATTA: That is correct, yes.

Q: And then it goes on to say, "Mr Kenyatta, when he got up said, "Once again KAU is not Mau Mau, it does not like wickedness, and that all those who were associated with KAU——

A: Yes.

Q: "should leave off those evil ways of burning people's houses like porcupines"?

A: Yes.

Q: "Like porcupines." Is that right?

A: Not, it is not like a porcupine. Here the translator may be off the track a little bit. It means when you burn a porcupine, you do not take a porcupine and burn it, you put the porcupine in the hole, and you put fire——

Q: You burn out its house?

A: You burn him or her inside the house, so it means "Do not burn the people".

Q: People in their houses like porcupines?

A: Yes, do not burn the people. Here you burn the huts as well as the owner of the hut inside, so do not do to the human being as you do to the porcupine, because the burning, the word is called "guchinirira".

By the sixth day of cross-examination Crown reached the point where Kenyatta cursed Mau Mau at Kiambu. A Swahili journal in reporting the Mikongoe tree curse had translated it into a phrase which could be rendered: "Kenyatta told Mau Mau to go and be hanged." Counsel produced a Swahili dictionary in an attempt to show the phrase could have meant "go underground". Kenyatta who had been speaking in Kikuyu called the question "absurd". In any case the speech was recorded on magnetic tape, "so do not beat about the bush, bring the record and you can hear what I did say".

MAGISTRATE: Of course it would be the best evidence of what he did say.

Defence at once asked the Court to grant a subpoena for the recordist to bring the tape-recording.

The meeting at Mombasa interested Crown because of a reported reference in Kenyatta's speech to a ship called *Jesus*. Witness said:

I was referring to historical events, and, well, I have not got the reference with me, but there was a captain or somebody called Hawkins, and he had a ship down at Mombasa, which was known as—I think—*Jesus* or something to that effect— the name of a ship, and if you want a reference you can read *Black Man's Burden* by Morel, an Englishman. I do not remember the pronunciation of his name but the title of the book is called *Black Man's Burden*. If you want to know more of our slavery I will recommend it to you, sir.

SOMERHOUGH: And did you go on to say in this historical excursion that Fort Jesus, Mombasa Prison, was named after the English ship *Jesus* which used to take the slaves away from the country?

A: I was not so ignorant as to refer to that, nor did I talk about Fort Jesus down in Mombasa. I was talking about slavery, but not about Fort Jesus down in Mombasa.

Cross-examination continued vigorously on this point for some time. At last Defence interjected:

PRITT: I would like to object quite shortly. The charge is that these various gentlemen have various things to do with Mau Mau in a period beginning on August—some date in August 1950. Is it really relevant to that, sir, what part the British took in the abolition of the slave trade?

MAGISTRATE: As I have said before, Mr Pritt, so many of these questions, as I see it—I may be wrong of course—so many questions go to this witness's credibility.

PRITT: Apart from the objection about that under Section 159, [of the Kenya Criminal Code] can it go to the witness's credibility what part the British took in abolishing the slave trade?

MAGISTRATE: No, his credibility is raised, as I see it, to some extent by the fact as to whether he answers the questions or not, but he has not answered the questions.

PRITT: Then he can be asked any questions in the world to see whether he answers or not?

MAGISTRATE: I did not say that Mr Pritt . . . I think you said before I reminded you before, when you were cross-examining the Prosecution witnesses, there are almost no limits to cross-examination, it is a very wide thing.

PRITT: Yes, and I did remind you, sir, that these persons are accused persons, and that Section 159 applies to them. I did remind you, sir.

MAGISTRATE: I did not know there was any difference between the latitude in cross-examination against a person that is, I did not think there was any distinction between accused persons and any other——

PRITT: Very good, sir, I will write that down.

SOMERHOUGH: Within, of course, limits.

MAGISTRATE: Within, of course, limits.

SOMERHOUGH: I am not quite sure whether my learned friend has withdrawn the objection or whether he has——
MAGISTRATE: I have overruled it.

This passage was regarded both by the Defence and—though in rather curious terms—by the Supreme Court, as a moment of some significance in the trial. The question raised, the rights of accused persons under cross-examination, is obviously important. This part of the law of Kenya is not taken from India, like so much of Kenya law, because in India no accused can ever go into the witness box. In fact the relevant article of the Criminal Procedure Code of Kenya is taken direct from English law. The old rule in England was like that in India—accused should not give evidence. It was changed here in 1898, with much anxiety and many safeguards for the accused.

Defence Counsel put the legal position, so far as it applied to this case, in terms which were accepted by Crown. These can be summarised like this: (1) Accused *may* be asked questions tending to incriminate him of the offences charged; (2) He may not be asked *and must not answer*, any question tending to show that he has committed or been convicted of, or been charged with, any other offence, or that he is of bad character. (To this rule there are certain exceptions which Crown agreed did not apply to the present case.)

The net result is that any questions to an accused person must necessarily fall into one of three categories, viz: (1) questions designed to prove that he is guilty of the offence charged; (2) questions to credit; and (3) irrelevant questions. Of these (1) is admissible, (2) is inadmissible because it goes to character, and (3) is inadmissible for obvious reasons. The only exception to (2) is that accused may be cross-examined on any evidence he has given in chief, with a view to testing his veracity.

Defence Counsel illustrated his points. For example a question as to polygamy, in a colony where polygamy is permitted but bigamy is also a crime, will fall either within (2) or (3); and so will most other questions which cannot be shown to be in (1)— above all, questions on wanting to drive out Europeans, questions about land grievances and so on. The broad general point in layman's language is that you can't in general cross-examine an accused to credit, whereas you can of course cross-examine any other witness to credit, up hill and down dale. And, what Defence

F*

claimed in effect, was that a principle, known to every lawyer's clerk in England, was ignored by both the Magistrate and Crown Counsel.

The cross-examination continued.

SOMERHOUGH: Right. Well, then, I am asking you this question again. Do you know as a matter of historical fact whether or not the English abolished slavery?

KENYATTA: I will say that the English took part in abolishing slavery . . . I say first: (1) Our land was taken away: we were subjected then to those early days of forced labour; (2) The wages which were given to our people is such that most of them lived in a kind of serfdom. While formerly a man could walk and feel like a man we were subjected to the humiliation of the colour bar, and everything. We were underdog. So in spite of the fact that slavery was abolished, a new form of slavery was introduced.

PRITT: Just a minute——

KENYATTA: And I dare say when you have taken the land from a man or a nation——

PRITT: Just a minute——

KENYATTA: He has finished—when you have taken a man, some-one, his land, which is a livelihood, living with—sorry, I do not want to——

SOMERHOUGH: Go on, I am hanging on your lips, go on.

KENYATTA: All right. I hope you will not fall. (Laughter in Court.) I say when you have taken somebody's land, leaving him with nothing, depending on a very low wage, subject him to all sorts of laws, some of which are most——

SOMERHOUGH: That must be terrible. Yes, go on.

KENYATTA: Well, it is terrible, if I were to change with you, sir, and you be an African, occupy an African position, and I occupy your position, I bet you will not stay one week or even two days in the African position. You do not know it, and you think he is happy, but he is not happy.

SOMERHOUGH: Your Honour will indicate when Your Honour has had enough, because this is not really an answer to the question.

MAGISTRATE: I think it is interesting——

SOMERHOUGH: All right. Go on.

MAGISTRATE: —but I do not want any more of it. (Laughter in court.)

Cross-examination finally came back to the charge:

SOMERHOUGH: You know, do you not, that Mau Mau is anti-European?

KENYATTA: We cannot say it is anti any particular race. It is anti-people, many people, it has killed many Africans, Asians, Europeans, so I think it is anti-society, but not anti any particular——it would not be right to say it is anti only one particular group of people.

Q: Yes. But its principal object is to drive the European out, according to what we have heard about the oath?

A: What we have heard about the oath, yes, but in practice we do not find it so. . . . What I say, they have been anti African and in practice they have killed Africans, they have killed Europeans, they have killed Indians, and therefore I say it is anti-society, anti-people, as a whole, not anti a particular group, African, European or Asian.

Q: My question was, according to the oath, the principal object was to drive the Europeans out?

A: According to what we have heard.

Q: And do you not agree that the conditions for driving Europeans out would be considerably improved if Africans, ignorant Africans, could be persuaded that it was the English who made them slaves?

A: I do not think so, sir, unless you are anti-truth.

During the sixth and seventh days of cross-examination witness was taken through the translation of some of the songs in the so-called "hymn books". From this nothing new of importance emerged. The songs were often parodies. One had the phrase "Come unto Jomo" to the tune of "Come unto Jesus". Another seemed to be set to the tune of "God Save the Queen".

A week-end intervened, cross-examination continued on Monday morning with a series of questions put formally—that is to say without much interest in what answer the witness would make—with the apparent object of producing a revised outline of the Prosecution case.

SOMERHOUGH: The Prosecution case is that from your return to Kenya in 1946 you led the Association which was then called the KCA.

A: I do not agree to that, sir.

Q: And that you imposed into the KCA a form of oath similar to that which was continued in the society commonly known as Mau Mau.

A: That is not true, sir.

Q: And the Prosecution case is that you did this because as a result of your own knowledge of your own people and the studies you had made, you realised the very binding force an oath of that nature would have upon the Kikuyu.

A: That is not so, sir.

Q: And that the case of the Prosecution again is that the main purposes of that oath were: (1) to bind people to the Association which was under your control——

PRITT: By the "Association" you mean?

SOMERHOUGH: Whether known as KCA or later as Mau Mau, it is the same continuous Association. (2) To foment trouble in the pursuit of your ideas about regaining the land for your people by driving out, if necessary, using the maximum violence against Europeans as holders of that land?

KENYATTA: That is utter nonsense.

Q: The Crown say further that you took an active part in 1950—in early 1950—in the imposition of this type of oath, that is to say with the blood and earth and banana-leaf arch accompaniments.

A: That is false—there is no truth in that.

Q: And that the Crown case is that as a result of prosecutions which took place in 1950 for taking the KCA oath, namely that of Dedan Mugo, the society's name was changed to Mau Mau.

A: Not to my knowledge, sir.

Q: And that ultimately to drive out the Europeans and obtain land and use violence.

A: I know nothing about that, sir.

Q: The Crown case is that all through the period covered by the charge you were in substantial control of Mau Mau or the society then commonly known as Mau Mau.

A: That is not true, I led KAU and not such an organisation as Mau Mau.

Q: And that you elevated Mau Mau into the position of a religious cult.

A: I have not done anything of that kind, sir.

Q: And that you were at all times aware of the existence of this Nyimbo song book in which you replaced in the songs, in some cases, the Deity.

A: That is not true.

Q: And that the Black Manuscript Book, found in your house, which contains similar and slightly similar, and apparently the original in one case of hymns in these three books, shows not only your connection but your inspiration of these hymns?

A: That is not true, sir.

Q: And that the Crown case is further that gradually through the influence of these hymn books you began to adopt or attribute to KAU policies of Mau Mau—driving out the white man and so on and so forth as stated in these hymn books.

A: That is a lie, sir.

Q: And the effect of this hymn book is threefold: (1) To propagate the religion of Mau Mau with yourself as object of worship; (2) To secure and increase membership of KAU as evidenced by the hymns; and (3) To introduce through the songs the aims of Mau Mau.

A: No, sir, KAU have nothing whatever to do with those hymn books.

Q: And that at all times your object was to seduce or induce members of KAU to join Mau Mau.

A: That is a false allegation.

Q: That you were well aware of the force and methods used to induce people to enter Mau Mau and to get money from them.

A: I did not know, sir.

Q: And that only in the middle of 1952 when you were alarmed at the increasing violence of Mau Mau did you seek to put any restraint on it at all, as evidenced by what you said at Ol Kalou.

A: I do not think that is true, sir, I will not take that to be true. I fought before that. . . . We started to denounce Mau Mau way back in 1950.

Q: The Crown case on that is that at no time have you denounced Mau Mau at all with any intention to be effective.

A: That is not true, I have denounced Mau Mau in the best way possible. I do not think there is anyone who has done more than I have done.

Q: And that in general the most that you did, the Crown say, is to deny the connection of Mau Mau with KAU which of course you had to do as Mau Mau was a proscribed society.

A: That is not true, I have denounced Mau Mau in the most strong terms I could use.

Q: And that when on occasions such as Kamirithu and at Kiambu you were forced into a position where you had to say something more definite than a denial of the connection of Kau and Mau Mau, you used such terms and with such double meaning and in such form that——

A: That is a lie.

Q: Let me finish my sentence—that your hearers were not deluded or deceived for one moment as to your true views.

A: If you are doubtful I ask you to call this 40 to 50,000 people to come here and tell you if they did not understand what I said: and at Kiambu I was not forced, I was one of the organisers of that meeting, therefore I could not have been forced to say what I said.

Q: You will agree will you not that your so-called denunciation had very little effect at all?

A: That is a lie.

Q: You think it has?

A: It has, yes.

Q: You think Mau Mau is much better since you started denouncing it?

A: You people have audacity to ask me silly questions. I have done my best and if all other people had done as I have done, Mau Mau would not be as it is now. You made it what it is, not Kenyatta.

Q: What—"Europeans", The Crown, or who has made it what it is?

A: The Government in not handling Mau Mau in the proper way, and you blame it to me.

Q: It is the Government's fault that Mau Mau exists and goes on?

A: Well, I say yes.

SOMERHOUGH: I will take that answer. Thank you.

Re-examination by Defence Counsel led to an expansion of the last point.

PRITT: You answered my friend—I think it was what purists call a responsive answer—that the Government is to blame for the present virulence of Mau Mau. Will you tell us why you think that; what is it the Government has done wrong or omitted to do?

KENYATTA: I blame the Government because knowing that the Africans have grievances they did not go into these grievances; such as shortage of houses in places like Nairobi, and land shortage and many other such things—poverty of the African people both in towns and the reserves—and I believe that if the Government had gone into the economic and social conditions of the people they should have done something good. Rather than that, the Government—instead of joining with us to fight Mau Mau, they arrested all the leading members of KAU, accusing them of being Mau Mau, whereas it would have been the Government's duty to co-operate with KAU to stamp out anything that was bad, such as Mau Mau. But instead of doing that they have arrested thousands of people who would have been useful in helping to put things right in the country, and it is on these points that I blame Government, that they did not tackle the business in the right way. They wanted to, I think, not to eliminate Mau Mau, sir, but what they wanted to eliminate is the only political organisation—that is KAU—which fights constitutionally for the rights of the African people, just as the Electors' Union fights for the rights of the Europeans, and Indian National Congress for the rights of the Asians. And I think and believe that by the activity of Government in arresting all the leading members of KAU who are innocent people, doing ordinary business, and putting them in concentration camps—I do not think that is the right way of combating Mau Mau because most of these people who are behind bars today are people who would be helping to adjust things and eliminate Mau Mau in the country. But instead of Government co-operating with these people they put false allegations on the Union that they were Mau Mau, whereas we do know pretty well that the reason for our arrest was not Mau Mau, but because they think we are going ahead uniting our people to demand our rights. The Government arrested us simply because when they saw we could have an organisation of 30,000 or 40,000 or more Africans demanding their rights here, they say, "We've an excuse—Mau Mau".

Q: Now I can pass to another topic, Mr Kenyatta. You expressed a desire of giving your explanation of the origin of a particular Kikuyu curse which you used at the big Kiambu meeting on the 24th August. State it shortly will you.

A: The story goes that from the early times when the Kikuyu was put on the Kikuyu land by the Lord of Nature, he sent to him two messengers, one was the chameleon, and his companion was a bird called in Kikuyu *Nyamindigi*. Their message was to inform the Kikuyu that there shall never be death as we know it today, in other words that people when they die they will just go to sleep and wake up again, or resurrect again, or come to life. Now they found Kikuyu sitting under a thick tree, and after exchanging greetings, they told him that they had message from the Lord of Nature. Now the first to give the message was Chameleon, who said, "I will start to tell the Kikuyu that there shall never be death", so the chameleon started telling Kikuyu: "We were told by Lord of Nature this, we were told this, were told this" and after the chameleon had been repeating this in Kikuyu *Twiriruo atiri atiri* three times, the *Nyamdinigi* was angry with his friend for forgetting so quickly, and he said,

"You fool, do not keep saying *Twiriruo atiri atiri,* we were told that when people die they should go to *miri ya Mikongoe!*" which means we were told that when the people die they are never to come back again; so that is *miri ya Mikongoe,* when people die they shall never come to life again, they will go to *miri ya Mikongoe.*

Q: And the curse is a curse which calls upon people to go to that?

A: The curse is the origin of death, that you die and you go somewhere where you can never come back again.

21

First Defence Witnesses

KENYATTA'S seven-day cross-examination being over the Defence called a witness to deal with Incident No. 1. Chief Charles Kigwe said he was with Rawson Macharia in Joram Waweru's shop. He and Macharia had been sitting all day in an arbitration case before the Supreme Court concerning a dissolution of partnership. The case was between witness Chief Kigwe and another, and Kigwe had chosen his friend Macharia as arbitrator. After the case they called in the shop where they found Kenyatta. They all sat and drank beer for half an hour and then went home. There was no oath-taking. They never went to Joram Waweru's house—where Macharia had described the ceremony as taking place. Macharia spent the night in Chief Kigwe's house, and next day the arbitration case continued.

Joram Waweru, the owner of the shop, confirmed Charles Kigwe's account of the evening's entertainment, adding a point against Rawson Macharia's story in which the entertainment had been divided between Joram Waweru's shop and his house which was some two hundred yards away. Witness said in 1950 he slept in his shop and not in his house. "I do not leave the shop because I am the only one there and I am afraid of thieves, so I do not leave the shop to go home. . . . Until the day I was arrested by the Government, I was sleeping there." Asked in cross-examination how he remembered this simple drinking-party so long afterwards, he said, "Because it was the only time Mr Kenyatta came to my shop." The honour was memorable.

George Waiyaki, a builder, swore he was present and confirmed the account of the other two witnesses. He was present on a latter occasion when negotiations were conducted for buying sheets of corrugated iron from Prosecution witness Gichungwa.

This witness said, "We talked about the corrugated-iron sheets, about the Age Groups who were to pay for the iron, and other things". This was the time when Kenyatta was alleged to have invited Gichungwa to join "my society", by which the Prosecution witness supposed him to mean the then unnamed Mau Mau. This witness swore there was no such passage in the conversation.

Harrison Gachukia, a clergyman of the African Pentecostal Church of Kenya, produced his diary for 1950. He was among those mentioned by Rawson Macharia as being present at the oath-taking, but his diary showed he was that night at Gichuki which is a long way from Nairobi. He was cross-examined.

SOMERHOUGH: What is puzzling me is this: that over these vital dates, the 14th, 15th, and 16th you have written out in full "Go to Gichuki: Spent the day at Gichuki", and, on the 16th you have just got "Gichuki" have you not? "Gichuki" and then a note about pineapples—is that right?

GACHUKIA: About the pineapples. I met a man at Thika. He told me he wanted to buy pineapples, so I wrote it down "Thika" because he wanted to buy pineapples.

Q: Wrote what at Thika?

A: I wrote "Thika" because Daudi stays at Thika.

Q: On what date did you write it?

A: I wrote it at Gichuki where I met him.

Q: Then there is another thing puzzling me—the ink on the date of the 16th—the pineapple entry—is quite different from the ink on the other two days.

A: You put ink in a pen and it is finished, and you put different ink.

Q: It happens to change colour between the 15th and 16th. Do you agree with that?

A: I see the ink on the 16th March is different from the ink on the 17th March as I wrote this at Gichuki. It may be that someone lent me a pen.

Q: The 14th and 15th is different from that of the 16th?

A: I see they are different. If I write and the ink is finished I get a pen from another person.

Q: What is the indelible pencil entry on the 15th which has been written over in ink and is only just visible?

A: I tried with a pencil on the 15th March which is attached to the diary but it would not write so I got a pen.

Q: You are talking about three years ago—you realise that don't you?

A: Yes, I know that.

Q: What is the word written in pencil?

A: I was trying to write the word "gutinda"—that is "to stay". It is a long time ago and I only suppose that I was trying to write that word.

Q: I want to put the fact to you that that writing on the 15th is with an indelible pencil, not a black lead.

A: I say it truly that I wrote this in pencil. It is a long time ago. I do not know whether with this one or another one.

Q: What I am going to suggest to you is that you were at Gichuki on the 15th and possibly on the 14th but not on the 16th.

A: I do not want to seem as if I am repeating this too often but we were a committee of six to go and spend three days in Gichuki—one person from Embu, two from Fort Hall, one from Nyeri—and it was agreed that we should stay there until we fully understood the Beecher Report.

Witness had explained, when examined in chief by Defence Counsel Kapila, that this committee of the Kikuyu Independent Schools Association had been called together for a three-day conference on the Beecher Report on Education. Defence were to argue later that the clergyman's alibi was either perjury plus forgery plus conspiracy—or else conclusive.

Thiongo, son of Waithaka, described in Macharia's story as giving the Mau Mau oath, swore, "That is sheer lies". There were no Mau Mau cuts on his hand.

Stephano Kamugu (also among those present in Rawson Macharia's story) denied all knowledge. He had never been in Joram Waweru's house or shop. Samuel Kihara swore he was not present though he too was on Macharia's list.

The next witness dealt with Incident No. 2—Muthondu, the tea-shop proprietor. Waira, son of Kamau, was present at the Age Group meeting in Gathundu in 1950 of which Muthondu had spoken, and afterwards he went to Kenyatta's house where he found only "Jomo's brother's wife and her children and Jomo's workmen". To all of these witnesses the Defence put a standard question:

Q: Have you made a statement to the police?

A: No.

This last witness, Waira, son of Kamau, had also been to the

Kiambu meeting—the meeting organised by an *ad hoc* committee to denounce Mau Mau. Afterwards he spoke to the District Commissioner for Kiambu. Crown Counsel at once objected to hearsay evidence.

SOMERHOUGH: The objection is it cannot be evidence what the DC said to the man.

PRITT: The way I put it is this, sir. A big meeting was held at Kiambu with the approval of the Government. According to a good deal of the evidence the meeting—to put it quite shortly —was a successful anti-Mau Mau meeting. According to the proposition put forward by the Prosecution—I say no more than that—the thing was a fake, a fake in which the 30,000 people were in the secret to fool all those who were foolable into the belief that it was an anti-Mau Mau meeting when in truth and in fact it was—the tongues were in the cheeks and they were really speaking in favour of Mau Mau. Sir, in my submission, the view of the Government at that time—and I am putting it very broadly—first, the view expressed by the Government at that time of approval of the meeting is evidence in favour of the accused and against the Government's what I might call tongue-in-the-cheek suggestions: and, in my submission, we can take as part of the view of the Government the expressions of a limb of the Government, who is actually the the proper person to go to for a permit for meetings, and in my submission, sir, this ought to be permitted.

[The Court upheld the objection. What the DC said remained unheard.]

The story in Incident No. 14 of oath-taking in the house of Prosecution witness Njui, "the season-ticket witness", was denied by William Kibera who took Kenyatta to the house in his car that day. He had later been questioned by a chief on Njui's report of these events and had been just as firm in his denials then as he was now. Morris Karuki, one of those present in Njui's story told of a quarrel. Njui, who runs a car-hire business, had backed his car into witness's bicycle and there had been a law-suit which made bad blood between them. In May 1950 Njui's tale to the chief resulted in witness being arrested, but on investigation the case was dropped.

Mwangi Wanjigi gave evidence of the meeting at Thika. Crown Counsel cross-examined on references Kenyatta was supposed to have made in his speech to the former Governor of the Colony Sir Philip Mitchell, who had announced his decision to retire to a farm in Kenya and spend the rest of his life as a settler in the territory he had governed. This point had not been mentioned in any earlier evidence and Defence objected to what they considered to be an attempt to smuggle in matter prejudicial to the accused. All this led to words between Counsel and sorrowful comment by the Magistrate. Crown Counsel threatened to abandon the case and report Defence Counsel to the Bar authority but subsequently agreed to wait till the transcript of these exchanges was available for reading over, perhaps in a calmer mood. Meanwhile Defence Counsel, getting on with the case, went back to the question of the tape-recordings. He reported that the Defence was in touch with the Director of African Information Services for the Colony, who had a recording plus a verbatim transcript of Kenyatta's speech at Kiambu and was willing to bring his apparatus to the Court. He would be called not as a witness but under what is called *subpoena duces tecum*—a summons to bring the relevant material with him. The Magistrate hesitated, saying, "I am afraid of short cuts and departing from the rules of evidence. . . . I have never come across anything like this".

PRITT: I have only had it four times; it won three cases in a quarter of an hour each, and made no difference to the fourth.

While the Magistrate still hesitated and Crown Counsel argued that a recording is not a document (nor could its identity as a true recording of the speech be legally proved) Defence Counsel let it be known that he felt himself to be in a strong position if he was able to make it clear "that this meeting which is of the greatest importance to the case, is the meeting about which all the available evidence has been given by my clients and not by the Prosecution, and when I tried to improve on it by getting an impartial, irrefutable piece of evidence to show what happened, the Crown succeeded in stopping it. I will accept that quite happily", he said.

Now it emerged there were two recordings, one on film, another on tape. The Magistrate hesitated about the film. A document is something with recognisable marks on it, and perhaps one might stretch the definition to include a film sound-track. But he felt that a piece of magnetic tape on which there are no marks that any microscope can make visible, could hardly be squeezed in. "From Mr Pritt's description", he added with simplicity, "From Mr Pritt's description of this scientific invention there seems to be considerable doubt whether these two things or either of them does come within the meaning of the word document." And naturally the Indian Evidence Act of Queen Victoria's day, while it paid a good deal of attention to documents, is silent about tape-recordings. The Magistrate decided to take a week-end to think it over and the rest of this Friday session was devoted to a close legal argument on the subject of the earlier dispute between Counsel. This was about the cross-examination of a witness who had volunteered evidence on some of the passages in Kenyatta's speech at Thika—not the speech recorded on the film and magnetic tape, but the other speech in which it was now being urged Sir Phillip Mitchell had been mentioned. Witness had not given evidence about this alleged passage in the speech, but he was cross-examined on it on the strength of a newspaper report which Crown Counsel held in his hand. Legally, unless it has been proved, a newspaper report is not evidence, and Defence argued that nearly all the cross-examination was inadmissible. Argument was prolonged, and, of course, in a case in which Crown laid so much stress on speeches in public meetings, and what the newspapers reported of them, newspaper cuttings cropped up in the hearing with some frequency. Arguments on their use in cross-examination punctuated the hearing, and this one had roused feeling.

The rest of this Friday afternoon session was devoted to a formal speech of complaint by Crown Counsel against the Counsel for Defence. Crown Counsel complained of "studious rudeness" and "a barrage of asides". Feelings had a little subsided by now, and the verbatim transcripts had been studied with legal care.

One of Crown Counsel's complaints had arisen when he overheard an aside between leading Defence Counsel and Mr Chaman Lall. Defence Counsel had whispered "Let him tell his own lies". and to this Crown formally objected in a moderate and studied speech. Defence replied in similar style, dividing the offences into two categories: remarks and asides made in the heat of the moment, for which he apologised and would try to curb; and another category of objections not so easy to curb, his objections to methods of adducing evidence and asking questions which in the eye of Defence Counsel seemed "utterly inexcusable in a professional sense", although, as he added, since His Honour had ruled in so many instances that the questions "were actually inadmissible, to that extent I must have been wrong".

The Magistrate replied at length. "If there are any more scenes in which I consider that either Counsel is to blame, and I confess I have never seen Mr Somerhough responsible for any of them initially, if there are any more scenes I shall adjourn as a lesson, and I shall adjourn until such time as I see fit to resume. Let that be understood." He added with what in retrospect looks like a pathetic note: "It isn't so much the scenes but what is possibly not considered by some to be important, that from 10 a.m. until 4 or 4.30 I am sitting on the edge of a volcano not knowing when these scenes are going to happen."

It is well known that irritability is usual in hot climates. In remote Kapenguria everybody was getting on everybody else's nerves. The trial had been going on for a long time.

The Magistrate adjourned the Court till Tuesday—this was Friday afternoon. When he resumed after the long week-end he brought a written ruling that the sound recordings of Kenyatta's speech were not admissible as evidence.

He announced also that on Saturday: "I attended on the Chief Justice in his Chambers at the Law Courts, Nairobi, in the forenoon I was received by him." He put to the Chief Justice a question suggested by Crown Counsel: "Were members of the Bar who come from overseas and who obtain an *ad hoc* licence to appear before a Court in this Colony—were such lawyers subject to disciplinary action?"

The Chief Justice made a very cold reply "which I took down in his presence and was checked as correct by him: 'The Chief Justice is not the legal advisor of the Deputy Public Prosecutor and he is not prepared to answer any theoretical questions submitted to him through you, the Magistrate, or otherwise.'

"I have no comment to make," said the Magistrate. "I pass the words of the message to you exactly as I received them." The Court turned its attention back to its prisoners and heard Kubai.

Fred Kubai came into the box and outlined his own career. He was brought up in Mombasa, was not a member of the Kikuyu Age Groups, worked in Government Posts and Telegraphs from 1931 to 1946 at a salary beginning at forty shillings a month, rising to a hundred shillings a month at the end of his fifteen years. Later he took a job as executive officer in the Transport and Allied Workers' Union, and was in fairly close touch with the Government Labour Department. He joined KAU in 1951, became chairman of the Nairobi branch, and dropped his trade union work. In 1952 "some Europeans came to our office", and left literature about the Oxford Group which interested him so much that he was invited to a Moral Rearmament Conference at Caux in Switzerland to which he travelled by air in September 1952.

The eating-house proprietor's story that witness attended a Kikuyu Age Group meeting at Gathundu market in 1950 was ridiculous since "not having been circumcised according to the rites of the Kikuyu" he could never have attended any meeting of this kind. He was present at the committee meeting in the Nairobi headquarters of KAU when the three men from Limuru came to criticise and be criticised. He confirmed Kenyatta's account of this meeting. At Ol Kalou (Tabitha's meeting) it was Kubai's job to collect money from newly-enrolled KAU members and to give them a receipt for their five shillings. In this he was helped by Jesse Kariuki and enrolments had been so numerous that they were busy counting the money and making up their books till 9 p.m. Then food was brought and a woman addressed by others as Wambui took him to her room. "She prepared a bed for me and a fire because it was cold and at that moment an inspector of police George Kipture came in. He took Wambui and they went away and I slept in that room alone."

Mnuyi, the self-styled "oath askari", had told of Fred Kubai holding an oath-taking ceremony and a series of Mau Mau study-group meetings with Willie George. Fred Kubai said he knew Willie George as "the leader of the trade union of Night Watchmen" but "it is over a year now since I sat near him in friendly way". Witness gave a brief account of the quarrel. Willie George and Fred Kubai had been in bitter antagonism over trade union politics. Kubai said he had opposed a strike called by Willie George's union whereon Willie George broke away "from the leadership of the Trade Unions of East Africa", he registered a new union, and, witness added, the quarrel developed into litigation between the two union officials. Jomo Kenyatta had tried in vain to compose differences and bring the two men together. Their quarrel was a matter of public knowledge.

PRITT: It has been said in this court that during the months of
August and September 1952, on Saturday nights, you went to
the house of Willie George and there both of you instructed
people in the administration and policy of Mau Mau.

KUBAI: It is all absolutely lies, and I have never heard such a lie
and I have never seen such a lie.

Witness went through the Saturdays of August so far as he
could remember them. One of them he remembered because he
was in the office stamping receipts for tomorrow's meeting, and
preparing the loudspeaker, when the police came to fetch Kaggia
who was helping him in these chores. "He was taken by the
police to be interrogated about hats which were snatched from
people." (It will be remembered that KAU policy disapproved
both of English hats and English beer.) Another Saturday there
was "a tea party and a very big concert in my honour in the
Kaloleni Hall". It went on till midnight and was Kubai's send-off
to Moral Rearmament and to Switzerland, Kubai said he was
placed under detention under emergency regulations in the early
hours of the morning of the 21st October 1952.

Cross-examined he agreed he organised "the big transport strike
of 1949". He was editor of *Sauti ya Mwafrika*. This led into a
close cross-examination, which later drew from the Defence the
hint that to show a man was not a very competent editor did not
prove anything against his moral character. Indeed it emerged
that *Sauti ya Mwafrika* was not really edited at all, a familiar
enough state of affairs with many more or less amateur journals.
When Kubai was away, as he often was, the paper was put together by anyone who happened to be in the office. Reports of
meetings were received from local KAU members, and put in
more or less as they stood. Matter in the paper, said the editor,
was not necessarily in accordance with KAU policy. "A paper is
like a ground on which people argue and debate. A person may
say something very dirty and another person will answer him and
that cannot be the policy of the KAU."

SOMERHOUGH: I am going to put it to you that you have actively
promoted strikes which have led to violence?

KUBAI: I say that nothing of the kind happened. That was a
peaceful strike.

Q: You organised the taxi-drivers' strike did you not?

A: I did not organise it, the members organised it.

Q: You organised the big general strike of the East African TUC did you not?

A: The strike I think you are referring to is that which took place after my arrest.

Q: I said you organised it. That is what I put to you.

A: I did not organise that strike because I was in prison.

Q: I put it to you that strike led to considerable violence, did it not?

A: I was not there.

Q: Do you know or don't you?

A: I do not know.

Mwangi Wanjigi was recalled for cross-examination.

SOMERHOUGH: The question I am going to put to you is that when you say the Mikongoe curse used at Kiambu is a very bad curse, that is not true.

MWANGI: I am a Kikuyu and know that it is so.

Q: And when you go further and say there was no stronger expression Kenyatta could have used, that is equally untrue?

A: I do not agree with you. Even if you go to Kikuyu country and ask all people and especially old people who are approaching death they will tell you it is a most serious curse.

In re-examination he was asked:

PRITT: You said a few minutes ago that you do not recollect this curse being used in a public ceremony?

A: Yes.

Q: But you heard it used at Kiambu?

A: Yes.

Q: Was it less impressive or more impressive used at Kiambu because it is something not normally used in public ceremony?

A: Unless he was a very brave person he could not have said that in public meeting because he must have been suffering from the bottom of his heart.

The cross-examination of one Elifas Mutheki produced a story of cleansing. Witness, who was one of those mentioned by Muthondu, the eating-house proprietor, was arrested in November 1952 and by his own account forced to go through a cleansing ceremony with "a white witch doctor" in Thita River, along with about twenty others under a certain Chief Kibathi. He protested vigorously in cross-examination that such forcible cleansing "was a dirty thing which should not be done to a Christian". Witness

was member of the African Pentecostal Church. Re-examination,
and a set of questions put by the Magistrate, brought out further
details.

MAGISTRATE: Who arrested you?
ELIFAS: The headman.
MAGISTRATE: Were you tied up?
A: No, and I was not beaten.
MAGISTRATE: Were you locked up in a room?
A: Yes.
MAGISTRATE: Where?
A: At a place called——
MAGISTRATE: In what sort of a building?
A: A stone building.
MAGISTRATE: And the door was locked?
A: Yes.
MAGISTRATE: Were you there by yourself, or were others with
    you?
A: There were many of us.
MAGISTRATE: How many?
A: More than fifty, including fifteen women.
MAGISTRATE: How long were you in this stone building?
A: We slept there for two nights.
MAGISTRATE: Never allowed out?
A: If a person wanted to answer a call of nature, he was taken
    outside by an askari.
MAGISTRATE: Were the askaris armed?
A: Yes.
Q: With what?.
A: With rifles.

   Willie George, an Embu, said he had known Fred Kubai "when
he was a leader of the trade unions. He was my superior and I
was like his boy". In 1951 they quarrelled and "since that time
to say that we should drink from the same glass or eat together
—no".

PRITT: On Saturday, when you are supposed to have held some
    kind of Mau Mau meeting in your house—what time would
    you go to work on Saturday?
GEORGE: I was going on duty always at 4.0, 5.0, or 5.30.
Q: In the afternoon?
A: Yes.
Q: And remaining on duty until when?

A: Until 7 a.m.

[It will be remembered that Willie George ran the night-watchman's union.]

Next came Tabitha's friend Wambui.

Penina Wambui said she lived at Ol Kalou with Police Inspector George Kipture. She went to Kenyatta's meeting in the afternoon and after food she and her policeman walked round "to the shop of that man called Owoko" to drink beer. From here she was called out by a woman named Muthoni who asked her to put up a visitor, Kubai. "We went to Muthoni's house, we collected Kubai and went with him to my house."

PRITT: Did you remain there?
WAMBUI: Yes, making the bed for him.
Q: Did you sleep there?
A: No . . . as I was making the bed for Kubai the Inspector came. He asked me what I was doing. I told him I was preparing a bed for a visitor who had been brought to me by Muthoni. He told me to go in to him and we went up to the police lines.
Q: Where did you sleep that night?
A: At the Inspector's house.

She did not know Tabitha's aunt Muthoni Nganga (not to be confused with Muthoni who introduced her to Kubai). She never borrowed a coat. Shown Tabitha's coat Wambui was indignant. "I have never seen this coat and I could not wear such a coat. If I knew the owner I could give them a better coat . . . I have a greatcoat, and I have got many at home."

She swore she was not present in the room of Daniel Mbugwa on the evening of the meeting. She had been questioned by a European police officer called Tempest, and again when she was brought by plane to Kapenguria.

Cross-examined, Wambui said she was 20, she was born at Thika, both parents were dead. After her mother died in 1950 she stayed with relatives but "suffered very much" and ran away to Ol Kalou. Why Ol Kalou? "I was travelling by train. I met a man on the train and he told me to go with him." He was Njuki, an Embu.

SOMERHOUGH: How did you propose to live at Ol Kalou? What were your plans?
WAMBUI: I was going as a prostitute.

She lived with Njuki for about a month. "When we parted I made a friendship with the Inspector."

Q: Were you sleeping with a lot of men before you left Thika?
A: If I loved a person I had to go with him.

The woman who lived in the same house was also a prostitute. George Kipture, the policeman, paid the rent.

Wambui told how she was brought by the police to Kapenguria, and at this point Crown's cross-examination elicited a point of interest.

SOMERHOUGH: Did you make three different statements which you either signed or thumb-printed?
WAMBUI: Twice and once at the police station and once when I was——
Q: I am talking about the 31st December—the day you arrived by aeroplane.
A: That was when I was threatened I would be thrown from the plane and I was forced to thumb-print a statement.
Q: Are these the two European policemen?
A: Yes.
[Mr Henderson and Mr Baker enter the court-room.]
Q: And did they both threaten to drop you from the aeroplane on the hills?
A: Yes. This one (points to Mr Henderson) threatened me first. And that one (points to Mr Baker) came later and sat down, but he found the first one telling me that I would be taken away in the plane and be dropped and my urine would flow away.
[Her statements to the police were read to her.]
Q: Did you say this: "That same evening, I remember seeing a woman called Muthoni wife of Nganga who is Tabitha's aunt"?
A: No.
Q: She asked me if there was anyone sleeping with me that night?"
A: No—not Muthoni wife of Nganga but Muthoni daughter of Wakaba.
Q: Did you say, "She then told me that she would bring along Fred Kubai and ask me to sleep with him"?
A: No.
MAGISTRATE: Would you clear up the ambiguity as to which Muthoni it was?
WAMBUI: It was not Muthoni, Tabitha's aunt, but Muthoni the daughter of Wakaba.

[Witness continues to answer the previous question.]

WAMBUI: She did not ask me that. She asked me if at my house there was a room because I was not sleeping there.

Q: And then did you say, "I agreed and Muthoni later brought Fred Kubai to my room".

A: I told him that we went to Muthoni's.

Q: Did you say, "I made the bed and then sat down"?

A: Yes.

Q: Did you say, "Fred Kubai got on to the bed"?

A: Yes.

Q: "Shortly after this Inspector Kipture came along to my room"?

A: Yes.

Q: "Then he told me to leave the room and go with him"?

A: Yes.

Q: I went with Inspector Kipture and I spent the night at his house"?

A: Yes.

Q: "I cannot remember how many times, nor can I remember if I saw Tabitha again that evening"?

A: No.

Q: Did you say, "I was very drunk"?

A: I did not tell him that I was drunk.

Q: Did you say, "I never heard of Mau Mau—I know nothing about it"?

A: Yes. . . .

Q: When Mr Henderson was questioning you, did you see him writing down?

A: Yes.

Q: When he had finished questioning you, something was interpreted to you. Was that done immediately?

A: Yes.

Q: Did you then put your thumb-print on it?

A: I refused to sign the statement because I told him I did not know what he had written down and I could not read so he told me that I must thumb-print it.

Q: Did you thumb-print it?

A: Yes.

Q: Did this take place in the afternoon, in broad daylight?

A: Yes, but I do not know what time it was.

MAGISTRATE: This was at Kapenguria?

WAMBUI: Yes, where the witnesses stay.

SOMERHOUGH: Did the place have four poles with an awning over it, and some chairs and a table?

WAMBUI: Yes.

Q: Were there lots of Africans—men and women—moving about all round the whole time?

A: Yes, most of them were staying up there and also the cooks were there.

Q: What exactly are you saying? Are you saying that Mr Henderson put in things in that statement that you never said?

A: Yes.

Q: Are you saying that anything you said in that statement was said because of these threats?

A: Yes.

Q: All of it or any of it?

A: I just told him exactly what I had told the Indians and then he told me if I annoyed him he would do something to me.

Q: Are you saying that any or all of that statement on which you put your thumb-print was said by you because you were threatened?

A: There is some which resembles what I said, but some of it I do not know.

Q: You do not think you said it even?

A: No. I did not tell him that I was drunk.

Q: Are you saying that you would not have made a statement to him at all if you had not been threatened?

A: I would have made a statement to him according to what I knew but not according to what I did not know.

MAGISTRATE: I must get this clear before we adjourn. I am so uncertain as to what she really means. Where does the force come in? Did the force compel her to make the whole statement, or part of it?

WAMBUI: Because my hand was held by force and I was told to sign.

SOMERHOUGH: You mean your thumb was actually forced on to the paper?

A: Yes, when he was taking hold of my hand he was threatening me, and he told me that it was not a bad affair—he would never call me to court.

MAGISTRATE: But some of it was true?

WAMBUI: Yes.

MAGISTRATE: Well, then, force had nothing to do with that, did it?

WAMBUI: He forced me because he added some things which I was not telling him.

SOMERHOUGH: Why did he have to use force to make you sign the things you did say?

WAMBUI: Because he was telling me this: "That what I want you to tell me you are not telling me."

MAGISTRATE: I think she is trying to rely on the double defence that he is putting things she never said and compelled her to execute the document by force, and the second line of defence is that she never said this. It is the same as the first. I cannot follow the African mind.

Q: Did you really believe that a European Inspector of Police could take you in an aeroplane and throw you out of it?

A: Well, I was not in his heart and I could not tell what he meant. He was telling it himself——

Q: Was it read over? Was something read over to you in Kikuyu —what I just put to you?

A: It was brought to me and he wanted me to say that these people and Kubai are Mau Mau, and I told him, "I can't say it because I don't know it".

From the simple prostitute who when she "loved a person had to go with him", the evidence moved, as so often happened in this case, to the extreme contrast, the evidence of an African religious reformer. This was the accused Kaggia.

He began his evidence with a small but to him significant act. Instead of taking the oath he elected to affirm.

Kaggia said he was thirty. He left school in 1939 and was then employed in the District Commissioner's office in Fort Hall. In 1942 he joined the army where promotion was rapid. He became a Staff-Sergeant and finally Quartermaster-Sergeant. He was Christian by religion, he said, but—the word had been heard before from Kenyatta—"undenominational", though he had been baptised and brought up an Anglican, in the Church Missionary Society.

DAVIES: How did you come to lose your denomination?

KAGGIA: While I was in England I came into contact with many kinds of Christians.

Q: Such as?

A: So many movements and denominations and in my experience I found that Christianity in England was different or a bit different from what we had been taught in this country.

Q: Before you go further I would like you to explain in what respect—is it from the administrative point of view or from the practices of Christianity?

A: The practices of Christian churches in this country were different from those in England and for that reason I decided to study the Christian theology and practices. When I came to find there were so many practices which were practices in Christian churches in this country which were not supported by holy scriptures.

Q: Did you do anything about that?

A: In pursuance of that study I also found that our Kikuyu Bible was not properly translated.

Q: Am I right in taking it that you mean that the Kikuyu Bible was not a correct translation of the English Bible?

A: There were some mistranslations. Therefore I took the question of mistranslation up with the British and Foreign Bible Society in London, who referred the matter to the Christian authorities in Kenya. As to the question of practices, I did not take any action till I returned to Kenya.

Q: What did you do when you returned?

A: I saw several church leaders and pointed out to them my objections to various practices.

Q: As a result of your discussion did anything happen?

A: The discussion took a long time and there were so many arguments of their translation, and they promised me that most of them would be adopted when the Bible is revised, but as far as the practices were concerned they told me that, although they agree I am right, they are not prepared to make any change to the already established practices and traditions of the Church.

Q: Could you give examples of these practices?

A: One of them which I strongly abhor and hate is the colour bar practised in the African churches in this country. In every African church there are some chairs which are always reserved for a small European community in that particular church. Another one was the practice of teaching people in classes before they were baptised and which is contrary to the scriptures because the scriptures say people should be baptised after believing, not after passing examinations.

Q: Did you carry the matter further than that?

A: I did not, but I started preaching what I knew was right.

Q: Did you have your own body?

A: Yes, I have got a group.

Q: You still have it?

A: Yes.

Q: Did you have any particular name for your group?

A: No, I did not believe in denomination.

Q: How do you meet?

A: In our own houses.

Q: Has the history of that been peaceful?

G

A: No. We believed in doing whatever was right to us and we were always ready to suffer any consequences or pay any sacrifices. In fact when the movement grew up and when the churches could not stand our arguments they asked the Government to intervene and I was told to stop preaching and not hold any meetings anywhere.

Q: What was your reaction to that?

A: I refused that and told the DC that I believed in freedom of worship and I believed what I am preaching is right and have got the commandment of God to do so.

Q: Were you left alone?

A: No, from that time onward myself and my other people in my group have been arrested and imprisoned several times and we have been accepting that willingly in the way Jesus Christ himself took that sort of persecution.

Q: How many times have you been in prison in connection with this?

A: Four times.

Q: Are you a member of the KAU?

A: Yes.

Q: I would like to ask a rather difficult question. How do you reconcile your religious convictions with your position in politics?

A: Jesus Christ himself was always fighting for the rights of his people by every peaceful means or way and he stood for the rights of human kind and as a Christian I stand for the rights of my people.

Q: Do you believe in violence as a political weapon?

A: No, all the time when I started my movement I have been a believer of non-violence and I still maintain that belief in my political activities because I could join the practice of Jesus Christ and that of Mahatma Gandhi which I consider as the two very good examples of Christianity and that is what I believe and practice.

After the lunch break Defence Counsel produced a copy of *Kenya Weekly News*, complaining of a passage in its leading article. In discussing transit camps in various parts of the country the newspaper said: "The overwhelming majority of the inmates are already Mau Mau in any case and it is equally improbable that they will be won over so long as there are gangs of Mau Mau terrorists at liberty and there is any prospect of Jomo Kenyatta being set at liberty." On another page the newspapers mentioned "terrorist gangs", adding: "I am sure that they are stimulated by

the conviction that Jomo Kenyatta will be released and that he will
lead the Kikuyu to victory over the white men." Defence Counsel
handed a copy of the newspaper to the Magistrate who undertook
to give the matter consideration over the week-end. Later, the
newspaper sent someone to Kapenguria to apologise.

Kaggia, questioned about the EC meeting with the branch
officials from Limuru, was able to throw fresh light on the Association of Those Who Wait.

PRITT: Now I would like to ask you to explain within your own
   knowledge what you know about this body called Etereri?
KAGGIA: This body is well known, I think in Central Province, it
   is a group which believes in certain words which are given by
   Jesus Christ to his disciples after resurrection when he told
   them to go to Jerusalem and wait until the spirit or the power
   comes from on high, and so this group stands on those words
   and they do gather and say they are waiting for the power on
   high and that is where their name derives from.
Q: I suppose they have some local Jerusalem?
A: No, they do not take Jerusalem literally, they just gather and
   they wait—they just wait for the power that may be.
In cross-examination a letter was produced which he wrote to
Kenyatta in 1950.
SOMERHOUGH: I am suggesting that in paragraph four of that
   letter you are saying three things: that when you went to
   Europe you abandoned the CMS religion and all those other
   religions which have been brought here; I understand you to
   say that you only meant denominations?
KAGGIA: Yes.
Q: Then you say that when you returned to this country in 1946
   you refused to have anything to do with any of the religions of
   the Europeans and you were left simply standing on the Bible?
A: Yes.
Q: And in the last paragraph, did you say that the third stage
   of your spiritual development was to abandon the whole of
   the Bible?
A: If you read the last paragraph properly you will see it says
   that I came to find that the Bible contained the customs and
   laws of the Jews and that I abandoned those.
Q: But that is not what the letter says. I will read it again. "I
   realise it contained the laws of the Jews and so I abandoned
   the teaching of the Bible?"
A: Yes, as far as the laws and customs were concerned which

are in the Bible. That is my meaning. I would like to explain
the parts of the Bible. The Bible contains one part prophecy, one
part Moses' laws; another part is of Jewish customs; and the
fourth is the teaching of Jesus Christ. And when I talk of laws
and customs which I abandoned, those are the things which
were meant solely for the Jewish people; but when we come to
prophecies and the teaching of Jesus Christ, they are meant for
the whole of mankind, which I, too, believe and practise.

Q: I am going to suggest to you formally that the Government
never banned any religious group with which you have been
associated, or that the Government had ever intervened in that
way at all?

A: It has . . . I can prove that once when I was imprisoned in
Fort Hall Prison the missionary in charge of Kahuhia, Mr
Cantrell, came up and saw the DC, and after seeing the DC
the missionary came to the prison and told me personally that
he had spoken to the DC about me, and they agreed that if I
would only join the CMS he would ask him to stop persecuting
me and my movement, but that if I refused they would see that
I lived in prison. I can also give another incident.

MAGISTRATE: Did you ever appeal against any of these convictions?

KAGGIA: No, I believe in passive resistance and I did not trouble
to appeal.

SOMERHOUGH: What is your other incident?

A: The other incident was in 1947 or 1948 when a European
missionary, Mr Newman, came to me once when I was living in
Nairobi. He told me that the police had been to the Rev. Bewes
asking where I worked and where I lived. I asked him why the
police should go to the Rev. Bewes to look for me. He could
not tell me that but it turned out that the Rev. Bewes had sent
him to ascertain where I lived. I told him that I was working in
the National Bank of India, and the next day two police inspec-
tors came to the office in the National Bank of India and
arrested me. They took me for questioning in connection with
the murder in the Gathundu area of Inspector Mortimer and
two other askaris. When they told me that they had been
reliably informed that I was a member of the *Dini ya Jesu
Kristo*, I denied that, and I informed them that I had nothing
to do with that movement, and that my movement does not
believe in any sort of violence. After so many inconveniences
they found that their allegations were completely untrue and
unfounded. These two instances and others show that the missionaries were always behind my persecution.

Q: Your suggestion is that the missionaries had you arrested?
A: Yes.

The sect witness referred to, the Dini ya Jesu Kristo, is, in fact, another proscribed organisation in Kenya.

Prolonged cross-examination on what happened in the KAU head office at Nairobi, where a prosecution witness had said Kaggia proposed that he should be a local leader of Mau Mau, added nothing new. Crown Counsel suggested that "there is no such thing" as the "Association of those who Wait". The answer was it was widely known amongst the Kikuyu. Kaggia also gave fresh details of the quarrel between Willie George and Fred Kubai and the vain efforts by himself and others to compose it.

Finally the Magistrate had a theological question of his own.

MAGISTRATE: I have one question which arises out of your examination-in-chief. You said Jesus Christ himself was always fighting for the rights of his people in every peaceful means or way and he stood for the rights of human kind. Rights —that is the word I want to emphasise—where in the scriptures do you get authority for that?

KAGGIA: I get it in this way. Whatever He believed or knew was right, he stood on that and would not be shaken. His disciples took his example. What they knew was right they did. For instance He believed it was the right of mankind to worship in the way they like, but it was forbidden in some cases, but He stood on that and preached as His right and the right of human kind.

MAGISTRATE: Don't you think he also pointed out the duties of humanity as well?

A: Yes, but it won't take Him from the right of human kind.

MAGISTRATE: You give me the impression that all which you are concerned with, and all that Jesus Christ was concerned with were rights.

A: That is only one point I gave, but if I was asked about His preaching I could tell that he pointed out in many ways the duties of what they should and should not do.

MAGISTRATE: I put it to you that Jesus Christ stood more for the duties of humanity and human kind. He advocated and pointed out the duties of mankind rather than telling them what their rights are.

KAGGIA: Don't you agree he stood for both?

Paul Ngei will be remembered as the prisoner who had the shouting row with District Officer Pedraza and sang "Bless 'em all". He had had a varied career, including film acting. He was in the army from 1941 to 1946, held an exemplary certificate, the African Star, and the Burma Star. He had appeared in the film *Where No Vultures Fly*. He told among other things of the affair with Mr Pedraza. "He pushed my wife who had a baby two days before. She fell about six feet away from where I was, on top of some Jerusalem flowers."

The letter about "Bless 'em all" was read.

DEAR MULLI AND DORIS AND FAITH,
    You had heard at last I was put in clink, or rather sent to rest in Kingi Georgii Hotel to be a prime boarder for a period of three months.

DAVIES: Were you trying to make light of the term of imprisonment or just joking about it?

NGEI: I was trying to relieve myself in that way.

Q: About eight lines down. "At last I got in for three months simple imprisonment. On 7th October I had gone to see Emma and see the new baby and I was arrested at Talla by Uku together with Fredie Mbitia and three others. They were kept in custody until the 14th October at Kangundo. On the 8th October, the following day, I was brought to Nairobi to hear my judgement. On the 9th October I was in pingu from Kangundo." ... What is "in pingu"?

A: Handcuffed.

Q: So from Kangundo to Nairobi you were in handcuffs?

A: Yes.

Q: "I had slapped the DO at Kangundo and threw a pail at him with several other abuses?"

A: That is not true. Actually here I remember, if I can recollect a little bit. I had said that "Barazi" newspaper had reported that I had slapped the DO and threw a pail, altogether my mother was slapped.

Q: Now you said: "When I arrived from Nairobi at Kangundo more than 1,000 people (decent, mostly rich people) had gathered to hear our case. When I arrived they burst into cheers—hurrah, and clapping." What happened?

A: People knew of my arrest at Talla. I found a very big gathering at Kangundo Court awaiting the hearing of the case and they cheered me. Pedraza was also there as witness in this case for which I was fined a hundred shillings.

Q: Now you said "the DO—to whom did you refer?

A: Mr. Pedraza.

Q: "The DO had a shock and drove to Machakos saying that there was an element of Mau Mau at Kangundo.' Is that right? Did you say that?

A: Yes, I did.

Q: Who told you that he used that expression?

A: The President of the Court, Stephen Kilomo Kikubi announced it, that Mr Pedraza had said that those people were Mau Mau and they shouldn't be there and told those people to go away because they were Mau Mau.

Q: You used the expression "element of Mau Mau". Did you coin those words?

A: Yes, they are my words, but there I meant by saying "element of Mau Mau" I did not know those people. It is just like Mr Winston Churchill, before the December recess, referred to elements of Mau Mau in the Labour Party but it was not proved that the Labour Party was Mau Mau.

Q: When you went on and said "it was not far from the truth" were you being serious?

A: No, I was not serious at all, and I do not think I used the word "not".

Q: Now you went on about the song which came in your letter and you said, "Do you know what I sing daily in my small cell?" and there follows: "Bless Mau Mau, Bless Mau Mau", etc. Did you compose that song?

A: No, this is what happened. I was in one of the small cells, not allowed to talk to other people. A Seychelloise or South African man was working in the prison as a painter and he was brought into the next cell from mine, and this chap started singing George Formby's song "Bless 'em all". Later he changed "them all" to "Mau Mau", and started singing it. He did this for a day or so.

Q: When you wrote to your friends and said, "This is what I sing in the cell every day" were you turning Mau Mau?

A: No, it was only a sort of comic. Also in the prison it was not serious at all.

Q: What was not serious?

A: Mau Mau. The Superintendent used to call us, "You Mau Mau, come here."

Q: In other words are you saying that Mau Mau was a sort of standing joke in the prison?

A: Yes.

Q: You said: "The Governor has proclaimed a State of Emergency"?

A: Yes. I wrote something of that sort.

Q: "Just like Malaya—White Massacre plan is coming up"? Did you write that?

A: I am not actually very sure of those words which I see here. . . . But I said something about white massacre.

Q: Will you explain to His Honour what you mean by "white massacre"?

A: This is what I had in mind, or actually what I had read. Some time towards the end of August 1952, I think it was either the 30th or the 31st—I had seen a publication in *The Citizen*, a newspaper in Nairobi. This piece of news, which took about a quarter of the paper, had written about a white massacre plan or plot, and I remember very well buying a copy of *The Citizen* and also because *The Citizen* said they had got the news from the *Sunday Dispatch*. I remember I went and bought a copy of the *Sunday Dispatch* from Woolworth Ltd., in Nairobi. I remember very well reading those two newspapers and I also saw Mr Kenyatta about it. I think we were in Executive Committee, but I cannot remember. Then we went to see Mr Patwa, the editor of *The Citizen*. He interviewed Mr Kenyatta and myself. Mr Kenyatta denied that he knew anything about it and that it was nonsense.

Q: How did the words "white massacre" come to be in your letter?

A: This plot had been published in the paper, and now the Battalion of the Lancashire Fusiliers, the 1st Battalion from Tanganyika and also another one from Uganda had come to Kenya—how are these Mau Mau who are in the minority going to compete with machine-guns? There would be killing and murder and massacre. That is what I had in mind.

The accused Kungu Karumba was called last. He said he was aged about 50, the owner of a shop and a transport business, chairman of the Chura Divisional Branch of KAU but not on the Executive. He said on the day the Limuru people came he happened to look in the office to inquire "about the money that had been collected at the Wangigi market meeting on the 19th"—he found there was a meeting in the office, so he simply put in his head, shook hands with Ephraim and went away. The rest of the story he had heard in court for the first time. His evidence on the Waweru story—Incident No. 10—was interesting.

PRITT: When did you last have anything to do with Waweru?

KARUMBA: My shop is near Waweru's home and I supplied his

wife with a permit for sugar. I saw Waweru last in November 1950 when their land case was in the appellate court and I was a member of the Court.

Q: Waweru said here that either in June 1951 or June 1952 you took part in administering a Mau Mau oath to him?

A: That is a very big lie and a false story, and I don't know anything about it. From 1949 I had my own business and I was elected to the ADC [Appellate Court for the District] in 1950 and then during that year my business grew up and his [Waweru's] brother joined me and I was very busy during that year and the following year, and he can't possibly have seen me in the day for a long time. I was fully employed during 1950 and during 1951 as a member of the ADC. We were visiting places like Mkweni, Yatta, Meru, and Gong in the Masai, at the same time I was busy with my big business, so if anybody says that he saw me during those months at Ndeya he would be telling lies.

Q: Did you ever administer an oath to him or to anybody else?

A: No.

Q: Now, one other question. Waweru said in this court that after the alleged administration of the oath he went to a witch doctor and he found with the witch doctor a man called Kimani Kihio. Do you know Kimani Kihio?

A: Yes, I know him.

Q: Is Kimani alive or dead?

A: He died on the last day of December 1950, and he was buried on the first day of January.

Cross-examination touched on his activities in the Chura branch, and the series of meetings he organised in 1950. "The first meetings were ordinary meetings," Karumba said, "but towards the end of the meetings we realised that Mau Mau had sprung up at Navasha. Then we started making arrangements to denounce it, because it would ruin the country."

Then the DPP went through Waweru's story with the witness, putting it to him sentence by sentence.

SOMERHOUGH: He says you said, "It is I who have ordered you to be seized because we want you to take the oath?"

A: That is a very big lie.

Q: "The oath for the Kiama of the country which has been organised with a view to driving out the Europeans?"

A: That is all lies. I do not like such things.

G*

Q: And then he goes on to say that you said that he, Waweru, belonged to the Government and went about and about?

A: That is a lie.

Q: "And Waweru is a policeman and he lives at the place of Major Buxton and the Chief is there and the Headman is there."

A: If a man said that to him, he, being a policeman, would report it.

Q: Did Waweru leave the police in 1942?

A: I know he left the regular police in 1942. He was then taken over by Major Buxton and lived with him. The first time I came to know him was in 1943.

Q: I wanted to ask you one more question. You have told us about this man Kimani who you say died on the 31st December 1950.

A: Yes.

Q: Do you know the witch doctor to whom Waweru went?

A: No.

Q: There seems to be a year's difference between you. You are quite sure this man died in December 1950?

A: Yes.

Q: Do you know him so well—Kimani?

A: His sons are my friends, and I am a partner of Waweru's brother, and the land about which there was a dispute in 1943 —the case which I heard with the other members—belonged to Kimani son of Kahui, who was half-brother of the father of Waweru, and I divided that piece of land between them, and Kimani was a very old man, and from Ndei to Kikuyu he always came by motor-car.

Q: You seem to know him very well. You are quite sure of the year of his death?

A: When we were hearing the case in November 1950 Kimani was a very, very old man, and very sick, and he could not move, and a very rich man.

Last, cross-examination once more elicited something about the strength of the KAU in 1952. Karumba was asked what was the amount of this collection he came to inquire about at KAU head office when the Limuru people were there? He said about 2,000 shillings. In re-examination Defence produced a report in *Sauti ya Mwafrika* which showed a collection of 2,187 shilling 98 cents: that is to say a collection of over £109 at an ordinary afternoon meeting in an African market, from an audience who would consider themselves tremendously well-paid at £5 a month.

After all Defence witnesses had been heard and cross-examined, Crown Counsel recalled the first witness after Kenyatta to be heard for the Defence. This was the Chief Charles Kigwe, whose evidence-in-chief is on page 177. His evidence had been heard on 9th February; he had been released to go back to his official duties on 11th February. Now on 2nd March 1953 he was brought back to Kapenguria.

SOMERHOUGH: You were telling us when you were last here about the case you had in the Supreme Court in which you appointed Rawson Macharia as your arbitrator. Do you remember that?

KIGWE: Yes.

Q: Did you in fact have a quarrel as a result of that case with Rawson Macharia?

A: What sort of quarrel?

Q: Did you in fact refuse to pay him his arbitration fee?

A: In fact I had paid him but later he said that I had not paid him and based that argument on the fact that he did not give me a receipt.

Q: Did he in fact complain to the Registrar of the Supreme Court about your failure to pay him?

A: Yes, he sent me a letter and sent a copy of that letter to the Court.

Q: Right, that is all about that. And the second thing is this: you told us you were in business before you were made a chief on 20th December last year?

A: Yes.

Q: Did your business in fact include the receiving of stolen goods?

A: No.

Q: Were you in fact convicted on two accounts of receiving stolen goods in 1945 before the first-class Magistrate, Nairobi, in Criminal Case Number 2634 of 1945, the date of the conviction being 2nd January 1946?

A: Yes.

Q: And found guilty on both counts and sentenced to six months' imprisonment on each count?

A: Yes.

Q: And fined a thousand shillings for the further six months in default? The charge was receiving whisky stolen from the NAAFI, was it not?

A: The facts were not as deposed in court, but I was found guilty.

Q: And you served how long in prison?
A: I think about nine months.

[Witness was re-examined by Defence Counsel.]

PRITT: With regard to your conviction in 1946, were you guilty
or not guilty in your own mind?
CHIEF KIGWE: No, I was not guilty.
Q: And this seven-year-old story dragged up by the Prosecution
at this stage was not, apparently, sufficient to prevent the
Government appointing you as a Chief last December?
SOMERHOUGH: Does that arise out of cross-examination and
would it be relevant to the case?
MAGISTRATE: I think so.
SOMERHOUGH: You think it does—what the Government knew
or did not know, why they made him Chief?
MAGISTRATE: I think it is relevant that he was appointed to
Chief. I am afraid I have not got that down, but I did hear
something about it, but I think it is relevant—in December?
SOMERHOUGH: December 20th.
PRITT: This old story—seven years old—did not prevent the
Government appointing me as Chief last December.
SOMERHOUGH: He has not answered it yet, but I presume he
will answer it that way.
KIGWE: No.

And now Defence had marshalled its witnesses. It remained to
put its final case.

22

Final Speech in Defence

DEFENCE COUNSEL was on his feet. "I want to begin by recalling at the time when the Prosecution case closed, and I and my friend made some fairly long speeches, that being the moment at which the Prosecution's case should have been at its strongest. I submit, or perhaps remind Your Honour that I did submit then, that it was—either looked at as a whole or looked at in its separate parts —an extremely weak case." Thus Defence Counsel opened his final speech.

He had a twofold submission about the Prosecution case. First it had never been properly prepared at any stage, either in the weeks which preceded the launching of the charges, during which time the accused were already in detention, nor during the period of the trial itself "which has lasted approximately as long as Napoleon took to get from Elba to Waterloo". It had been noticeable during recent weeks that the Prosecution "up till two or three days ago was still trying to build up its case from the Accused and Defence witnesses", said Counsel, and he added, "Of course there is nothing improper about it but it is unusual for a Prosecution to be reduced to that."

The second submission was "that it does not seem that the Prosecution has ever really made up its mind as to what the essence of the charge against the accused is. It is difficult to believe," said Counsel, "that the Prosecution ever really has had faith in its own case. The whole root of the business is that there never was seriously a real case against my clients at all."

A flippant story was once current about a defendant in the dock who was making out a very good case for himself when the North Country magistrate looked at him and said, "Now then, thou must a' done summat or thou wouldn't be there". Yet, Counsel said,

"Speaking as objectively as I can, and purely professionally, I fail to understand how such charges can be made on the evidence". So Counsel came back to his original claim that there was in reality no case.

"Managing Mau Mau. Well, where? Not why, of course, but how? In what fashion, with what assistance, in what office, with what policy, with what documents? Never, never anything." Sticking to the evidence and avoiding either hysteria or newspapers, "I think we can all agree that Mau Mau exists on a substantial scale and in a terrifying form." The difficulty of the Prosecution was to be found in the very weight of what they had set themselves to prove.

The difficulty of the Prosecution, the difficulty not in the least created by their own failure to prepare a case, but by the inherent facts of the case, is that you have got to prove something very grave and terrible indeed. You have got to prove that these six gentlemen participate in terrorist organisation in respect of which incidentally there is a large body of evidence that the body in which they are most prominent, the Kenya African Union, is a plain and outspoken enemy of that organisation. The loose talk of this being Mau Mau, and the leaders of Mau Mau being on trial, the talk of the Stern gang, the militant wing, are, of course, things by which (whatever the public may do) a court will not allow itself to be led astray. The famous agenda or alleged agenda of one of Cromwell's Council meetings, "Item the King, to be tried, condemned and executed", is not part of Kenya or English legal procedure.

The first moment when the Prosecution explained its case was not unnaturally the opening. "The last moment was on 9th February at a moment of no particular significance in the case except that it was the end of a cross-examination of Mr Jomo Kenyatta spread over seven days, and more significant, the 9th of February was a Monday and somebody had a week-end's reflection, and towards the close of the cross-examination Mr Somerhough appeared to put to Mr Kenyatta a case which when I come to examine it will be almost an abandonment of everything that had been put in the case before." The first version had been "that Mau Mau is the militant branch or the Stern gang of Kenya African Union". But this idea was utterly inconsistent with "the pedigree that Mr Somerhough developed on 9th February—that it was a mere alias for the Kikuyu Central Association".

February 9th witnessed a *volte face*, a reformulation of the Crown case, a new case under nineteen heads.

They give the general impression that they are the product of a week-end's anxious reflection by somebody who, whatever he does know, knows very little of the mental discipline which lawyers have to impose on themselves, of limiting themselves to the evidence—and I hope it is not in any way an offensive thing to say. It is not meant to be offensive, but it looks as if it was something presented by some lay adviser to Mr Somerhough and accepted possibly, or possibly not, against his better judgment.

The first of these heads was put to Mr Kenyatta "From your return to Kenya in 1946 you led the Association which was then called KCA?"

You can see, so to speak, what is coming. Now my comment on that is it is an effort to make a case which is in essence, I think, this: "The Kikuyu Central Association was proscribed in 1940, lingered on with more or less vigour underground for a period which—after all—would be something like a decade, and then decided to rename itself Mau Mau."

The first comment of course on such a proposition is that the opening, as I have already pointed out, is wholly silent upon it, and the evidence is almost equally silent. I shall analyse the evidence later, but it could all be put in a thimble, and if anybody spilt it out of the thimble one would hardly notice it reaching the ground. One comment I will make is that if that sort of story were going to be made the Prosecution would have presumably called some evidence about it, and one particular thing that would be important would be why the Kikuyu Central Association was proscribed. . . . There is practically no evidence as to why it was proscribed. There is a vague statement that it was something to do with the war, and one could well imagine that a proscription in 1940 for war reasons might or might not have any pertinence to the conditions of 1950 to 1952.

Again, if the case was this story of Kikuyu Central Association and Mau Mau being a fairly continuous life of one organisation in substance, "there would be no rhyme or reason whatever" in having limited the charge here to the period beginning on 12th August 1950.

I feel sure that, however badly this Prosecution was prepared, however little evidence there ever was to support it, if this suggestion that the real case is that Mau Mau is a development or an alias of the Kikuyu Central Association, if that had ever been thought of before the week-end of 7th to 9th some evidence would have been produced to tell us what the Kikuyu Central Association was, why it was banned, and to link it with Mau Mau.

The second step in the Prosecution's new case was: "You imposed into KCA a form of oath similar to that which was continued in the society commonly known as Mau Mau." But there was no evidence that either Mr Kenyatta or any of the accused had anything to do with the taking of the KCA oath "and no evidence indeed in the case of any KCA oath having existed later than early 1950, when Dedan Mugo is said to have been convicted of taking a KCA oath." The third step: "You did this because as a result of your own knowledge of your people and of the studies you had made, you recognised the very binding force that an oath of that nature would have upon the Kikuyu." There was no evidence that Mr Kenyatta did this and no evidence of the nature of the oath. Fourth step: "the main purpose of that oath was: (1) To bind the people to the Association which was under your control, whether known as KCA or later as Mau Mau ... and (2) To foment trouble about regaining the land for your people." Fifth: "You took an active part in early 1950 in the imposition of this type of oath, i.e. with earth, blood and banana-arch accompaniments." This turned on the evidence of Macharia, Muthondu and Njui, and Counsel submitted that "these incidents on the balance of evidence already are as dead as the proverbial doornail." Sixth step. "As a result of a prosecution in 1950 for taking the KCA oath, namely of Dedan Mugo, the society's name was changed to Mau Mau." This again depended on the argument—without evidence—from continuous existence of KCA and Mau Mau. Step seven: "The objects of Mau Mau and the KCA were the same, ultimately to drive out the Europeans, to obtain land, and to use violence."

Answer: "Unfortunately for the Prosecution there is no evidence whatever from beginning to end of the case what the objects of the KCA were and not a very great deal of what the objects of Mau Mau were." Step eight: "Through all the period covered by the charge you were in substantial control of Mau Mau." There was no evidence that Mr Kenyatta was in substantial control, but

"it is interesting that the high-water mark is not a charge of
management but of substantial control, as if what they really
believed was that someone else was managing, but that Kenyatta
was able to give orders".

Steps 9, 10, 11, 12, and 13 were grouped. "You elevated Mau
Mau into the position of a religious cult: you were at all times
aware of the existence of this Nyimbo in which you replaced in
the songs in some cases the Deity; the Black Book found in your
house contains apparently in one case the original of hymns in
these books: gradually through the influence of the Nyimbo you
began to adopt or to attribute to KAU the policies of Mau Mau.
The effect of the hymn books is threefold (i) To propagate the
religion of Mau Mau with Jomo Kenyatta as the object of worship; (ii) to secure and increase membership of KAU as evidenced
by the Hymns; (iii) to introduce through the songs the aims of
Mau Mau."

Defence comment: "It is interesting once again that the Prosecution puts its case as low as 'well aware'. It does not say he had
anything to do with it. . . . Because X is aware that someone is
publishing a song book, X becomes criminally liable as manager
of an illegal organisation which is not mentioned in the song book,
but he is criminally liable for managing the illegal organisation,
since some of the songs in the book advocate a policy which is
also advocated by the illegal organisation in question—and this
is the sort of nonsense that develops in modern political repression."

You get an illegal organisation that demands equal pay, and
then it is discovered that some responsible organisation demands
equal pay for equal work, then you include, say, the Liberal
Party in England with the demands of some subversive political
organisation. You will remember that the Union of South Africa
had put the definition of Communism in a statute, that is to say
anybody who advocated anything Communistic or opened his
mouth about anything was technically a Communist.

There is no evidence of any songs being sung from these
books. There is not much evidence of any singing at all, and
and one has to remember that of the three song books one was
only published a month before the emergency and another three
weeks before that, and there is no evidence of the date of
publication of the other at all.

With regard to the Prosecution's case for the effect of the hymn books, "if there had been anything in this part of the case at all, the Prosecution could have found a witness somewhere who could have said in the witness box: 'I heard the song sung and I liked the idea of violence and accordingly I joined Mau Mau.' I am sure he would have been delighted to say that if anyone had asked him to say so."

Step Fifteen: "That only in the middle of 1952 when you were alarmed by the increasing violence of Mau Mau, did you seek to put any restraint on it at all, by the evidence of what you said at Ol Kalou."

> The first comment I have to make is that it is a funny way of describing a man who is charged with being the manager of Mau Mau, giving him this rather detached view of being alarmed by the increase of violence which after all he is running himself. . . . You have got to convince everyone here that Mr Kenyatta is in fact and in secret the manager, the controller, the runner, the driver of this huge terrorist organisation which incidentally has been going from strength to strength while Mr Kenyatta has been out of active life for something like five months.
>
> The suggestion is: So here you are, running a terrorist organisation, you are alarmed by the increase of violence of some of your supporters you can't control, so you say to one or two of them one evening quietly: "When you administer the oath don't use so much force or someone will tell the police." Really, that is a perfectly fair description of a piece of absolute rubbish and that is the sort of thing we have to face in this case.

The last three steps in the new argument asserted that accused at no time denounced Mau Mau with any intention to be effective, at most accused denied any connection between Mau Mau and KAU, and on such occasions when forced into a position of saying something Kenyatta had spoken with double meaning.

It was the Prosecution case that Kenyatta had deliberately neglected to condemn Mau Mau. On this they relied first on meetings at Thomson's Falls and Nyeri. These petering out, they were left with Limuru.

> The whole Prosecution case about everything he said was confined in the end to perhaps the smallest meeting he had ever addressed, and a case which broke down completely because

when Ephraim Gichereri was cross-examined he had to admit that Mr Kenyatta had condemned Mau Mau very strongly.

Counsel characterised the witnesses briefly. "My criticisms of the Prosecution witnesses were fully made in my earlier speech and nothing has happened since then to make them any better or worse, except that of course they have been refuted by a number of witnesses—our witnesses." Endless cross-examination by putting newspaper reports to witnesses and getting their denial "produce in my submission exactly nothing". A young and enthusiastic politician rushed to his father saying, "Father, the newspaper reported my speech last Saturday incorrectly, can I stop them?" Father sagely replied, "If you worry them they will report your speech correctly and that will be the end of you".

Defence witnesses had taken risks in appearing.

Mr Kigwe might easily lose his chiefship and I do not suppose he felt any happier when the Prosecution elected to have him brought back specially to ask him whether he had been convicted of a criminal offence nearly seven years ago. The witnesses in my submission gave their evidence pretty well. Many of them suffered from an inability to say yes or no, an inability which I think affects ninety per cent of all witnesses. Some of them were loquacious; that is irritating to lawyers, but it does not mean that they are not speaking the truth.

In general "when one looks at the history and the records" the accused were not the sort of people who would be likely to join in the leadership and management of an underground terrorist organisation.

Counsel now had something to say about each one separately, beginning with Jomo Kenyatta.

The first thing he did in the evidence-in-chief is something very much more important and very much less simple than appears at first sight. The first thing he did was to take up a general policy attitude for KAU and himself.

Now I say that is very important but not so simple for a number of reasons.

We have so often seen in history, in many countries, leaders of a great movement or organisation charged with some violent activity. They come into a dock or witness box, with the public or the press having already convicted them, and they get up and say, "Well, you accused us of all sorts of violence, but our policy, attitude, character, actions, and conduct does not match with the violent things that have been suggested. Anybody who says that has been deceived, and we proclaim our faith and our policy and you can see it in our constitution. It is orderly and not subversive. . . ."

It is not easy or practicable or possible for leaders of any great organisation to say that sort of thing if it is not true. . . . There are limiting factors preventing any excuse of that type and I would like to state them. I think they are two in number and the first is this. You cannot "get away" with it, and by that, I mean if any man in fact leads or takes any active part in any movement or organisation which is known and carries on work publicly and he advocates in the course of his leadership the policy of that movement, he can never thereafter give any incorrect or modified version of that policy because he will have gone on record in scores of speeches and documents, pamphlets, and even in the constitution itself, so that it is impossible for a person in that position to come into the witness box and say that his line of policy is what it is not. If a man is a leader of any organisation and denies, Judas-like, the policy of that organisa- tion, then he destroys for ever his own position in that organisa- tion which would say to him when he came out: "You have lied yourself out of this court, you have lied yourself out of this organisation too."

It is obvious in my submission that if Mau Mau is anything like what it is shown to be, then it must be bitterly hostile to the one great African organisation with a large membership and capable, as the evidence showed, of recruiting in open and broad daylight at one single meeting 4,000 new members of KAU, individual members putting down their subscription then and there in hard cash, and getting a receipt for it.

After all KAU is seeking to travel constitutionally some way down the road along which Mau Mau want to travel by terror, and every time KAU can enlist a member Mau Mau loses the possibility of recruiting a member. Obviously the KAU leaders stand in some danger and in my submission Mr Kenyatta's state- ment of policy is one that must be taken as genuine.

Of the Limuru incident Counsel said, "The central point can be put like this, that Mr Kenyatta was pressed at a public meeting to deny or denounce Mau Mau and that he evaded it, and in effect refused to do anything of the sort. . . . The answer to this central point is extremely simple. Gichereri proved beyond any doubt whatever in his cross-examination that Mr Kenyatta had denounced Mau Mau in emphatic terms. . . . The Prosecution say that the tailors asked us to denounce Mau Mau and we did not. The answer is that the master tailor has proved that we did."

The office bearers of the Limuru branchlet had complained of the Chura branch. "The Chura branch has approximately 7,000 members, and one would have thought that with or without assistance of informers or trap applications the Prosecution would have been able to get at any rate four or five people to come forward and say that they had been in touch with the Chura branch and had been told they would have to join Mau Mau if they wanted anything to do with it."

Of Ol Kalou: "What on earth does a responsible Prosecution mean by starting as part of their case an incident of this kind without first ascertaining what Wambui has to say? They based their sensational and highly improbable story on Tabitha alone."

They went over this story, they took Tabitha's evidence some time, I think the evidence shows various times from perhaps as early as July, certainly August, and on up to the end of November, and then, of course she came and gave her evidence, and then comes the adjournment in the latter part of December, and up to that moment there is no sign whatever that the Prosecution ever had any intention of, let alone calling Wambui, but even asking her for a statement.

Then, sir, what happens? Some people described as "the Indians" went to call on her. Then knowing that the Indians had called on her, and they at any rate knowing—well, of course Your Honour could not know until you were told—that the Indians were not the police, the police or Prosecution authorities (I do not know which I ought to say—it does not matter) without informing us—I do not make much complaint of it—proceeded then to question her. She was questioned at Ol Kalou, she was questioned at Nakuru at least twice, and ultimately they brought her to Kapenguria, and they got one statement after another out of her, and every statement they got except the last was of no use whatever to the Prosecution, and the last was only of the purely negative use that it could be used against her in cross-examination to a moderate extent. Presumably all those statements, except perhaps the last, were obtained from her with a view to seeing whether belatedly they could put her into the box. It was too late to consider her statement from the real point of view, that they should have been considering in the previous November, namely, is her evidence such that we ought to run this point at all?

I want to say a little about her allegation that she was threatened by the police. I ask you to accept it. It does not make a very great deal of difference to the essence of the story whether you do or not, but I submit that it is plain from her conduct and demeanour that there were threats. . . . I submit that the story of threats is also strongly supported by the fact that it seems to have taken so many weeks and so many days to get any statements out of her at all, because she is obviously a young woman of the intelligence of simple people. She is not an elaborately educated woman, but she is obviously intelligent, and obviously spirited, and quite capable of answering back in the witness box. . . .

They told you, sir, they decided not to call her because they decided she was unreliable and untruthful. I think this is the most magnificent example of sheer impudence I have ever heard in a court in my life. Unreliable witnesses! The people who called Rawson Macharia! The people who called Njui! The people who called Waweru! The people who called Munyi! And they started suddenly becoming, if you please, fastidious about witnesses. I leave it to the amazement of the multitude.

Thika—the incident in which Kenyatta was alleged to have told people that they could take some snuff—came next.

Now this Thika story is inherently silly because it is a picture of a big political leader putting forward an anti-Mau Mau policy which would put him in some personal danger from Mau Mau, putting it forward apparently, as a bold and clear part of the policy of his great party, and then in half a dozen words destroying his own prestige, his party's policy, any hope of reasonable treatment for his party from the Government, by just saying, "Well, gentlemen, that is what we say, and please do not believe a word of it". It is a sort of double suicide and the achievement of the impossible by getting the worst of both worlds. The Prosecution themselves have deprived the point of any plausibility by the evidence of the admirable Mr Philp, who comes forward as a Kikuyu expert, and says perfectly correctly that he never head of any such phrase or any particular meaning for it; and our evidence destroys it, in my submission quite thoroughly.

The Kiambu meeting was taken separately. The Prosecution must have considered it at the beginning, they had to make up their minds what to do. Here was a meeting organised by Kenyatta and others for the express purpose of denouncing Mau Mau, a meeting at which Kenyatta was the principal speaker, it was lengthily reported in newspapers, it was photographed, it was recorded on film, it was recorded on tape. Against this the Prosecution case was that Kenyatta never denounced Mau Mau.

They had to make up their minds what to do. They could explain it away, bring it forward as part of the Prosecution case and explain it away—like the famous story in England when it was suggested that the Italian Garibaldi would be greatly helped by marrying an English princess. And when the quite Victorian objection was raised that he was married already, it was suggested that Mr Gladstone would be able to explain that away quite easily. So no doubt the Prosecution would be able to explain it away. They would somehow, I suppose, think of the idea of destroying it . . . or they could have said, "We had better give up all idea of saying that Mr Kenyatta has not denounced Mau Mau, and that means dropping Limuru".

The actual course adopted by the Prosecution was to conduct their case as if the meeting had not happened.

And when in due course, whilst we have not the resources to prepare everything as we would have liked, we have the resources to prepare that much, and we prove that the meeting was held, and that it was attended by 30,000 people, that it was accepted as a genuine and important step in the fight against Mau Mau, that it was broadcast, then the Prosecution found themselves in the pit, I will not say which they dug for themselves because that would involve some form of active thought, but the pit which they must have known was there. . . .

All they can do is to cross-examine and then, making up in courage for what they lack in foresight and preparation, they produce the childish suggestion that the whole of this great meeting was, so far as Mr Kenyatta was concerned, a swindle.

Then as soon as it became known that there were or had been in existence some semi-official recordings of the Kiambu meeting "naturally it occurred to most people that that would be the best possible evidence."

You, sir, speaking of course, not, so to speak, with Woodroffe[1] in your hand, but as a Magistrate using common sense, said it

---

[1] Woodroffe on *The Indian Evidence Act* is the standard text-book.

would be the best evidence, and as it was too late for the Prosecution of course to get the evidence I said I would get it, and brought up on *subpoena* the correct witness, and then ensued an incident, perfectly lawful, though whether it has ever been applied with such strict technicality by a Prosecution against the Defence I cannot recall, but at any rate Mr Somerhough left what I might call no page of Woodroffe unturned to persuade Your Honour that I could not obtain the material from the witness on *subpoena duces tecum,* and so all we know is that recordings were taken, some were destroyed, some were available, and we shall never know what they said.

I submit that the Kiambu meeting has clearly established a complete refutation of the Prosecution case.

Basically there were nine items against Kenyatta.

Item 1. First half of Limuru. Mr Kenyatta is clearly established to have done this, that in answer to a demand that he should denounce Mau Mau he denounced Mau Mau.

Item 2. Second half of Limuru—at head office. This in my submission can now be put much more strongly. In my submission it is no longer possible on the evidence to find that Kenyatta told these people not to worry about Mau Mau.

Item 3. Ol Kalou. In my submission on the evidence it is no longer possible to believe, if it ever were possible to believe, that Mr Kenyatta made the observations that Tabitha attributes to him.

Item 4. Nyeri. It remains true that Mr Kenyatta in a speech disclaimed knowledge of Mau Mau and that the crowd applauded him for doing so.

Item 5. Thika. It is in my submission sufficiently established that Mr Kenyatta never said a word about taking snuff. It is quite clearly established that if he had said anything about taking snuff it would not have had any secondary meaning whatever.

Item 6. A Yellow Song Book, not shown to be his property or to have any connection with him, lay in his house.

Item 7. A Black Exercise Book, of which the same observations may be made, lay in his house.

Item 8. There lay in his house the draft of a letter now five years old, which he did not send out and which if he had sent out would have been concerned with the legitimate task of reporting upon his efforts to persuade the Governor of the Colony to remove the eight-year-old wartime ban on the KCA.

Item 9. Somebody had a Grey Nyimbo and in some of the verses, in some of the songs, in that Grey Nyimbo, there was praise of Jomo Kenyatta.

That is the whole case against the principal accused in a very important political prosecution, and it is apparently suggested that that establishes that he is the manager of an underground terrorist organisation.

Counsel dealt in turn with the Prosecution case against each of the other five accused, and then: "Sir, that is the end of my task, and I thank you for patient hearing and hope that by this speech, even if it was not as long as I feared, I have been able to assist Your Honour's labour which will now be intensified."

23

The Crown's Final Speech

CROWN COUNSEL began his speech on the afternoon of 3rd March 1953, and on 10th March he was still speaking. A week-end intervened, and another day the Court was adjourned on account of His Honour's indisposition, otherwise the days were full. Counsel had remarked on the comparative brevity of Pritt's final speech. "The case has according to my reckoning lasted fifty trial days, and the closing address for the Defence has taken approximately one trial day, that is to say just about two halves of a day, and the manuscript which has been covered has reached approximately 2,000 pages ... I cannot guarantee, in fact I do not intend to take so little time." He kept his promise.

The speech began with asperities. "As far as possible I shall follow the course set by what has been described as the leader of the Defence." Pritt had by now set off for London and was not present to hear himself described in such neuter terms. Crown Counsel now embarked on an analysis of the case occupying some 80,000 words, which flowed more or less evenly over the next week.

By now Crown Counsel was ready to assert that it had been a political trial, but he thought only on one side. "It has been a fighting campaign in this case—a political trial—and it would be a far easier retort to make when one reads the record that it has been a political defence, but it has never been a political Prosecution."

Defence Counsel had cried rhetorically, "Management of Mau Mau—how? Where?" Crown Counsel replied: "How? Well, the answer to that is fairly simple. It follows from the evidence that the control of Mau Mau was exercised undoubtedly partly by propaganda, and by the very constant assertion that the Africans had been robbed of their land which appears in the Nyimbos. The encouragement to drive out the Europeans which again appears in the Nyimbos, and the sometimes fantastic allegations which have been made about slavery, and that sort of thing: that also is part of the geared propaganda machine to force on the simpler African the idea that he is a victim suffering from immeasurable grievances which can be put right if a certain policy is followed.

"It is common ground between the Defence and the Prosecution that the effect of an oath on this particular tribe is extraordinarily potent—of a certain type of oath, that is to say, administered in a certain way and accompanied by some apparent great fear. The word Defence used was 'terroristic'. With that term I do not quarrel at all... That was the method by which it was done, and the actual evidence that has been given, in two of the most important instances, was to coerce KAU members into a situation where they would have to take this oath and would then be bound."

Defence Counsel had asked another rhetorical question. "In what office" was Mau Mau managed? Crown Counsel replied. "The office was the head office of KAU; and, with regard to documents, when I opened this case I said of course it was a society of the type that did not keep its list of members, and had no insignia, and whose records really appeared to be more or less non-existent. But as to documents we have at least obtained from the lips of the defendants and from witnesses that the policy of Mau Mau appears to be enshrined in the Nyimbo hymn books."

The Defence had asserted that Crown Counsel changed his case as he went along and some of the points which later were stressed most heavily were not even hinted at in his opening. To this Somerhough made a two-pronged answer: (1) "Persons experienced in criminal law will know that an address is always kept substantially low and you hope to close high"; and (2) It was in fact the Defence case which had been in process of constant change. Certainly the Crown had put to Kenyatta in cross-examination a nineteen-point challenge. But "what the Crown say in this case does not vary at all. We say that it is obviously quite possible to be a member of KAU and not a member of Mau Mau, but that certain people—that is to say the accused who were running KAU at the material time—were exerting pressure, and did exert pressure on one of the branches, the Limuru branch, till they were forced into the position where they might have to take the Mau Mau oath. We say that the accused were propaganding on the lines of Mau Mau, that they were saying that Mau Mau was a religion and that it was not to be interfered with". Through speeches and actions persons in KAU were being brought over to Mau Mau. The real point the Crown hoped to establish "is that the leopard has not changed his spots. The effect of the oath and the taking of an oath is something upon which he (Kenyatta) relied in Mau Mau, and what we have done is to say 'And not for the first time! You have ample experience of the effect of an oath, and how it can bind people, in your connection with KCA'".

Crown Counsel touched on the arguments about the "pre-proscription period". "Some criticism was made that Mau Mau was lawful until the 12th August 1950. That of course is not so. I actually cannot trace a Mau Mau case before 12th August 1950" but, Crown Counsel stressed, the Mau Mau oath was *de facto* unlawful all the time, though it might only be said to be unlawful *de jure* after proscription.

He turned now to the arguments about "failure to denounce" Mau Mau.

By itself, not denouncing Mau Mau does not mean very much. It is odd or curious that a man who takes up a position that Kenyatta says he was in, did not denounce it, if he did not, but there are many other bodies, no doubt, of which the same thing could be said, and, by itself, a failure to denounce Mau Mau was not a part of the Prosecution case, and that is why we did not lead it.

It only became a matter of interest to the Prosecution when, with what wisdom I leave other people to judge, the Defence decided to make it part of their defence that Kenyatta had always denounced Mau Mau at all his meetings, and proceeded to lead details of the six Kiambu meetings and details of the Rift Valley series, and finally the 24th August meeting to show that he did denounce Mau Mau. Now that is a challenge, of course, which the Prosecution cannot refuse, and we therefore attacked him in cross-examination on other things that he said, merely with a view to attacking his credit. . . . A final observation was that putting newspaper reports to people produces nothing. Well, sir, the answer to that, of course, is that putting newspaper reports, as was done in this case, eventually produced a situation where the witness may be regarded, quite frankly, as incredible. The situation in general, which was the result of putting newspaper reports, was that nobody had, apparently, read the reports. Nobody ever corrected them. The politicians did not read the reports of their own speeches. The editor did not read his newspaper. Consistently the reports were wrong, even when the editor was present at the meeting which was reported.... What the Prosecution contend about that is that a situation was produced in which the accused appeared, we submit, to be quite unworthy of credit. It became quite impossible to accept what they said."

Crown Counsel had come to the evidence of the accused.

Now the first of the accused to give evidence was Kenyatta, and he took three days, and as I said before without complaint, he went through his evidence-in-chief fast, in fact very fast, without any real delays, and he painted a picture of himself, and he gave a history of his activities since 1922. Now there were two pictures really which it was open to Kenyatta to paint of himself. One was a tough, fighting politician who had certain strong views; disliked Europeans intensely and did not care who knew it; was fighting for the rights of his own people; and, in fact, said "Yes, I wanted you out of it, I wanted certain rights and certain things, land and things like that for my people, but I am prepared to go about it in certain ways. I do not advocate throat-cutting and arson and things like that, but I dislike anybody being in this country but the Africans, and I do not care who knows it'. That would have been one picture, the other picture, that was in fact painted, was an extraordinary picture of a rather saint-like figure who abhorred violence, who thought everybody should lie down like the lion and the lamb, and that we could all be brothers and sisters who would never do anything except by constitutional means; never be associated with anybody who did anything except by constitutional means, and really was a sort of curious cross between, say, Gandhi and a boy scout, and that was the picture which he elected to paint of himself.

The Crown regarded Kenyatta as hypocritical.

There are many politicians who have taken up a line of policy and have been quite hypocritical about it. There is nothing new in that at all. There is nothing to bar persons who take part in public life from advocating one thing in one place and with one class of audience, and another in another place with another class of audience. It seems to make no difference to their positions. In this particular matter, the Crown say, it would have been impossible for Kenyatta to advocate openly the known policies of Mau Mau. He would come fairly close to them in the policies of KAU and his public attitude, as long as it was kept within the ostensible aims of KAU and would not bring him into any clash with the law. What the Crown say is that that would not in any way prevent him privately and secretly and furtively advocating a much stronger policy, and, indeed, more than advocating it, ensuring that it was put into force.... Moreover, in my submission, his Mau Mau—or any Mau Mau adherents—would well understand the necessity of public denials, and for public objuration, so long as that objuration was kept in moderate bounds.

Crown justified its cross-examination of Kenyatta on racial enmity.

The Crown's contention, of course, is that Mau Mau, or a society like Mau Mau, can only flourish in an atmosphere of hatred between races. It is no good telling Africans to drive out Europeans if they like Europeans.... If you can get the idea into people's heads that they are victims of theft, the victims of ill usage, you prepare the ground, and the next step is, "Well, let us turn out the thieves, let us turn them out, let us, if necessary, kill them".

Counsel laid emphasis on Kenyatta's letter written in 1948 to "former leaders" of the proscribed KCA. "Now, the unfortunate fact is, and it cannot be disputed, that the KCA was banned as dangerous to good order. But in 1950, at the material time when Mau Mau was just beginning to show its head, KCA would appear to have been operative by the conviction of Dedan Mugo for taking oaths, and we have been told that KCA and Mau Mau were simply other names for an oath-taking association, that it never died.

"You get all sorts of queer insights", Counsel said, "into Kenyatta's mind" in the course of his evidence and cross-examination and re-examination, "his curious ideas about the Crown Lands Ordinance, about which he has been petitioning for years without knowing very much about it, in fact when we asked him a few questions about it, it was quite hopeless, because it was quite obvious he did not really know what it contained, and had not appreciated that the African land had not been Crown Land for

about twelve years, and so on and so forth". Kenyatta's state of
mind was one "of great bitterness, and, indeed, fallacious bitterness to a great extent, which might well be a state of mind of a
man accused of what he is accused of doing."

So much for the general section of Counsel's speech. The rest
of his time he devoted to a point by point analysis of the twenty-
one incidents, beginning with Rawson Macharia. Here his object
was to analyse the stories of the ten Defence witnesses, and first
that of the Chief Charles Kigwe who had said he was with
Macharia that day.

> Kigwe is one of the few witnesses called by the Defence in
> this case who was apparently respectable at first—*apparently*
> respectable—and he came down here and he had been made a
> Chief on the 20th December, while the case was going on, and
> not unnaturally, carried a sort of aura of respect with him. But
> he did corroborate Macharia, so that no one could say that this
> is an absolute invention from beginning to end. You have got
> all the actors, or some of them, the principal actor Kenyatta, at
> the place, the time, and Rawson doing the things he said he was
> doing, and what has got to be accepted, if you hold that Raw-
> son Macharia's evidence has been refuted, is that for some
> reason of his own he has made up the oath-taking ceremony.

Of Charles Kigwe, the Chief, "Well, I said that he was apparently respectable, because afterwards, as you know, I recalled
him, and he established that there had been some dispute between
him and Macharia about the payment of Macharia's fees as arbitrator, and that in fact Macharia had made a complaint to the
Supreme Court about it, which had been forwarded to his lawyers
and had been dealt with there. And then, of course, he also re-
vealed the fact that far from being the respectable businessman
of unsullied reputation, he had been convicted of receiving stolen
goods in 1946, on two counts, and was therefore a person who was
an ex-convict, and for that particularly dishonest and unpleasant
form of crime, as a receiver."

Another witness against Macharia was the Reverend Harrison
Gachukia.

> He was a Minister of this indigenous Church and obviously
> worked for the now proscribed organisation KISA (The Kikuyu
> Independent Schools Association). His diary, which should have
> been his strong point, was attacked by the Crown on several

grounds, one was the difference in the colour of the inks over the dates. Secondly, the extraordinary detail into which he entered for the only time, "staying at Gichuki" putting the matter beyond all doubt—the only time in that diary that he wrote "staying at Gichuki". Thirdly, the fact that on the 15th something was overwritten, there was another indelible-pencil entry underneath and the ink was over it, and then he said he had written it with indelible pencil and the Crown say that it is obvious that it is not written in indelible pencil.

He was cross-examined at some length on his association with KAU.... He is from the local church, the church in Kenyatta's village, and therefore in that curious geographical circle of Kiamwangi, the school at Gichuki and Kahiu, coupled with Gathundu. [The strongholds of KAU and the Independent Schools Association, as well as the Teacher's Training College, were round Kenyatta's home.] In view of all that, and the state of that curious diary, and his connection with KISA, and his evasive and indeed untruthful answers about all his connections with KAU, the Crown submit that he also is not worthy of credit.

The Crown turned to Muthondu and his tea-house.

Now Muthondu's story—and it is very important this story— was that there was a meeting of the Age Groups of the Kahaguini school close to his house, that is also of course next door to the church of the Reverend Harrison Gachukia—that there was a party there—Dedan Mugo was there and Kubai and Kenyatta.... It is a story of inference, hymn singing all night until dawn, the KISA people being retained there, and the inference arising from the slaughter of the goats.

Now the refutation of this was twofold—one was distance, because he said it was a quarter of a mile away and Defence put in a plan which showed it was more than three-quarters of a mile away... but the important thing, is whether you can hear a lot of people singing, and, in my submission, this is very possible especially in mountainous country where there is a ravine which carries sound.

The cuts on the hands described by Muthondu, "according to the evidence of Mr Henderson are characteristic of Mau Mau, and indeed there is no evidence that they are characteristic of anything else. And we know from Rawson Macharia that the cuts were inflicted by a razor blade. Although a number of people have been asked whether they have any cuts or scratches, they were apparently lightly inflicted with a razor blade and one would not expect to find anything left, or that people were permanently marked".

(Perhaps the editorial comment should be made here that anthropologists may not find this argument conclusive. Ritual incisions are common to many African ceremonies, and, as a rule, means are found of making them permanent, or nearly so, by filling them with earth, or some of the components of whatever magical brew forms part of the ceremony. On page 42 Rawson Macharia describes this being done.)

Crown went on to the case of "the season-ticket witness" Njui.

Now there are various factors about Njui which are peculiar to this particular incident. The first one is that the Defence say that he has transferred the allegations that he originally made against Dedan Mugo to Kenyatta. Secondly, they claim that they have some grievance that we did not produce the statement made to the police by Njui. Well, now I will deal with the latter first.

Your Honour, a search of the cases will indicate that the most that has ever been decided in law is that the Defence have a right to call for statements. It has never been decided as a matter of law that there is a duty on the Prosecution actually to hand over statements. In practice, if we abandon a witness because he is deviating from a statement he has made to the police, we do, but at least that situation does not arise until, if it is our witness, until after the evidence-in-chief, and, consequently it cannot possibly arise until cross-examination, and this grievance they now claim, in my submission, is merely prejudicial, and without any foundation at all. . . . They say now that only by the diligence of their cross-examination did they discover the existence of an earlier statement, but if you look at the statement that he made to the police in 1952, you will see that it reveals at once that he has given evidence before in the case, and anybody who has this particular statement, the 1952 one, knows at once that there is an earlier one, and, of course, as soon as they called for it, they got it, and I handed them the 1952 statement before their cross-examination began.

If you compare what he said in 1950 you have the story just the same, the names of the policeman, the driver of the car, and William Kibera and Jomo Kenyatta there, and you have the distance they walked, and then he goes on to describe what

H

happens in the house, which is almost exactly the same: "the lamp burning low", he said here, "and when I went in it was turned down, right low, practically out, and I was asked, 'Are you Njui?', I felt myself having my hand seized by a man, and I was told by that man, 'Take off your boots, and if you have any money take it out'." Then he was asked by me, "Can you tell us who said this?" He said, "It was some visitor, I did not recognise his voice". In chief he would not recognise it, but when he came to be cross-examined it was put to him that he had said that it was—that he had actually named a person. "Did you say last week it was Jomo Kenyatta who said that? Do you remember giving an account last week of being told to take off your shoes, and being told it was a simple matter, and not to make a fuss?" Answer: "Yes". "Did you say last week it was Jomo Kenyatta who said that?" Actually he had not, he did not say it at all, he did not know who it was. When he was asked if he said that, he said, "Yes". "Did you say in your statement you signed in May 1950"—and we know it was not May 1950—"that the person who said it was Dedan Mugo?" He said it was not, "I was being threatened before I made the report". If you look at the statement, and, of course, you are supposed to put passages of the statement to the witness when you put in statements like that, you will find that he does not say so at all, he says quite plainly, "I heard the voice of a man say in the room, 'You, Njui, take off your shoes and if you have any money in your pocket, take it out and put it on the table'."

MAGISTRATE: Is the position this then with regard to him, that in the 1950 statement he does not implicate Jomo Kenyatta except that he was there?

SOMERHOUGH: He brings him to the house, but never brings him into the oath ceremony.

MAGISTRATE: In 1952 he substitutes Jomo Kenyatta for——

SOMERHOUGH: No he does not substitute, with respect, Your Honour, he added Jomo Kenyatta to the persons who were present——

MAGISTRATE: He brought him in in the 1950 statement?

SOMERHOUGH: As far as Kariuki's house, but never into the actual oath-taking ceremony.... The story that he has given in Court, the story he gave in 1952, is exactly the same as he gave in 1950 with the addition of Kenyatta as taking him through the arch.

CHAMAN LALL: May I correct my learned friend in one particular, Your Honour? Since Your Honour has asked this question about substitution, I think my learned friend will find in the original statement, it was Dedan Mugo who compelled him to go through this business.

MAGISTRATE: Which do you call the original statement?

CHAMAN LALL: The 1950 statement. Later on it was Jomo Kenyatta who was doing what Dedan Mugo was supposed to be doing.

SOMERHOUGH: No, they are both there. It is Dedan Mugo plus Jomo Kenyatta, but there are no words substituted as was claimed in the Defence that were originally put into the mouth of Dedan Mugo and are now put into the mouth of Jomo Kenyatta. You will not find that in the evidence at all.

CHAMAN LALL: I think my learned friend will find in the original statement that he was running away and it is Dedan Mugo who stopped him, whereas when he comes to this Court he says it was not Dedan Mugo who stopped him but Jomo Kenyatta who stopped him. That is the substitution.

Crown Counsel in his final speech put strong emphasis on the Limuru incident.

Now it it essential, Your Honour, to look at the cross-examination of these witnesses, because the way the Defence dealt with this, in my submission, is a particularly flagrant example of the tactics that they have adopted of the developing of the defence after the defence has opened, rather than before. The defence to the story is to discredit Ephraim, Johana and Stephano, and the line that is taken is that all they say is quite untrue, and moreover, they are persons who belong to a religion called the Etereri, which, at the last minute we hear was the same as a religion called the Aroti, or the Arumai, and that their whole object in visiting the head office was to complain about the misreport in *Mumenyereri*. That is the only reason they came.

Now their story is perfectly consistent. They told you how they were called up to the head office, and, indeed, that appears in the very newspapers of the Kenya African Union themselves, that they had been summoned to head office. They say they went there first with their books, and they made an appointment. Now, the importance of the meeting-place is that it leads up remorselessly to the Committee affair. Without it, you could not really understand the story. There had been this third meeting, Kenyatta turned up, they put to him the request to disassociate himself from Mau Mau. In the submission of the

Crown he dodged it completely, merely abused the local office-bearers and told them to come to KAU, said he did not know what Mau Mau was, referred to it as an animal to have a rope or chain put round its neck and be hit on the head with an axe handle and disappear.

The three office bearers from Limuru duly turned up bringing their books with them, and the money they had collected. Then they arranged to go there again on the 21st... Kenyatta took the chair, and he opened the meeting by asking them who had given them permission to start the branch, and they told him Tom Mbotela. They were asked about why they held three meetings and they showed their letter of permission, and then come these three phrases. Kenyatta said, "You have been given permission, of course, but you were enemies of the people and want to fight against the black people instead of the Europeans". He then repeated what he said at the meeting that they had sent a petition to England about self-government and that "we"—that is the Limuru branch—"definitely ought not to be fighting against the other people, the Mau Mau, because Mau Mau was a religion". Then he went on to complain that the branch was opened wrongly and they ought to be under Karumba's leadership....

Now the Crown case is that the whole of this is what might have been expected. First of all, you have the meeting, and the row at the meeting. You have—and it is not disputed—that they were told to come up to head office, and they do go up to head office, as you might expect, and again as you might expect, they are called over the coals.... Then come these very illuminating remarks about Mau Mau being a religion and so on.... The first line the Defence took, which they now cheerfully describe as a red herring... is that they were never a branch of KAU at all. So these, presumably, were the instructions then given for the Defence—"I suggest that your so-called branch was not a branch at all. Do you know it was never registered or recorded in the books of KAU as a branch?" Now on that, of course, the Defence were absolutely and completely and utterly defeated, because not only did they produce their books but they even produced the official KAU receipts, and the letter written by the late Tom Mbotela with even a KAU Head Office reference at the top....

Later on... all the accused... said... that these people arrived purely fortuitously, happened to arrive at the Committee, happened to ask for the president, were shown in, and all the Committee meeting stopped while they were dealt with, and that their sole object was to complain about a *Mumenyereri* article which had reported them as taking the "chicken oath", and they were given certain advice and went away contented. . . .

Every one of these accused persons has elected to take his stand on this particular account of what happened at the meeting and it is quite impossible in my submission to separate them in that respect. Achieng has told precisely the same story as Kenyatta—you could not part them. So either you believe Ephraim, Johana and Stephano or you believe the accused, and if you do not believe the accused you have to disbelieve them all, because their story is almost word for word the same.

When he came to Ol Kalou, Crown Counsel had something to say about Wambui.

The final witness was the much-disputed witness Wambui. She is the girl mentioned by Tabitha for the first time in the statement she made when she went into police protection in November. . . . On Tabitha's statement about Wambui she is coming out of the room where this particular meeting is being held, and she would therefore appear to be very closely compromised with Mau Mau activities and not a very likely source of useful and truthful information. However, she was eventually found by the police, and in December it was they found she had already been approached by the three Indians. The police then took a statement from her and at Kapenguria. Now it has been said in the evidence that she was examined off and on for weeks. In actual fact all that happened was that she was seen, asked some questions, and went back to her home. Later, on the 30th December, she was questioned again and brought here on the 31st when she made certain statements and was handed over to the Defence on 2nd January. Therefore the "weeks and weeks" resolves itself down to about four days, during only three of which was she questioned in any shape or form. . . .

She comes into the witness box and makes her statement which of course completely disagreed with that of Tabitha, and she is then cross-examined as to the previous statement she has made, and, of course, they become quite different, and we get the story that (*a*) she was forced to make this statement by physical means, having her thumb forced on the paper; (*b*) that she was threatened to be dropped out of an aeroplane unless she told the police what they wanted, and (*c*) the police have forged her statement, and have added things to it, and got her signature by force.

Now the astonishing part of that, and in my submission I am not going to mince my words, is that the two officers who were accused—Mr Baker and Mr Henderson—were in the witness box being cross-examined by the Defence on the 6th January— Wambui was in the hands of the Defence on 2nd January—on the 6th they had Mr Henderson and Mr Baker here in the witness box. Do they ask one single question about Wambui and what they are supposed to have done? They do not. They do not mention Wambui. The tactics are to say nothing to Mr Henderson and Mr Baker but to get Wambui in the witness box where she can tell her story without fear of being rebutted in any shape or form. . . .

Another criticism which arises—if these people are so ready to make these allegations against the police—when they read this statement would they not ask themselves the question: Supposing the police are the sadistic torturers, forgers and perjurers they are supposed to be, would they not get a really useful statement out of her?

She deals with the story of her life and how she came to Ol Kalou—which she admits was true. She says she remembers Tabitha coming up and she says that she does not remember a thing about the final part of the 10th because she was drunk. That is how she tries to get over it—"I do not know, I was drunk"—that is what she tells the police, and it is not an uncommon sort of lie for persons who know more about things— she can hardly say she lost her memory. She also gets the aunt of Tabitha completely muddled and suggested that the aunt of Tabitha arranged for her to sleep with Kubai. That is the respectable old Muslim woman! Why she did that I do not know. It is curious that she fell into the same defects as the Defence who actually made some suggestion in court that someone had switched the aunts. . . . Bearing in mind what she said and her conflicting statements, the most the Crown can do is to say that she should be regarded at utterly unreliable, a witness upon whom no credit can be placed whatever.

Counsel had something to say about the claim that Tabitha took the police to the wrong shop.

Well, as we know the building consisted of two rooms, and all we know about her pointing out in October, when she went up with Alleyne, was that she did point out the building, and he apparently went into the shop and spent about one and a half minutes there, and that was the shop which was occupied, but she did not point out the wrong building. . . .

If it is suggested that Tabitha has had the story put into her mouth by the police it is not a strong story. It involves Kenyatta in the more violent Mau Mau activities because it purports to show Kenyatta trying to put the brake on his followers, in the sense that he is controlling Mau Mau, but if it suggested that it is some wicked plot on the part of Crown or the police—if that is suggested it is never suggested why such a comparatively temperate line was being used, because the picture she paints is not Kenyatta inciting his followers to greater excesses, it is Kenyatta trying to restrain his followers from the excesses they are committing. He is not trying to stop them administering the oath, but it is suggested that they should not use so much force because it is getting them a bad name with the police and will do their political aims and objects no good. The accused deny that there is any such conversation. . . . Then they bring three witnesses to support Kenyatta—one is Jesse Kariuki. He is the perfect type of the Kenya agitator. As he himself admits he starts in the East African Association—banned. He goes to the KCA in which he becomes a very big noise—he is interned and kept interned for some time. Out he comes and in he goes to KAU as a travelling inspector, and with KAU from the beginning. At the present moment he is detained under an Ordinance having been found in the full hearing of a Court to be high up in the Mau Mau movement. One would have thought that would be the most unfortunate evidence.

CHAMAN LALL: Is there any evidence?

SOMERHOUGH: He admitted it.

CHAMAN LALL: He did not agree.

SOMERHOUGH: Having been found, he agreed he had been so found. No doubt it may be said by anyone that everyone who is found guilty in this Colony is wrongly so found, but nevertheless the fact was put to him that he had been so found and he agreed that he had been so found. A rather unfortunate witness one would have thought to have called when one was defending oneself on a charge of being concerned with Mau Mau.

Crown Counsel touched on the vexed question of whether or not the tape-recording and sound-film could have been called in evidence.

The true position you will recollect perfectly well. The document he had to produce must be identified so that Your Honour knows what it was—whether it was the original record, the record added to—if so how much, or if anything was cut out. You must know in other words what it is. A thing was to be dropped on the table in front of you and that was all this court was allowed to know, and unless I would give an undertaking not to cross-examine, and a more extraordinary request for anyone with experience in law to make in a criminal case I have never heard. So much for Mr Reiss. So neither did we have the reporter from the *East African Standard* nor did they call or put in the record this denunciation, and they have made it an incident, and its only value is purely credit. It was only introduced by the Defence to establish their credit.

Counsel referred in shocked tones to the so-called "hymns".

They are, as Your Honour knows, in a small hymn book published and sold for a small sum of money particularly in 1952 apparently—there may have been earlier ones but we do not know. But the ones we are dealing with ... contained four features. One, they contained praise of the KAU leaders. Two, they contained all sorts of injunctions to KAU. Three, they contained something more than praise of Kenyatta—the Crown put it as high as worship. They are actually Christian hymns lifted from the Church of Scotland and other hymn books, with the name of Kenyatta substituted for that of the deity. They contain certain objects which are known to be the objects of KAU—self-government and getting the land back. And finally they contain certain objects and certain references which the Crown say are those of Mau Mau.

In his peroration Crown Counsel provided a summary of his analysis of the case.

May it please your Honour I have finished dealing with these incidents and with the evidence from which I have read certain passages here and there to illustrate the points that I was trying to make, and this is the fourth day on which I have addressed you in a case, the transcript of which exceeds 2,000 pages and the trial days are now somewhere between fifty and sixty. It now really remains only for me to connect up the threads of the case for the Crown and present it to you in as compact a form as I can do.

First of all I would remind Your Honour respectfully at this stage of the heads of the Prosecution. They are these. Kenyatta for managing the unlawful society commonly known as Mau Mau in Kenya between the dates of its proscription in August 1950 and the date of his detention under the Emergency regulations. The others accused jointly for assisting him as a joint enterprise in that management. That is what the charges amount to and they are compassed within narrow walls. We say Kenyatta is the manager and these other accused were assisting in the management. There is no suggestion of anybody else managing but Kenyatta. No evidence at all to that effect, and so what it really comes to is that you have to decide whether or not these are the Mau Mau.

The accused are in this position that they are all members, and Kenyatta is the manager, and the other accused are his assistants. Now Your Honour the evidence has fallen into three classes, that is to say, the direct incidents upon which the Prosecution place their greatest reliance; the pre-proscription incidents upon which the Prosecution place reliance, if you accept them, merely in so far as they assist you in deciding whether Kenyatta was still managing the society; and finally the collateral incidents which are really the Nyimbos and what was being said in speeches, what was handed out to the public, a part of which was introduced by Crown and partly by the Defence. In those three sets of incidents the Crown places its greatest reliance on the Ol Kalou and the Limuru office-bearers incidents, because we say that our submission is that these incidents, if you believe them, are incompatible with anything else but the management and the assisting to manage and the membership of Mau Mau.

Therefore the main ingredients are questions of credit, pure and simple and can be resolved in the submission for the Crown by these two questions: (1) Do I believe the witnesses for the Crown or the witness for the Defence? (2) If I believe the witnesses for the Crown then do the incidents lead me to an irresistible conclusion and without any reasonable doubt that those things can only have been said or done by persons who were managing Mau Mau?

All the accused were involved in the Limuru incident in the capacity of members of the Executive Council of KAU with the exception of Kungu Karumba whom the Crown say was called in *ad hoc* for that particular meeting.

At Ol Kalou only Kenyatta, Kubai and Achieng are involved.
H*

The pre-proscription incidents are these: Macharia, Muthondu, Gichungwa, and the KCA letter.

Those incidents—I cannot again stress this too strongly—are only relied on by the Crown so that you can say, if you find any of them are true, that helps you to decide whether a man behaving like this with Macharia, Muthondu and Njui in 1949 and 1950 was in fact still leading a society and still making importance of it in 1952.

The collateral incidents are really the Nyimbos and the Black Book and those are incidents which have to be considered in relation to the accused and what they said in their defence and in relation to what you have learned about the objects of Mau Mau of which we have learned a great deal in this case. The Ngei incident, the incident with regard to Munyi, Kaggia and his attempt to introduce Mau Mau into the Kilungu Youth Association, Waweru and his initiation into Mau Mau—those are all, subject to the same test, straight questions of fact, all the direct incidents are straight questions of fact.

Now Your Honour this trial has lasted a long time. It has taken place under special circumstances, that is to say it has been placed as far as possible out of reach of any outside interference. We have all suffered some inconvenience therefrom, the Crown no less than the Defence, but looking back there has been no real suggestion that justice has failed during this trial. The machinery has worked with extraordinary speed, sometimes papers and documents have arrived within 24 hours, and I think one can dismiss from one's mind any suggestion in any way beyond minor and temporary inconveniences, not being able to get a book at an hour's notice and that sort of thing. Nor has the administration of justice been affected by the fact that we have been so far from the centre of things.

A trial of this nature is bound to arouse considerable passion and prejudice in the country. It must do so. Looking at Mau Mau quite dispassionately and quite objectively and quite outside this trial, there can be no one who can say that it does not do the most appalling criminal things and that it appears to be a purely barbarous movement negative in everything it does and accompanied by circumstances of revolting savagery.

That does arouse strong feelings in everyone, and when you have a trial in which persons have taken a leading part in political agitation, are charged with managing that wicked organisation and being concerned in it, naturally their fate and their trial arouses a great deal of passion and prejudice. We, I think, can pride ourselves that those waves of passion have beaten in vain against the walls of this court. We have dealt with the case to the best of our abilities and endeavoured to exclude as far as possible—evidence is always a matter of opinion—but we have endeavoured to exclude matters which should not weigh with this court and outside—it is right that accused persons in the position of these accused should be defended vigorously and skilfully, and it is right that it should be so, and must always be so, where British justice obtains.

24

Judgment and Kenyatta's last speech

On 8th April 1953, the Magistrate delivered judgment. He found all the accused guilty, though the Supreme Court later acquitted one of them. With the exception of the evidence about the hymn books, the Magistrate accepted the Crown case in its entirety.

In his summary and analysis of the evidence the Magistrate came to a number of conclusions which the Defence were later to characterise as "perverse", though no-one can complain that they are obscure. One by one he went through the incidents on the chart which the Defence had produced in Court.

Rawson Macharia. Although my finding of fact means that I disbelieve ten witnesses for the Defence and believe one witness for the Prosecution, I have no hesitation in doing so. Rawson Macharia gave his evidence well.

Muthondu, the tea-shop man. Although again this is a case of seven witnesses for the Defence against one for the Prosecution I have no hesitation in accepting the evidence of Muthondu as a true version of what happened.... All the Defence witnesses were evasive on this matter.

Limuru. The three Limuru officials gave their evidence very clearly, frankly and fearlessly, and were amongst the best witnesses to whom I had to listen.

Tabitha. I observed very closely the demeanour of Tabitha, and I am satisfied that she is telling the truth, and that it was possible for her standing outside the shop door to have heard a person speaking inside the room, and I believe her evidence that Kenyatta made the remarks to which she testified.

Mr Pedraza. I am satisfied that the evidence given by Mr Pedraza is accurate and truthful; that Ngei did say the things attributed to him.

"Bless 'em all". There is no dispute that Ngei sent this letter.... Ngei writes: "Do you know what I sing daily in my small

cell? Here is the tune—'Bless Mau Mau, Bless Mau Mau, Bless all the adherents of Mau Mau, Bless all the oath-takers of Mau Mau. Oh, cheer up my lads of Mau Mau.' It is George Formby's tune; sing it, Hennie, and remember me in the cell." Later, he writes: "Yesterday, 21.10.52, all the leading KAU officials have been arrested. The Government has proclaimed a State of Emergency just like Malaya. White massacre planned is coming up." Later: "Nairobi . . . is steaming up now." Now this letter suggests that Ngei knew there was an element of Mau Mau at Kangundo. It would also appear to display sympathy with the Mau Mau movement, its adherents and oath-takers. It also shows that Ngei thought or heard or knew that a white massacre was going to take place. . . . To say the least it shows that Ngei, if not a member of Mau Mau was very sympathetic towards the movement.

Jomo Kenyatta's attitude.   Kenyatta replied to the question "Was any plan known in 1949 concerning any organisation known as Mau Mau?" "No; the best person to answer that question was John Gichungwa and his associates." Not a clever or convincing reply, but one rather typical of Kenyatta. Kenyatta further went on to say that he first heard the word Mau Mau used in 1950, when he found the expression used in the *East African Standard*. Some of Kenyatta's answers in cross-examination upon this point, and generally, are of interest. When asked, "What do you know of Mau Mau?" the answer was, "Just as you know". Again, "I know what I read in the paper, what I have heard in a court like this, and I mean I know just what the general public know about Mau Mau".

Again, "I think everybody knows the activities of Mau Mau. From what I have heard, that is, forcing people to take oaths, killing people, burning huts. From what I have heard from the papers, and from this court it is being said with the aim of driving the Europeans from Kenya". Kenyatta was unable to say how many members or office bearers of KAU had been involved or convicted of Mau Mau activities, and blamed the restrictions on public meetings for not being able to investigate this matter."

Fred Kubai and Willie George.   "Willie George was a some-what vague witness—at times endeavouring to act like a comedian, and at other times being rather insolent.

The evidence of the Prosecution was given by the self-styled "oath askari" Munyi. "I believe he was telling the truth, but it would not be safe in these uncorroborated circumstances, to find that his evidence is true, although it may well be so."

Njui, the "season-ticket witness". It may well be that both Njui and Kimani were too terrified to mention Kenyatta and I am not saying that their court evidence is untrue—it may well be true—but it would not be safe to rely on it or to find the incident proved beyond reasonable doubt.

Take a pinch of snuff. In the result I have no doubt that Kenyatta in his speech used this expression and it is equivalent to the English expression "Take a pinch of salt with it"; and that he intended his hearers to understand that when he said that he did not know what Mau Mau was he was not to be taken seriously, and that he intended them to understand that he did not know what Mau Mau was.

The draft note to former KCA leaders. It means that Kenyatta was, several years after the KCA had been banned, endeavouring or thinking of calling the leaders of it together and regarded himself as the leader of a proscribed society.

The Black Notebook. The book was important in one respect and that is on the question of Kenyatta's credibility. I confess that when he denied all knowledge of the book I was at once surprised, because the book was found in his house, and it is very difficult indeed, in fact it is impossible, to believe Kenyatta when he stated that he had never seen the book before and knew nothing of its contents or of the hand-writing. I consider that Kenyatta was badly advised to deny all knowledge of the book, as he has done, and that of course affects his credibility throughout the case.

The curse of the Mikongoe tree. I was left with the distinct impression that if it was any denunciation at all it was an extremely short and vague one, or not at all adequate or sufficient for one who whole-heartedly or sincerely wished to exhort his hearers to put down Mau Mau or to have nothing to do with it.

Witnesses in general. All the Prosecution witnesses impressed me as speaking the truth. . . . I now turn to the credibility of the accused and their witnesses. Here a very different state of affairs soon arose.

Kenyatta was inclined to be bombastic, and he was certainly vague when he wished to be. Very many of his replies were evasive, especially in cross-examination. I gained a strong impression that he was content to sit on the fence, as it were, and to refuse to be drawn into giving specific answers to specific questions. I came to the conclusion that on material issues he was not a truthful witness.

Kaggia spoke English very well, and much of his evidence was taken up in recounting his religious beliefs. Apparently he lived for some time as a Christian, but no longer relies upon the Bible, and is to all intents and purposes a Pagan.... I do not regard him as a truthful witness.

Ngei was ... flamboyant and self-assured ... Karumba was a loquacious and argumentative witness, and I do not regard him as truthful.

With regard to the other African witnesses called by the Defence on their behalf, I made notes at the time of the impression which their evidence made upon me. The adjective "evasive" can be well applied to nearly all of them. I am sure their evidence has largely been concocted and that it is not true.

One thing which runs throughout the evidence in this trial is the allegation that Europeans in the past have robbed the Kikuyu of their land. The allegation appears in the Nyimbos or hymn books, and there can be no doubt in anyone's mind that all these accused feel that they have a grievance and that they believe that Europeans have in the past robbed them of Kikuyu land. Kenyatta dealt with this matter in his evidence and prefers the expression "alienation of land" rather than the more extreme expression "robbing of land". There is no proof before me that any land has been stolen from the Kikuyu, and the most that Kenyatta has been able to put forward in support of his allegation is the Crown Lands Ordinance of many years ago, and it is quite unreasonable to suggest that this Ordinance affected anything in the nature of stealing or robbing of land by Europeans from Africans.

Another matter which stands out strongly in this trial is the objection by all of the accused to what is called the colour bar. Most of these accused have travelled overseas to Europe and have lived there. Kenyatta in particular is a most widely travelled man, having spent several years in different countries in Europe, and I feel some of the underlying causes for their actions, is their obsession about what is called the colour bar or alleged racial discrimination.

During the trial I watched with interest to see if any of the accused would whilst giving evidence denounce Mau Mau or repudiate it in such words as would leave no doubt in my mind of the sincerity of the denunciation or disavowal, and I came to the conclusion that not one of the accused made such a denunciation....

To sum up, I find all the accused guilty on all the charges brought against them. It is my opinion, after consideration of the evidence on both sides, that these accused functioned as

high officials of KAU over which they obtained control and in
their capacity as KAU officials attempted to persuade the outside world that they were pursuing constitutional methods in
their desire for self-government and the return of land which
they allege was taken from them by Europeans.

I further believe that at the same time, in secret, they planned
and organised and developed the Mau Mau society. They used
their positions in KAU as a cover for their real purpose, which
was to drive the Europeans from Kenya by force and violence.
They are all educated Africans, and undoubtedly have exercised
a great power and influence over the Kikuyu tribe. They have
taken advantage of the uneducated and primitive Africans in
order to further their own ambitious purposes and their lust for
power. They have chosen to take, as they think, the short cut to
personal power by the formation of the Mau Mau society, and
have preferred secretly to throw over all constitutional means
towards political advancement of the Kenya African: and have
regarded the secret society and violence as a quicker and more
effective way to achieve their objects.

Kenyatta addressed the Court on behalf of himself and the
other five accused.

KENYATTA: May it please Your Honour. On behalf of my colleagues I wish to say that we are not guilty and we do not
accept your findings, and that during the hearing of this trial
which has been so arranged as to place us in difficulties and
inconvenience in preparing our cases, we do not feel that we
have received the justice or hearing which we would have
liked.

I would like also to tell Your Honour that we feel that this
case, from our point of view, has been so arranged as to make
scapegoats of us in order to strangle the Kenya African Union,
the only African political organisation which fights for the rights
of the African people. We wish to say that what we have done
in our activities has been to try our level best to find ways and
means by which the community in this country can live in har-
mony. But what we have objected to—and we shall continue to
object—are the discriminations in the government of this
country. We shall not accept that, whether we are in gaol or out
of it, sir, because we find that this world has been made for
human beings to live in happily, to enjoy the good things and
the produce of the country equally, and to enjoy the opportu-
nities that this country has to offer. Therefore, Your Honour, I

will not say that you have been misled or influenced, but the point that you have made us that we have been against the Europeans, and, sir, you being a European, it is only natural that perhaps you should feel more that way. I am not accusing you of being prejudiced, but I feel that you should not stress so much the fact that we have been entirely motivated by hatred of Europeans. We ask you to remove that from your mind and to take this line: that our activities have been against the injustices that have been suffered by the African people and if in trying to establish the rights of the African people we have turned out to be what you say, Mau Mau, we are very sorry that you have been misled in that direction. What we have done, and what we shall continue to do, is to demand the rights of the African people as human beings that they may enjoy the facilities and privileges in the same way as other people.

We look forward to the day when peace shall come to this land and that the truth shall be known that we, as African leaders, have stood for peace. None of us would be happy or would condone the mutilation of human beings. We are humans and we have families and none of us will ever condone such activities as arson etc.

Without taking up much more of your time, I will tell Your Honour that we as political bodies or political leaders stand constitutionally by our demands which no doubt are known to you and to the Government of this country, and in saying this I am asking for no mercy at all on behalf of my colleagues. We are asking that justice may be done and that the injustices that exist may be righted. No doubt we have grievances, and everybody in this country, high or low, knows perfectly well that there are such grievances, and it is those grievances which affect the African people that we have been fighting for. We will not ask to be excused for asking for those grievances to be righted.

I do not want to take up more of your time, Your Honour. All that I wish to tell you is that we feel strongly that at this time the Government of this country should try to strangle the only organisation, that is the Kenya African Union, of which we are the leaders, who have been working for the betterment of the African people and who are seeking harmonious relations between the races. To these few remarks, Your Honour, I may say that we do not accept your finding of guilty. It will be our duty to instruct our lawyer to take this matter up and we intend to appeal to a higher Court. We believe that the Supreme Court of Kenya will give us justice because we stand for peace; we stand for the rights of the African people, that Africans may find a place among the nations.

The Magistrate asked each of the accused if they had anything to say why sentence should not be passed.
They replied:

KUBAI: I have nothing to say. You can impose any sentence.
ACHIENG: I have nothing to say at the moment. You can impose any sentence you are prepared to impose. I am only waiting to appeal to the Supreme Court of Kenya.
KAGGIA: I am in full agreement with what has been said by my colleagues and have nothing to add.
NGEI: I strongly associate myself with what Kenyatta has said. You can impose any sentence you like.
KARUMBA: Just as you like.

The Magistrate now addressed the prisoners in turn as follows:

You, Jomo Kenyatta, stand convicted of managing Mau Mau and being a member of that society. You have protested that your object has always been to pursue constitutional methods on the way to self-government for the African people, and for the return of land which you say belongs to the African people. I do not believe you. It is my belief that soon after your long stay in Europe and when you came back to this Colony you commenced to organise this Mau Mau society, the object of which was to drive out from Kenya all Europeans, and in doing so to kill them if necessary. I am satisfied that the master mind behind this plan was yours.

I also believe that the methods to be employed were worked out by you and that you have taken the fullest advantage of the power and influence which you have over your people and also of the primitive instincts which you know lie deep down in their characters. When they have made so much progress towards an enlightened civilisation, you have successfully plunged many of them back to a state which shows little of humanity. You have persuaded them in secret to murder, to burn, to commit evil atrocities, which it will take many years to forget. Some small part of the Mau Mau plan to kill Europeans has succeeded, but perhaps the greatest tragedy of all is that you have turned Kikuyu against Kikuyu. Your Mau Mau society has slaughtered without mercy defenceless Kikuyu men, women and children in hundreds and in circumstances which are revolting and are better left undescribed. You have let loose upon this land a flood of misery and unhappiness affecting the daily lives of all the races in it, including your own people. You have put the clock back many years and by your deeds much of the respect for your tribe has been lost, at least for the time being.

You have much to answer for and for that you will be punished. The maximum sentences which this Court is empowered to pass are the sentences which I do pass, and I can only comment that in my opinion they are inadequate for what you have done. Under Section 70 and on the first charge the sentence of the Court is that you be imprisoned for seven years with hard labour, and under Section 71 and on the third charge for three years with hard labour, both sentences to run concurrently, and I shall also recommend that you be restricted.

To the other accused, I would say this: You have intelligence, and, like Kenyatta you also have power and influence over the less educated Africans. You have not hesitated to join in with Kenyatta in this foul scheme of driving the Europeans from Kenya. Like him, you have thought that by murder, by arson, and by foul deeds of terror and intimidation you could achieve your evil objects. You could not have made a bigger mistake than to imagine that by such methods you could drive people from this Colony. Make no mistake about it, Mau Mau will be defeated, and although there may be more crimes of violence, more murders, more arson and more terror, the rule of law and the forces of law and order will prevail in the long run, even though the way may be hard and difficult.

His Honour then sentenced each of the other five prisoners in turn to seven years' imprisonment with hard labour under Section 70 and three years under Section 71, both sentences to run concurrently: and, as in Kenyatta's case, in each of the five others he recommended a restriction order to be made.

The effect of this last recommendation was not seen till some time later. On 8th September 1954 a news item in *The Times* announced that the restriction order had been made. "Jomo Kenyatta will probably spend the rest of his life in the remote northern frontier district of Kenya", added *The Times*, under the dateline *Nairobi Sept.* 7. "He is now serving a seven-year sentence there for managing the Mau Mau society, and the Governor of Kenya, Sir Evelyn Baring, today announced that he would have to stay in the area indefinitely.

"Sir Evelyn Baring said that the Government had made restriction orders which would mean that Kenyatta and his four lieutenants, Fred Kubai, Paul Ngei, Bildad Kaggia, and Kungu Karumba, must live in the northern province when they finish their sentences. . . .

"These are the first of such restriction orders made since the start of the emergency, and the Governor announced that they would remain in force indefinitely."

25

Crisis Develops

DURING the five months' sessions of the Court at Kapenguria, and in the period that again elapsed between the hearing of the appeal by the Supreme Court of Kenya the Emergency became steadily more acute.

After eight months of the Emergency, Mr Lyttleton had given the House of Commons figures showing that from 20th October 1952 to 6th July 1953, 1,300 Africans had been killed, 514 wounded, 2,673 captured and 112,529 taken into custody, and it was at once pointed out that the disparity between the figures of those wounded and those killed—the number killed is nearly two and a half times that of the number wounded—shows with what ruthlessness the operation had had to be conducted. By 7th June 1954, Mr Michael Blundell announced that 5,000 Mau Mau terrorists had been killed, and by this time the whole operation had become to all intents and purposes one against the whole Kikuyu population. In May 1954 in *Operation Anvil* the police rounded up almost the whole African population of Nairobi and detained 24,000 men of the Kikuyu, Embu and Meru tribes— about one quarter of the African population of the city. Mass executions followed and on 6th May in the leading article *The Times* declared that "anxiety cannot fail to be felt at the high number of executions". By this time 370 Africans had been executed by hanging and 150 more were under sentence of death. *The Times* went on to say:

Nobody would wish murderers, or the administrators of vile oaths binding others to murder to be spared. But the number of offences bearing the death penalty has been considerably increased. It includes consorting with terrorists, unlawful possession of arms or ammunition, and being present at oath-taking

245

ceremonies. Obviously in some cases these offences originate from a motive which can only be murderous; but it is possible also for them to be largely technical. Are the authorities always drawing this distinction? If they were not they would be building up in the name of Britain a terrible legacy of hatred and bitterness, for while deeds done in hot blood may be forgotten, the cold processes of law are apt not to be, in Africa any more than in Europe.

As if to add point to the anxieties thus expressed, Major-General Hinde, the Director of Operations in Kenya made a speech a month later, on 7th June 1954, in which he declared that "from a soldier's viewpoint it would be a good thing to expel Kikuyu tribesmen from their reserves for the rest of their lives. . . . What every soldier wanted was a kind of 'swill tub' in a large area where 100,000 Kikuyu could be put out of the way on works projects and told that they were there for life". Protests in the House of Commons brought an admission that the phrase 'swill tub' was not well chosen, but no correction of a policy which seemed to be carrying war to all the tribe of the Kikuyu.

Meanwhile anxiety was increased by a steady flow of evidence about atrocities by Europeans.

> Captain G. S. L. Griffiths (Durham Light Infantry) accused of murdering an African forestry worker, told a Company Sergeant-Major that he could shoot anybody he liked provided they were black.—*Manchester Guardian*, 26th November 1953.

Subsequently Captain Griffiths while acquitted of the charge of murder was sentenced by court martial to five years' imprisonment on six charges of disgraceful conduct which included "ordering a soldier in his company to cut off the testicles" of a prisoner, and "knowingly permitting" another prisoner "to be taken out as a guide with his ear pierced and with a piece of wire through the hole by which he might be led".

Mr Tom Driberg, M.P., quoted from the half-yearly journal of the Devonshire Regiment the following passages:

> We soon chalked up our first kill. . . . As "D" Company claimed a Mau Mau on the same day the Commanding Officer's prize of £5 for the first kill had to be shared.
>
> "C" Company was also lucky. In one area "the lack of Mau Mau was to a certain extent compensated for by an abundance of elephant, rhinoceros, baboons and all types of buck . . ." and

as a whole "our record up to date, of which we are justly proud, reads twenty-four killed, four captured."

There were also allegations of official connivance at brutality in screening.

> Sir Richard Acland has prepared a memorandum ... arising out of the verbatim transcript of the trial of Sergeant Keats and Police Officer Ruebens ... for beating up an African named Elijah. They were acquitted of manslaughter but found guilty of causing grievous bodily harm and were fined.
>
> The memorandum states that the report of these very light sentences (£50 and £100) had caused much concern ... but that the verbatim transcript "discloses far greater grounds for anxiety and further inquiry than any of us suspected at the time ... (it) shows beyond any possibility of doubt that the evidence against Elijah was obtained by an equally savage beating-up of another African to a point where he was too injured to speak and had to write his testimony against Elijah, and that proceedings were taken in relation to this action.— *Manchester Guardian*, 16th December 1953.

On the general question thus raised the Parliamentary Delegation wrote a cogent paragraph of their report.

> We were ... disturbed by the attitude of a section of European public opinion towards the sanctity of the law and the general question of police malpractices. For example, we were informed that a fund has recently been started with the object of paying the legal expenses of European members of the security forces accused of committing offences "in the course of their duty". Activity of this kind, taken in conjunction with protests in the press and elsewhere when proceedings are instituted against Europeans in the security forces, is tantamount to giving moral support to breaches of the law. Open displays of contempt for the law should be condemned just as sternly as breaches of it, for it is clear that once public opinion takes this course, no matter what the circumstances, the results are bound to be the disrepute and ineffectiveness of law and order.—(Cmd. 9081.)

At the end of this long and fierce campaign, Mau Mau in the opinion of the Parliamentary Delegation was not diminishing its influence but increasing it.

> It is our view, based upon all the evidence available to us, both official and unofficial, that the influence of Mau Mau in

the Kikuyu area, except in certain localities, has not declined; it has, on the contrary, increased.

In this respect the situation has deteriorated and the danger of infection outside the Kikuyu area is now greater not less than it was at the beginning of the State of Emergency. These are serious words and they are used with a due sense of responsibility, but that they are fully justified we have no doubt.

This was the conclusion of the report of the delegation led by the Rt Hon Walter Elliott and representing all parties in the House. Their report was presented to Parliament in February 1954. Later the same year an increasing number of reports told of Mau Mau spreading among the Meru, the Embu, in Nyassaland, and among the Kikuyu's ancient enemies the Masai. By July 1954 part of Masailand was declared a closed area in which unauthorised persons could be shot at sight.

The Parliamentary delegation summed up the political part of their report in these words: "We believe . . . that it is necessary to provide an outlet for African political thought . . . Africans should be encouraged to develop their own political organisations, thus filling the vacuum created by the banning of the Kenya African Union for complicity in Mau Mau."

This brings us to the period of the appeals, January and July 1954.

Appeals

THERE was an appeal to the Supreme Court of Kenya which heard the case in January 1954, acquitting Achieng but confirming the convictions of the other five.

The Supreme Court, in its judgment, paid careful attention to the intricate question of the status—"documents or not documents"—of tape-recording and sound-film. They quoted Mr Pritt's statement from the bar "as to the nature of the objects" and went on to express grave doubts whether magnetic tape should be considered to bear "marks".

> Thus in relation to the tape recording, having stated originally that it did not bear physical marks, he [Mr Pritt] went on to say that it might be contended that it bore marks by reason of the nature of the substance with which metal tape was coated having been changed by an electrical impulse. While this may be so, it would appear to us, in the absence of any technical knowledge, that it is at least equally possible that the effect of an electrical impulse on the magnetic tape is not to change the nature of the tape but rather to vary in some manner its properties; and we are by no means certain that a variation in the properties of a substance necessarily entails a variation in the substance or any marks upon the substance. In our view the term "marks" in the definition of "document" clearly connotes a physical mark upon the substance on which the document is recorded.

The learned judges felt, then, that magnetic tape was perhaps no document. Sound film, however, on which there were "visible marks which could have been seen by the Court upon inspection" —sound film might be another matter. Yet on consideration the learned judges had doubts. Should not the "marks" on documents

convey information "through the visual sense"? Mr Somerhough
had admitted, during the course of the argument, that a gramo-
phone record was a document, and this gave the learned judges
pause. But at last they came to the more or less firm conclusion
that "We do not consider that a sound track is a document within
the meaning of the Indian Evidence Act". Further they thought
that the exclusion of the sound film and the tape-recording was
not, as it happened, of great moment to the Defence.

In fact had they been produced and duly proved, they could
at the most have provided verbatim confirmation of Kenyatta's
evidence as to what he said at the Kiambu meeting. The Magistrate's finding in this respect, was not that Kenyatta did not use
the words which he alleged he had used at that meeting, but
that the terms in which Kenyatta denounced Mau Mau were
not such as to constitute a genuine and sincere denunciation.
That conclusion could in no way have been effected by the
tendering of evidence which merely repeated in Kikuyu what
Kenyatta had himself said were the words used by him.

On the critical question of the latitude allowed to the Prosecution in cross-examination, the Supreme Court referred to the contention of Defence that

... the number of inadmissible questions asked was so great
that their cumulative effect must inevitably have been to prejudice the mind of the Magistrate, more especially as, according
to the Defence, that mind was susceptible to be prejudiced. In
this connection, Mr Pritt referred *inter alia* to an observation by
the Magistrate in the following terms: "I did not know there was
no difference between the latitude in cross-examination against
a person—that is, I did not think there was any difference between accused persons and any others", which was subsequently modified by the addition of the phrase "within, of
course, limits". ... The limitations upon cross-examination of
accused persons are clearly established and need not now be
recapitulated and all that can be said as to the Magistrate's
observation above quoted, is that it is only explicable upon the
assumption that he had momentarily forgotten the provisions
of Section 159 of the Criminal Procedure Code, or did not
realise that Mr Pritt had this section in mind.

This somewhat unexpected comment on the Magistrate's
absence of mind was quoted by the Defence when they brought
their Petition to the Privy Council.

Under English law every person in a Colony has a right to petition the Privy Council for leave to appeal if he can make out a
case. There are several heads under which he may base his claim.
He can argue want of jurisdiction; he can object to the admission
of a large body of inadmissible evidence; he can argue from lack
of evidence to support conviction, or some other grave departure
from proper processes of law. The petition of Kenyatta and four
others was made on all these grounds, presenting as their Counsel
said, a very strong case of leave of appeal to be granted.

In their appeal the Defendants said:

The Magistrate accepted practically every application motion
or submission made by the Prosecution;

The Magistrate rejected practically every application motion
or submission made by Your Petitioners;

The Magistrate . . . accepted as truthful every witness called
by the Prosecution, no matter what their character or history,
how improbable their stories were, how gravely they contradicted themselves, or how badly their stories were shaken in
cross-examination or refuted by documents and found excuses
for any prosecuting witness who appeared to be evasive or
unreliable;

The Magistrate rejected as untruthful every witness called
by the Defence, no matter what their character or history, however fully they were corroborated, or however intrinsically probable their stories were.

Among other grounds for complaint was that the Magistrate
adjourned the hearing for rather more than a fortnight in December while the leading Defence Counsel was tried for contempt of
Court, his supposed offence being that he had sent to Members of
Parliament in London an attack on the action of the Kenya
Government in causing the trial to be heard in circumstances of
great inconvenience to all concerned, at a remote station on the
edge of the desert. The Supreme Court of Kenya quickly threw
out the charge of contempt.

The Petitioners claimed that the Magistrate admitted "such a
large body of inadmissible evidence as to make his findings of
fact untenable".

Thus the case moved from Kenya to Downing Street, where the
Judicial Committee of the Privy Council sits in London. In a
quiet room, more like the library of a cultivated eighteenth-

century gentleman than a court-room, with big windows giving on the trees of a London garden, their Lordships sat at a table to hear the petition from Kenyatta and his four remaining colleagues. This was in July 1954. The hearing attracted attention, the little crowd that gathered consisting largely of African and Indian men and women, students and missionaries, and it was clear that they came from all corners of the British Empire, and that they thought they were seeing history being made.

After a two days hearing their Lordships refused leave to appeal. Their decision was unexpected, and something of a shock to many, both in the Colonies and the United Kingdom, who had thought of this case as pre-eminently one of those which the Privy Council, far removed from the heat and dust of practical politics in Kenya, would feel bound to review. The conditions prevailing in the Colony—the Emergency and all that it entailed—seemed to be such that the very appearance of judicial calm was difficult to sustain, and therefore this case seemed to be one of those for which the reviewing function of the Privy Council was originally intended.

In rejecting the petition their Lordships could be said to have refused even to ask the question, Was justice done? or perhaps just as significantly, Does it appear that justice was done? Yet in a very clear sense their refusal was tantamount to a declaration that they were satisfied there had been no apparent injustice. It can be argued that British justice was itself on trial in this case—indeed it can be so argued of any case in the calendar: but in such a trial as this, where passions run high and the implications reach forward into the future history of the whole African Continent, it is at least as important that the unwritten British constitution permits an appeal, even beyond Her Majesty's judicial committee of the Privy Council, to the reader in his arm-chair, and to anyone who likes to take the trouble to examine the evidence for himself.

Index of Incidents

(in the order of the chart prepared by the Defence, which follows this index).